Textiles:
Concepts and Principles

Textiles:
Concepts and Principles

VIRGINIA HENCKEN ELSASSER

Delmar Publishers

I(T)P® an International Thomson Publishing company

Albany • Bonn • Boston • Cincinnati • Detroit • London • Madrid
Melbourne • Mexico City • New York • Pacific Grove • Paris • San Francisco
Singapore • Tokyo • Toronto • Washington

NOTICE TO THE READER

Cover photo by: Brian Sullivan

Delmar Staff
Acquisitions Editor: Christopher Anzalone
Developmental Editor: Jeffrey D. Litton
Project Editor: Eugenia L. Orlandi
Production Coordinator: Linda Helfrich
Art and Design Coordinator: Douglas J. Hyldelund

COPYRIGHT © 1997
By Delmar Publishers
an International Thomson Publishing Inc.

The ITP logo is a trademark under license.

Printed in the United States of America

For more information, contact:

Delmar Publishers
3 Columbia Circle, Box 15015
Albany, New York 12212-5015

International Thomson Editores
Campos Eliseos 385, Piso 7
Col Polanco
11560 Mexico D F Mexico

International Thomson Publishing-Europe
Berkshire House
168–173 High Holborn
London WC1V 7AA
England

International Thomson Publishing GmbH
Konigswinterer Strasse 418
53227 Bonn
Germany

Thomas Nelson Australia
102 Dodds Street
South Melbourne, 3205
Victoria, Australia

International Thomson Publishing-Asia
221 Henderson Road
#05–10 Henderson Building
Singapore 0315

Nelson Canada
1120 Birchmount Road
Scarborough, Ontario
Canada M1K 5G4

International Thomson Publishing-Japan
Hirakawacho Kyowa Building, 3F
2-2-1 Hirakawacho
Chiyoda-ku, Tokyo 102
Japan

1 2 3 4 5 6 7 8 9 10 XXX 02 01 00 99 98 97 96

Library of Congress Cataloging-in-Publication Data

Elsasser, Virginia Hencken
    Textiles: concepts and principles   /   Virginia Hencken Elsasser.
      p.   cm.
    Includes index.
    ISBN 0-8273-7686-3
    1. Textile fabrics.   2. Textile fibers.   I. Title.
TS1760.E47   1997
677—dc20   96-35771
                                                          CIP

Contents

Preface

This book is designed to be an introduction to textiles for students who are planning to enter careers that require a basic knowledge of textiles. These careers may include interior design, fashion design or merchandising, costuming, textile marketing, product development, buying, and retailing. Information relevant to both furnishings and apparel is included. Industrial applications are included but not emphasized.

This book offers the advantages of a textbook, laboratory book, and a swatch book template in one volume. The reader is encouraged to become immersed in the study of textiles through hands-on assignments which require investigation of the contemporary applications of textiles using current magazine and trade journals.

The information is presented in a readable, nontechnical style. The challenge was to present complex information in an easy-to-comprehend format which would allow students to gain an appreciation for the beauty and serviceability of textiles without a preponderance of technical information. Definitions of key terms in the industry are emphasized. The glossary provides easily accessible information which will make this text a valuable reference for the nontechnical student of textiles.

The organization of the book is based on the components of textile products: fibers, yarns, fabric formation, coloration, and finishes. Chapter 1 presents an overview of the global textile industry and introduces the components of textile products. The properties of the fibers, which are presented in Chapters 2 through 8, form the basis for the behavior of textiles. Each fiber is presented similarly with information on properties, care, and end uses. Since the properties of manufactured fibers can be controlled during production, the properties of these fibers are discussed in general terms. Yarn and fabric formation, coloration methods, and finishing processes are presented in Chapters 9 through 14. The interrelationship of the components of textiles and the contribution of each component to the final product are emphasized. It is important to remember that the appropriateness of a textile product must be evaluated in terms of the needs and desires of the consumer. The book concludes with a chapter on career possibilities.

Each chapter begins with objectives which guide the student through the chapter. Photographs, diagrams, and tables are included to provide visual reinforcement and to illustrate the information in the text. Key words are highlighted in the text.

The instructor's guide includes objectives, an outline, and key terms for each chapter. Additional learning experiences, suggestions for laboratory experiences, and sources for laboratory supplies are also included. Industry resources for visual aids and supplementary information are listed. The Instructor's Guide concludes with a test bank.

Delmar Publishers has also published the *Garment and Textile Dictionary* by George L. Conway, which is an excellent reference. It has over 3,500 terms with phonetic pronunciations. At the end of each chapter a defects section is presented underscoring textile problems and solutions.

I hope this book will provide students with an enjoyable learning experience and instructors with an enjoyable teaching experience.

Virginia Hencken Elsasser
July 1996

Acknowledgments

This book would not have been possible without the contributions of many people, several of whom deserve special thanks.

First, my family. I mention them first because they have encouraged me every day since the beginning of this project. My daughter Meghan's special sense of humor provided comic relief when needed; my son Christian patiently taught me the intricacies of word processing; and my husband Neil showed his unfailing kindness and continuing support by his willingness to accept additional responsibilities on the homefront. A special note of thanks goes to my mother, Jean Hencken, and my mother-in-law, Ruth Elsasser: the best cheerleading section an author could have. And, although they are not here to accept my appreciation for years of encouragement, I thank my father, Robert Hencken, and father-in-law, Cornelius Elsasser, Jr.

I sincerely appreciated the guidance and support from the editorial staff at Delmar Publishers. Jeff Litton, Developmental Editor, and Judy Roberts, Senior Editorial Assistant, were especially patient and helpful. I am also grateful to Doug Hyldelund, Art and Design Coordinator, and his staff for their skill and expertise with the visuals. Delmar also found the following readers who provided valuable feedback and constructive criticism: Lori Battistone-Obel, ICM School of Business, Pittsburgh, PA; Catherine Boyd, PhD., Mississippi State University, Mississippi State, MS; Nancy Bredemeyer, Indian River Community College, Ft. Pierce, FL; V. Merlene Lyman, Fort Hays College, Hays, KS; Rosa Lee Davenport, Indian River Community College, Ft. Pierce, FL; Judy Thacker, Fashion Careers of California, San Diego, CA.

Thanks also to the staff at PublisherStudio for providing expert copyediting.

My students and colleagues form a special group whose contributions are much appreciated. The questions and comments from my current and former students shaped not only this book but also my philosophy of teaching and learning. I have learned a great deal from them. Pat Keating was especially helpful as a reviewer for the first draft. Lyn Crouse provided lots of interesting ideas. The current and former Vice-Presidents of Academic Affairs at Centenary College have been particularly supportive of my efforts. Dr. Dorothy Prisco was a strong advocate of my early attempts and Dr. Anna Maria Moggio provided encouragement and sound advice. Leslie Littell, of Ashbridge Studios, brought unique perspectives and creativity to this text. She freely offered her boundless enthusiasm and knowledge of visual arts and textiles; I gratefully accepted.

Many individuals from universities, museums, trade organizations and journals, and textile companies were helpful in providing information, photographs, and illustrations. The following have been especially generous: American Fiber Manufacturers Association, Inc.; American Wool Council, Division of American Sheep Industry Association, Inc.; Amoco Fabrics and Fibers Company; Avondale Mills; Cotton Incorporated; Courtaulds Fibers, Inc.; DuPont, Wilmington, DE; Federal Trade Commission; Hagley Museum and Library; Hoechst Celanese; INDA, Association of the Nonwoven Fabrics Industry; International Silk Association; International Textile and Apparel Association, Inc.; MASTERS OF LINEN/U.S.A.; Metropolitan Museum of Art; Milliken & Company; Mohair Council of America; Monsanto Company, the Fibers Unit; National Cotton Council of America; Pendleton Woolen Mills; PPG Industries, Inc.; Springs Industries; Textile World; University of Chicago; Vanguard Supreme; W. L. Gore and Associates, Inc.; WestPoint Pepperell; and The Wool Bureau, Inc.

Several people deserve special recognition: Rita Fisk at DuPont, Gail Raiman at ATMI, Mary Doherty and Debi Jackson at the Metropolitan Museum of Art, Elaine Greten at INDA, Walter Lehmann at Hoechst Celanese, and Richard Dillard at Milliken & Company.

Virginia Hencken Elsasser
September 9, 1996

Chapter

1

Introduction to Textiles

OBJECTIVES

The student will be able to:

1. Begin to develop a working vocabulary of terms used in the textile industry
2. Appreciate the size and scope of the textile industry
3. Differentiate between industrial and consumer textiles
4. Define the term *product pipeline* as it relates to the textile industry
5. List and discuss the major components of a textile product and discuss how they interrelate
6. List and discuss five major laws that impact the textile industry

Textile Industry Terminology

In order to communicate effectively with people in the textile industry, it is necessary to develop a working vocabulary of basic textile terminology. Commonly used terms are defined.

Converter—Company that purchases unfinished goods, has them finished and dyed or printed, and resells them

1

Dye house or **dye plant**—Factory that dyes fabric

Finishing mill or **finishing plant**—Factory that finishes fabric

Generic name—Name of a manufactured fiber that is based on the fiber's chemical composition. Generic name categories are established by the Federal Trade Commission (e.g., olefin, nylon, and acrylic)

Greige goods—Unfinished goods. *Greige* is pronounced "gray." Alternate spellings of "gray" and "grey" are unacceptable

Jobber—Company that purchases fabric from large mills or converters and sells small quantities of finished fabric

Mill—Factory that produces yarn or fabric

Off-shore production—Use of lower-cost foreign labor to assemble and finish garments

Over-the-counter fabrics—Fabrics sold to retail stores for the home sewer

Print house or **print plant**—Factory that prints fabric

Quick response or **Just-in-Time**—Production and delivery that emphasizes speed and efficiency through computer use and automated manufacturing

Spinners—Factories that produce yarn from staple fibers

Trademark name—Name a manufacturer uses to identify goods sold or made by that company. Trade names begin with uppercase letters (e.g., Herculon®, Dacron®, Lycra®); generic names begin with lowercase letters (e.g., olefin, polyester, spandex)

Introduction

The purpose of this book is to help the reader understand the importance of textiles in society, appreciate the visual and tactile beauty of textiles, and identify the characteristics of textile products. With this knowledge the reader will be able to predict appropriate end-use applications more accurately and make informed design, merchandising, and retailing decisions.

Size and Scope of the Textile Industry

The textile industry, which encompasses every step from raw fiber production to final consumption of the product, is a fascinating blend of science and technology, art and design, and business. Textiles is one of the largest industries in the United States. Approximately 700,000 Americans work in the industry, and over 5,000 small to very large companies develop, produce, and/or distribute textile products in the United States.

Textiles is also an international industry. The United States trades textiles and apparel with approximately 130 foreign countries. Imported textile and apparel goods account for about 50 percent of the clothing market in the United States, but only about 20 percent of the furnishings market.

SCIENCE AND TECHNOLOGY

Science and technology have created an ultramodern textile industry that is capable of engineering products to meet specific demands. Wrinkle-free clothing, lightweight, bulletproof vests, and artificial replacements for diseased veins and arteries are examples of textile products that meet specific needs. Increased automation and mechanization have reduced production time and improved efficiency.

In addition to creating products, the textile industry is working to improve the environment. Some recent developments include improved methods for spinning manufactured fibers and reducing water, air, and noise pollution. Manufactured fiber producers have begun to recycle plastic bottles into fibers used in apparel and furnishings. Wellman, Inc., Fibers Division, New York, N.Y., produces Fortrel® Ecospun™ and Fortrel® Microspun™ polyester, recycled plastic-bottle fibers.

ART AND DESIGN

Textile and apparel designers create fabrics and garments that are both beautiful and functional. Computer-aided design, new classifications of dyes and pigments, and high-technology fibers and fabrics have provided designers increasing opportunities and challenges.

BUSINESS

The textile industry is profit driven and therefore must respond to the needs of each customer. The customer may be a final purchaser of consumer or industrial textile products or an intermediate purchaser along the product pipeline. Figure 1–1 illustrates the product pipeline for consumer textiles, from fiber production to final customer. Each step along the pipeline depends on and relates to every other step. Business management and marketing provide the framework within which the textile industry operates.

Difference Between Consumer and Industrial Textiles

The textile industry is divided into two main sectors: consumer and industrial. **Consumer textiles** includes apparel and home furnishings. **Industrial textiles** includes geotextiles for dam and roadbed construction, insulation, industrial filters, and materials for the space industry.

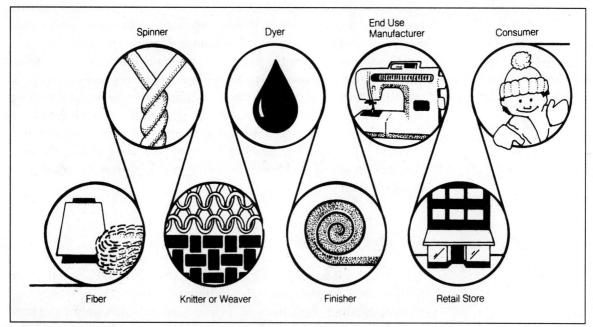

FIGURE 1–1

Product pipeline for consumer textiles. (Courtesy of DuPont, Wilmington, DE.)

Table 1–1 lists approximate percentages of fiber use in the United States. Table 1–2 lists a variety of end uses for textiles.

Major Components of a Textile Product

The major components of textiles are fiber, yarn, fabric, finish, and dyeing and printing. Although most textiles used for apparel and home furnishings include each component, not every textile product contains each component. For example, nonwoven products such as tea-bag covers lack a yarn structure.

TABLE 1–1 PERCENTAGES OF FIBER USE IN THE UNITED STATES	
Apparel	39%
Home Textiles	16%
Floor Coverings	22%
Industrial	19%
Exports	4%

(Source: September 1995 Fiber Organon)

TABLE 1–2 END USES FOR TEXTILE PRODUCTS	
Apparel	men, women, and children's clothing innerwear, sleepwear, and outerwear athletic wear, swim wear accessories including hats, gloves, scarves, belts, ties, handbags, umbrellas, some shoes
Furnishings	upholstery, slipcovers draperies and curtains table linens carpeting, rugs towels, shower curtains sheets, bedding, and pillows

Industrial	defense
	    uniforms, bulletproof vests,
	    helmets, parachutes, flags, tents, etc.

TABLE 1–2 (continued)

```
geotextiles
    road beds, soil erosion control,
    drainage, etc.
manufacturing
    belts, gaskets, tapes,
    filters, hoses, gloves,
    protective clothing and
    aprons, bagging
medical
    artificial arteries, blood
    vessels, and kidneys,
    bandages, sutures, casts,
    gowns, etc.
recreation and leisure
    outdoor furniture, some
    sporting equipment, luggage,
    backpacks
transportation
    tire cord, brake linings,
    hoses, upholstery and
    carpeting, etc.
space exploration
    heat shields, space suits, etc.
```

DEFINITIONS OF THE COMPONENTS OF TEXTILE PRODUCTS

The study of textiles begins with an understanding of the component of textile products. Each component will be presented in greater detail later in the book.

FIBER. **Fibers** are fine, hair-like substances. They may be natural or manufactured and are the smallest component of a textile product. Cotton is an example of a natural fiber. Polyester is a manufactured fiber.

YARN. **Yarns** are groupings of natural or manufactured fibers that combine to form a continuous strand which can be used to produce fabric.

FABRIC. **Fabric** is formed by assembling yarns and/or fibers into one cohesive structure. The most common fabric structures are woven, knit, and nonwoven. Fabric may be referred to as cloth, material, piece goods, or goods.

FINISH. **Finish,** or a finishing process, is any chemical or mechanical treatment or process that modifies the properties of a textile product.

DYEING AND PRINTING. **Dyeing and printing** add colors and/or patterns of colors to a textile product.

IMPORTANCE OF THE INTERRELATIONSHIPS OF TEXTILE COMPONENTS

The interrelationship of textile components is of primary importance when evaluating a product for end-use suitability. Each component must be considered as part of the combination of components that make up the final textile product, because each component can modify the behavior of the final product. Often undesirable characteristics can be overcome by finishing processes. Examples of finishes that improve performance include mothproofing, water and soil repellent finishes, and yarn texturing. A relatively low-strength fiber, like cotton, may be used in high-strength applications if suitable yarn and fabric structures and appropriate finishes are used.

The textile products manufacturer/producer evaluates the cost/ benefit of each component. Most manufacturers attempt to create products that meet customers' needs and desires while reducing costs.

Major Laws and Regulations Affecting Textile Products Sold in the United States

The purpose of textile laws and regulations is to protect the final consumers of textiles, as well as their producers, manufacturers, and distributors, from dishonest presentation of goods. It is important that professional and legal responsibilities are considered by each company along the product pipeline. The following laws cover products sold in the United States. Products manufactured overseas must be screened carefully.

TEXTILE FIBER PRODUCTS IDENTIFICATION ACT, 1960

The Textile Fiber Products Identification Act (TFPIA), which was most recently amended in 1984, requires that specific information on fiber content, manufacturer identification, and country of origin be included on a garment or home-furnishings label. The six main requirements of the TFPIA are:

1. The **generic name** of the fiber, such as cotton, nylon, or rayon, must be listed.
2. The percent of each fiber, by weight, must be listed vertically and in descending order. If a fiber composes less than 5 percent of the product, it must be listed as "other fiber" unless it has a specific function. The purpose of this provision is to prevent manufacturers from implying that less than 5 percent of a fiber will improve performance or appearance, which, in general, it does not. Exceptions are spandex, an elastic fiber, which provides stretch, and metallic fibers, which control static electricity.
3. The label must state whether the item was produced in the United States or imported. If the item was imported, its country of origin must be named.
4. The manufacturer's name or registered identification number must appear on the label.
5. The use of misleading names is prohibited.
6. Labels must be attached securely and conspicuously.

PERMANENT CARE LABELING RULING OF THE FEDERAL TRADE COMMISSION, 1972

The Permanent Care Labeling Ruling of the Federal Trade Commission (FTC), which was amended in 1984, requires that each piece of wearing apparel and bolt of fabric carry a permanent label describing its recommended care. The label must remain legible for the life of the garment. Figure 1–2 shows examples of care labels. Items that are completely washable and retail for $3 or less are exempt from this ruling. Totally reversible garments without pockets, some institutional products, shoes, hats, gloves, and nonwovens are also exempt.

FLAMMABLE FABRICS ACT, 1953

The Flammable Fabrics Act, which was amended in 1967, bans the sale and use of highly flammable materials for clothing, carpets, draperies, bedding, and upholstery. Flammability standards are

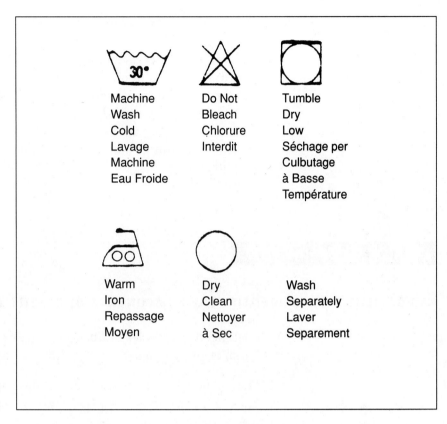

FIGURE 1–2

Example of a care label

established by the Consumer Product Safety Commission. The sale of flammable mattresses, carpets, and children's sleepwear (sizes 0–14) is also prohibited under this legislation. Some types of hats, gloves, and footwear are exempt.

FEDERAL TRADE COMMISSION RULING ON THE WEIGHTING OF SILK, 1932

The Federal Trade Commission (FTC) Ruling on the Weighting of Silk controls the weighting of silk with metallic salts. Weighting increases the body, weight, and dyeability of silk but also causes the fabric to break and disintegrate. Under the FTC ruling, all silk, except black, with 10 percent or more weighting must be labeled "weighted silk." Black silk, which can be more heavily weighted than other colors without disintegrating, may have 15-percent weighting.

WOOL PRODUCTS LABELING ACT, 1939

The Wool Products Labeling Act, which was amended in 1980, requires that recycled wool, except when used in carpet, rugs, mats, and upholstery, be labeled "recycled." The terms **wool, virgin wool,** and **new wool** refer to previously unused fleece of lamb or sheep fibers and specialty fibers such as camel hair. **Recycled wool** refers to fibers from woven, felted, or knitted wool products that have been returned to a fibrous state.

LABORATORY ASSIGNMENTS

ASSIGNMENT 1–1   IDENTIFY THE COMPONENTS OF TEXTILE PRODUCTS

Materials needed: samples of fiber, yarn, greige fabric, finished fabric, dyed and/or printed fabric

1. Mount and label a sample of each of the following:
   fiber
   yarn
   greige fabric
   finished fabric
   dyed and/or printed fabric

ASSIGNMENT 1–2   FABRIC CHARACTERISTICS AND PROJECTED END USE

Materials needed: six 3″ × 3″ fabric samples (suggested fabrics: corduroy, plissé, wool or wool blend, challis, dotted swiss, or flannel)

1. Mount the six 3″ × 3″ fabric samples.
2. Describe the texture (e.g., soft, fuzzy, harsh, stiff) and color of each.
3. Suggest an appropriate end use for each sample.

1. Fabric name   color
   fiber content   suggested end use
   texture

2. Fabric name   color
    fiber content   suggested end use
    texture

3. Fabric name   color
    fiber content   suggested end use
    texture

4. Fabric name   color
    fiber content   suggested end use
    texture

5. Fabric name   color
    fiber content   suggested end use
    texture

6. Fabric name   color
    fiber content   suggested end use
    texture

ASSIGNMENT 1–3   TEXTILE FIBER PRODUCTS IDENTIFICATION ACT

1. Identify which of the following labels conform to TFPIA requirements. Rewrite the label(s) that do not.

    A. 20% wool
         80% Dacron®
         Machine wash, line dry
         Made in the USA

    B. 70% Herculon®
         27% cotton
         2% silk
         Manufactured by the ABC Company

    C. 60% cotton
         40% polyester
         Made in the USA
         Manufactured by the XYZ Company

Fibers and Their Properties

OBJECTIVES

The student will be able to:

1. Summarize the major natural and manufactured fibers
2. List generic names for manufactured fibers
3. Describe how fiber properties affect textile product performance
4. Define and discuss the physical, mechanical, and chemical properties of fibers
5. Begin to relate the properties of fibers to the overall performance of apparel, furnishings, and industrial textiles

Textile Industry Terminology

Abrasion resistance—The ability of a fiber to withstand the effects of rubbing or friction

Absorbency—The ability of a fiber to take in moisture

Compressional resiliency—The ability of a fiber to return to its original thickness after being crushed

Covering power—The ability of a fiber to hide what is beneath it

Denier—Refers to the weight in grams of 9,000 meters of filament yarn

Dimensional stability—The ability of a fiber to maintain its original shape, neither shrinking nor stretching

Elastic recovery—The ability of a fiber to return to its original length after being stretched

Elongation—The lengthening or stretching of a fiber

Epitropic fibers—Synthetic fibers that have small particles of carbon imbedded in their surfaces to conduct electricity

Filament fibers—Long fibers measured in yards or meters

Hand—Refers to how the fabric feels, or the texture of the fabric

Heat setting—The controlled application of heat which allows creases and pleats to be permanently set in fabrics made from thermoplastic fibers; also improves the dimensional stability of fibers, yarns, or fabrics

Hydrophilic fibers—Fibers than can absorb moisture

Hydrophobic fibers—Fibers that do not readily absorb moisture

Hygroscopic fibers—Fibers that can absorb moisture without feeling wet

Loft—The ability of a fiber to return to its original thickness after being crushed; also called compressional resiliency

Luster—Amount of light reflected from a fiber

Manufactured cellulosic fibers—Fibers derived from cellulose (wood pulp and cotton linters) that cannot be used as textiles in their original forms

Manufactured fibers—Fibers that are created through science and technology, as opposed to fibers that occur naturally

Microfibers—Manufactured fibers that are less than 1 denier; also called microdenier fibers

Micron—One micron (or micrometer in S. I.) equals $\frac{1}{1000}$ of a millimeter

Natural fibers—Fibers that come from vegetable, animal, and mineral sources

Progressive shrinkage—Shrinkage that occurs every time the fabric is laundered. Rayon and wool are particularly susceptible to progressive shrinkage

Relaxation shrinkage—Shrinkage that occurs because fabrics are held under significant tension during manufacture and processing. During laundering, moisture encourages the fibers to relax and contract

Resiliency—The ability of a fiber to return to its original shape following bending, folding, or crushing; also called wrinkle recovery

Specific gravity—Comparative measure of the mass of a fiber to an equal volume of water; also called density

Staple fibers—Short fibers that range from less than 1 inch to 18 inches long

Striations—Longitudinal markings on manufactured fibers result from indentations or valleys in the cross section of the fiber

Synthetic fibers—Fibers that are synthesized chemically, frequently from petroleum products

Tenacity—Refers to fiber strength, usually describes the force needed to rupture the fiber

Tex—Unit of measure in the International System that refers to the weight in grams of 1,000 meters of fiber or yarn

Thermoplastic fibers—Fibers that melt or soften when exposed to heat

Wicking—The ability of a fiber to carry moisture along its surface

Wrinkle recovery—The ability of a fiber to return to its original shape following bending, folding, or crushing

Introduction

Textile fibers can be divided into two main categories: natural and manufactured. (See Table 2–1.) **Natural fibers** come from vegetable, animal, and mineral sources. Cotton and flax are examples of vegetable fibers. Wool and silk are animal fibers. Asbestos, a mineral fiber,

TABLE 2-1   MAJOR FIBER CATEGORIES

I. Natural Fibers
  A. Protein Fibers
      1. Silk
      2. Wool
      3. Specialty hair fibers

a. Alpaca	f. Llama
b. Angora	g. Mohair
c. Cashmere	h. Qiviut
d. Camel's hair	i. Vicuña
e. Guanaco	

      4. Fur fibers

a. Mink	d. Chinchilla
b. Fox	e. Angora rabbit
c. Beaver	

  B. Cellulosic Fibers
      1. Cotton
      2. Flax
      3. Ramie
      4. Minor cellulosic fibers

a. Coir	f. Piña
b. Kapok	g. Sisal
c. Hemp	h. Abaca
d. Jute	i. Henequen
e. Kenaf	

  C. Mineral Fibers—Asbestos
  D. Natural Rubber

II. Manufactured Fibers
  A. Manufactured Cellulosics
      1. Regenerated cellulosics—rayon, lyocell
      2. Derivative cellulosics—acetate, triacetate
  B. Regenerated Protein Fibers—Azlon
  C. Synthetic Fibers
      1. Major synthetic fibers

a. Acrylic	e. Olefin
b. Aramid	f. Polyester
c. Modacrylic	g. Spandex
d. Nylon	

      2. Special application synthetic fibers

a. Anidex	g. PBI (polybenzimidazole)
b. Carbon	h. Saran
c. Fluorocarbon	i. Sulfar
d. Lastrile	j. Vinal
e. Novoloid	k. Vinyon
f. Nytril	

  D. Inorganic Fibers
      1. Ceramic
      2. Glass
      3. Metallic

has little application in textiles because it is a known carcinogen.

Manufactured fibers have been available since the end of the nineteenth century. The two main categories of manufactured fibers are manufactured cellulosics and synthetics. Rayon and acetate are **manufactured cellulosic fibers** that are created from cellulose. **Synthetic fibers** are synthesized chemically, frequently from petroleum products.

Science and technology have allowed man to create fibers to meet specific end-use applications. For example, the nylon used in automobile tires is very different from the nylon used in hosiery.

The properties of a fiber determine how the fiber can be used. A weak fiber like rayon is suited to different end uses than is nylon, which is very strong. Rayon is frequently found in summer-weight apparel, while nylon is often found in long-wearing hosiery, carpeting, and upholstery fabrics. The physical, mechanical, and chemical properties

---

TABLE 2–2   FIBER PROPERTIES

I. **Physical Properties**
   A. Color
   B. Shape
      1. Length
      2. Cross section
      3. Surface contour
      4. Diameter
      5. Crimp
   C. Covering Power
   D. Hand (Feel or Texture)
   E. Luster

II. **Mechanical Properties**
   A. Abrasion Resistance
   B. Dimensional Stability
   C. Elastic Recovery/Elongation
   D. Flexibility
   E. Resiliency
   F. Specific Gravity
   G. Tenacity

III. **Chemical Properties**
   A. Absorbency/Wicking
   B. Electrical Conductivity
   C. Chemical Reactivity
   D. Effect of Heat
   E. Flammability

Physical Properties

of textile fibers are summarized in Table 2–2.

Physical properties are properties that can be evaluated with the naked eye or with a microscope.

COLOR

Manufactured fibers are usually white, while natural fibers vary in shade from white to brown, tan, and black. Camel hair, a natural fiber, is tan; wool may be from off-white to black. Natural fibers may be bleached if whiteness is desired. Both manufactured and natural fibers can be dyed to meet consumer preferences.

SHAPE

Physically all fibers have length, cross section, surface contour, and diameter. Some fibers also have crimp, which is waves or bumps. Covering power, hand, and luster are fiber properties that relate closely to the shape of the fiber. Whereas nature determines the shape of natural fibers, manufactured fibers can be produced in many different shapes. Manufactured fibers are shaped by forcing the liquid fiber through a spinneret. (See Figure 2–1.)

FIGURE 2–1

Spinneret. (Courtesy of the American Fiber Manufacturers Association, Inc.)

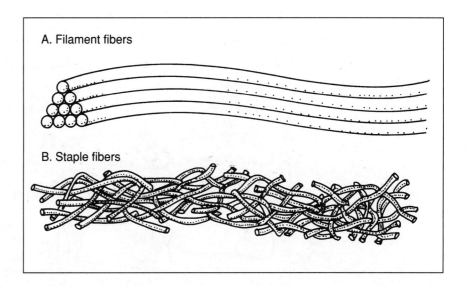

FIGURE 2–2

(A) filament fibers and

(B) staple fibers

LENGTH.   Fibers may be staple (short) or filament (long). (See Figure 2–2 to compare filament and staple fibers.) Staple fibers range from less than 1 inch to 18 inches long. **Filament fibers** are indefinitely long and therefore, are measured in yards or meters. All natural fibers, except silk, are staple. Silk and all manufactured fibers are produced as filaments. These filaments may be cut to staple length. Staple fibers are spun into yarns. (See Chapter 9 for a complete discussion of yarn formation.)

CROSS SECTION.   The cross section of a fiber is the appearance across the diameter of the fiber. (See Figure 2–3.)

SURFACE CONTOUR.   Surface contour is sometimes called **longitudinal appearance**. The surface contour of manufactured fibers results from the shape of a fiber's cross section. (See Figure 2–3.) The longitudinal markings on manufactured fibers are called **striations** and result from indentations or valleys in the fibers' cross sections. The distinctive surface contours of natural fibers, which affect their properties, are discussed in Chapters 3 and 4.

DIAMETER.   The diameter of a fiber is the width of the cross section. The diameters of manufactured fibers are traditionally measured differently than are the diameters of natural fibers.

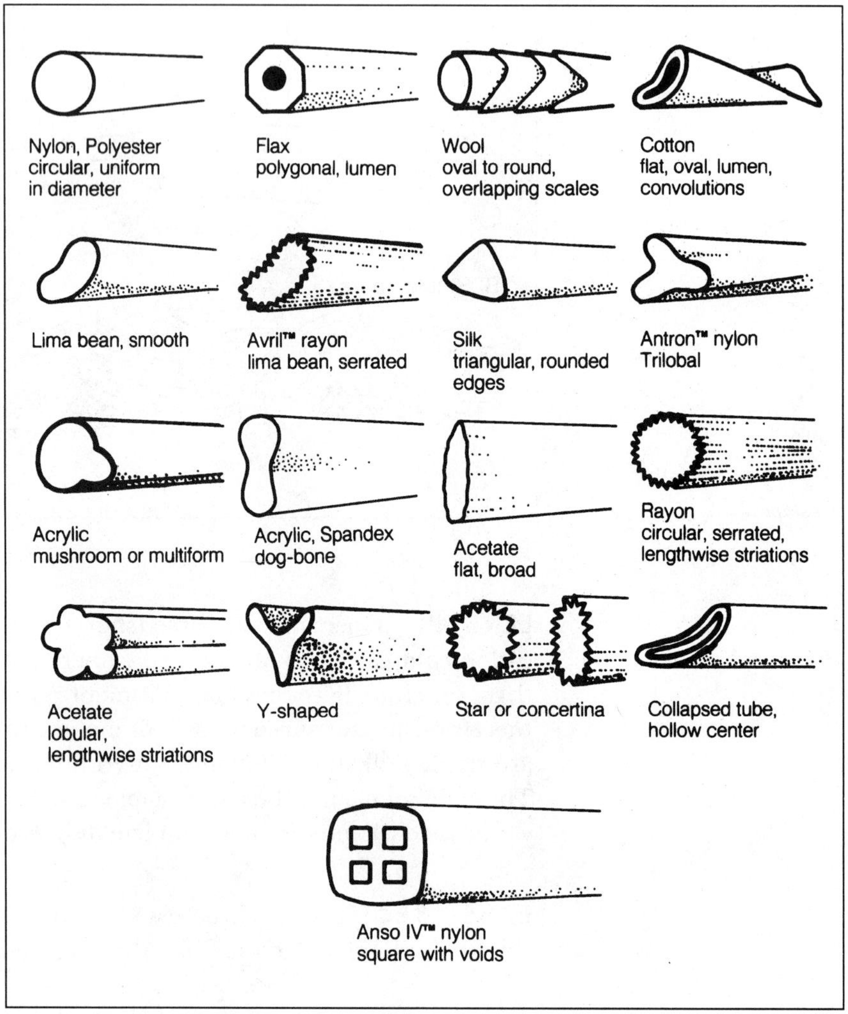

FIGURE 2–3

Cross sections and fiber contour

As mentioned earlier, manufactured fibers are formed when liquid fiber passes through a spinneret. The size of the openings in the spinneret regulates the size of the manufactured fiber. The end use of the manufactured fiber determines the fiber's diameter. Fiber diameter is measured by the denier system or by the International System (SI). **Denier** refers to the weight of 9,000 meters of fiber or yarn. **Tex** is the unit of measure in SI and refers to the weight in grams of 1,000 meters of fiber or yarn. Note that denier and tex refer to the weights of both fiber and yarn. The lower the tex or denier number the finer the fiber or yarn.

Large fibers tend to be coarse and stiff, while small fibers are fine and flexible. In general, fine fibers are more expensive than large fibers. **Microfibers**, or very fine fibers, have been developed for use in surgical and filtration applications. Recently, microfibers have found application in the apparel industry. See Table 2–3 to compare the diameters of manufactured fibers.

The diameter of natural fibers is measured in microns (micrometers in SI). One micron (μ), or micrometer, equals $\frac{1}{1000}$ of a millimeter. See Table 2–4 to compare the diameters of natural fibers.

CRIMP.   The waves or bumps of a fiber are called **crimp**. Some fibers, like wool, have natural crimp. Crimp may be added to manufactured

TABLE 2–3   DIAMETERS OF MANUFACTURED FIBERS

Denier	End Use(s)
Ultrafine fiber (0.01 or less)	Apparel, furnishings, medical
Microdenier (less than 1.0, usually 0.5 – 0.8)	Apparel, furnishings, medical
Less than 7	Apparel, very sheer hosiery
7-15	Furnishings
15-25	Carpeting
1000+	Fishing line, rope, some carpeting

TABLE 2–4   DIAMETERS OF NATURAL FIBERS

(Expressed in Microns)

Fiber	Diameter
Silk	9-11 μ
Wool	8-70 μ
Angora rabbit	13 μ
Cotton	12-20 μ
Flax	15-18 μ

fibers during the texturing process. Texturing produces a manufactured fiber that feels more like a natural fiber.

COVERING POWER

Covering power is the ability of a fabric to hide what is beneath it. Fibers with round cross sections tend to have poorer covering power than those with dog-bone or flat cross sections. (See Figure 2–3.) Fibers with texture or crimp have better covering power than smooth fibers.

HAND

The **hand**, or texture, of a fiber refers to the feel of the fiber. All the shape characteristics of a fiber impact hand. For example, filament fibers feel smoother than staple fibers, fine diameter fibers are softer and less stiff than thick fibers, and crimped fibers feel fluffier than untextured fibers.

LUSTER

Luster is the amount of light that is reflected from a fiber. Silk is a natural fiber with high luster. In general, manufactured fibers have high luster unless they are delustered with titanium dioxide or other delustering finishing processes. See Figure 2–4 for photomicrographs of chemically delustered nylon 6,6. The shape of manufactured fibers affects luster. Fibers with round, flat, and trilobal cross sections have higher luster than fibers with other cross section shapes. See Figure 2–5 for effects of cross section shape on luster.

Mechanical Properties

The mechanical properties of fibers are determined in a textile testing laboratory. Testing procedures have been developed by organizations such as the American Association of Textile Chemists and Colorists (AATCC) and the American Society for Testing and Materials (ASTM). These procedures make possible accurate evaluation of the qualities of textile products, such as the relative strength, or tenacity, of the fibers.

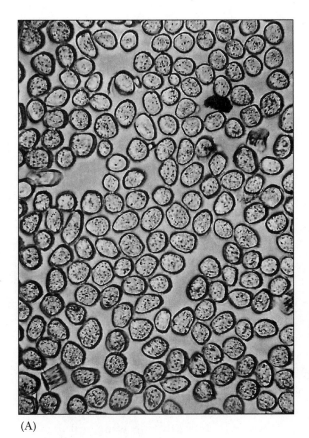

(A)

FIGURE 2–4

Photomicrographs in (A) cross-sectional and (B) longitudinal views of delustered nylon 6,6. (Courtesy of DuPont, Wilmington, DE.)

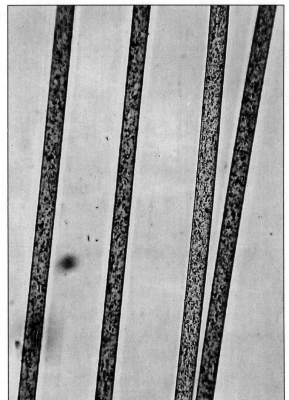

(B)

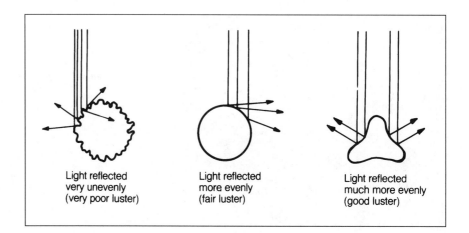

FIGURE 2–5

Light reflecting from the surface of differently shaped cross sections

Light reflected very unevenly (very poor luster)

Light reflected more evenly (fair luster)

Light reflected much more evenly (good luster)

ABRASION RESISTANCE

Abrasion resistance is the ability to withstand the effects of rubbing or friction. It is a significant factor in the durability of a fiber. It is important to realize that the overall durability of a fabric depends on the yarn and fabric structures, the dyeing and/or printing procedures, and the finishes, as well as the fiber. Nylon and aramid fibers have excellent abrasion resistance, while glass and acetate have poor abrasion resistance.

Pilling, the formation of little balls of loose fibers on the surface of a fabric, results from abrasion. Pills form during wear and may be found near pockets, on sleeves, and in the underarm areas of a garment. The tumbling action of laundering and automatic drying may also cause pilling. In general, strong fibers, like nylon and polyester, made into spun yarns exhibit the worst pilling because the broken fibers do not fall off but are held on the surface of the fabric. In contrast, weak fibers, like rayon and cotton, seldom pill.

DIMENSIONAL STABILITY

Dimensional stability is the ability of a fiber to maintain its original shape, neither shrinking nor stretching. Fibers placed under extreme tension during processing may create fabrics that shrink during laundering. This is **relaxation shrinkage** and is usually completed after the first few launderings. Cotton exhibits relaxation shrinkage. **Progressive shrinkage** occurs each time the product is laundered. Viscose rayon and wool shrink progressively. See Chapter 14 for a more complete discussion of shrinkage and shrinkage control.

ELASTIC RECOVERY/ELONGATION

Elastic recovery is the ability of a fiber to return to its original length after being stretched. Elastomeric fibers like spandex can be stretched 100 percent and return to their original lengths. **Elongation** is the lengthening or stretching of a fiber. It refers only to the fact that a fiber can be extended, not that it will return to its original length.

FLEXIBILITY

Fibers that bend or fold easily have good **flexibility**. The flexibility of a fiber contributes greatly to the drape of fabric. **Drape** is the ability of a fabric to hang in graceful folds, either on the body or some other form, such as draperies or curtains hanging from a rod. In general, flexible fibers result in fabrics with better drape. Stiff fibers are hard to spin into yarns and create fabrics with limited consumer appeal. Special-use applications in industrial, commercial, or home textiles may require stiff fibers, however.

RESILIENCY

Resiliency, or **wrinkle recovery**, is the ability of a fiber to return to its original shape following bending or folding. Fibers with good resiliency, like polyester, are often used in apparel when appearance retention is important. **Compressional resiliency**, or **loft**, is the ability of a fiber to return to its original thickness after being crushed.

SPECIFIC GRAVITY

Specific gravity, or density, compares the mass of a fiber to an equal volume of water. The specific gravity of water is 1.0. A specific gravity greater than 1.0 indicates that the fiber is heavier than water; a specific gravity lower than 1.0 indicates that the fiber is lighter than water. Most fibers have a specific gravity between 1.0 and 2.0. Olefin, a very light fiber, has a specific gravity of 0.91 while glass, a heavy fiber, has a specific gravity of 2.54.

TENACITY

Tenacity, or fiber strength, is important to the wear life of a textile product. In general, strong fibers last longer and provide more service than weak fibers. Nylon, aramid, and glass fibers are noted for their strength. Acetate and acrylic are relatively weak in contrast. Manufactured fibers are drawn, or stretched, after extrusion to improve their strength. Manufactured fiber production is discussed more fully in Chapter 5.

Chemical Properties

The chemical properties of a fiber determine how it will react when exposed to the many substances used in production and in cleaning. The chemicals used in production include finishes and dyes. Chemicals used in cleaning include soaps, detergents, and dry cleaning fluids.

ABSORBENCY AND WICKING

The **absorbency** of a fiber, or its ability to take in moisture, is an important component of wearing comfort. **Hydrophilic fibers**, those that can absorb moisture, are more comfortable to wear than **hydrophobic fibers**, which do not absorb moisture readily. Cotton and rayon are hydrophilic, while most synthetics are hydrophobic. Fibers with good absorbency generally accept dyes and finishes more readily. **Hygroscopic fibers** can absorb moisture without feeling wet. Animal hair fibers are hygroscopic.

Wicking is a fiber's ability to carry moisture along its surface. Micro-denier olefin and acrylic fibers have excellent wicking properties.

ELECTRICAL CONDUCTIVITY

Fibers that do not conduct electrical charges create static electricity. Hydrophobic fibers, because of their low absorbency, tend to have low electrical conductivity. Hydrophilic fibers are not likely to build up static electricity unless the atmosphere is very dry. Finishes, **epitropic fibers**, and metallic fibers are used to control static electricity. Epitropic fibers are synthetic fibers that have small particles of carbon embedded in their surface to conduct electricity.

CHEMICAL REACTIVITY

Dyes, pigments, finishes, soaps, detergents, and bleaches are examples of chemical agents used on textiles. Fibers have different reactions to these chemicals. For example, alkalis will destroy wool but improve the strength and luster of cotton.

EFFECT OF HEAT

Fibers also react differently to heat. Most synthetic fibers are **thermoplastic**, which means they melt or soften when exposed to heat. **Heat setting**, or applying heat and pressure in a controlled manner, permanently changes the shape and improves the dimensional stability of thermoplastic fibers. Fabrics made from thermoplastic fibers can be heat set to create permanent pleats and creases. Heat-set fibers, yarns, and fabrics are stable at lower temperatures than those at which they were set, but they may be damaged by higher temperatures. Although natural fibers are not thermoplastic, they can also be damaged by exposure to excessive heat. Cotton may scorch, and wool becomes brittle.

FLAMMABILITY

Flammability characteristics are important in determining the end-use suitability. The Flammable Fabrics Act of 1953 and its subsequent amendments require that certain flammability standards be met. The burning of small samples of fibers can also be used as a general guide in categorizing fibers. Burning wool fibers tend to smell like burnt hair and burning cotton fibers tend to smell like burning paper.

LABORATORY ASSIGNMENTS

ASSIGNMENT 2–1   **IDENTIFY NATURAL AND MANUFACTURED FIBERS**

Using purchased or teacher-provided samples, list each as a natural fiber or a manufactured fiber in the following table.

NATURAL FIBERS	MANUFACTURED FIBERS

ASSIGNMENT 2–2   **EVALUATE THE COLORS OF NATURAL AND MANUFACTURED FIBERS**

Using the fiber samples from Assignment 2–1, evaluate the color of each sample in the following table.

SAMPLE	COLOR
Cotton	
Linen	
Silk	
Wool	
Mohair	
Rayon	
Acetate	
Nylon	
Polyester	
Acrylic	
Modacrylic	
Olefin	
Elastomeric	

What generalizations can be drawn about the colors of natural versus manufactured fabrics?

ASSIGNMENT 2–3   **IDENTIFY FILAMENT AND STAPLE FIBERS**

1. Define the terms *filament* and *staple*.
2. Using the fiber samples from Assignment 2–1, determine which are filament and which are staple and enter them in the following table.

FILAMENT	STAPLE

ASSIGNMENT 2–4   **DETERMINE CRIMP IN FIBERS**

1. Define the term *crimp*.
2. Using a linen tester, determine which natural and which manufactured fibers in Assignment 2–1 have crimp and list them in the following table. Use of the linen tester is described in the Appendix.

NATURAL FIBERS WITH CRIMP	MANUFACTURED FIBERS WITH CRIMP

3. Draw a simple diagram of a crimped fiber.

ASSIGNMENT 2–5   **EVALUATE FIBER LUSTER**

1. Define the term *luster*.
2. Evaluate the luster of each fiber sample from Assignment 2–1 and indicate whether the sample has low, medium, or high luster in the following table.

SAMPLE	LOW	MEDIUM	HIGH
Cotton			
Linen			
Silk			
Wool			
Mohair			
Rayon			
Acetate			
Nylon			
Polyester			
Acrylic			
Modacrylic			
Olefin			
Elastomeric			

3. Name the chemical that is added during the production of manu-factured fibers to decrease luster.
4. Draw the cross section of a chemically delustered fiber.

ASSIGNMENT 2–6   **INVESTIGATE THE CREASE RECOVERY OF SELECTED FIBERS**

1. Define the term *resiliency*.
2. Perform the following crease recovery experiment.
   a. Gather the following materials:
      one sample (2″ × 2″) of each of the following greige fabrics:
        cotton, polyester, and acrylic
      one 1-pound weight
   b. Fold each sample in half lengthwise, and then fold it in half again crosswise.
   c. Place the samples under the weight for 5 minutes.
   d. Remove the weight and observe the creasing.
   e. Record your observations.
   f. Allow the samples to rest (or recover) with their creased sides up for 5 minutes.
   g. Observe the samples' recovery from creasing and record your observations in the following tables.

FIBER	AMOUNT OF CREASING UPON WEIGHT REMOVAL PRONOUNCED	MODERATE	MINIMAL
Polyester			
Acrylic			
Cotton			

	AMOUNT OF CREASING AFTER 5 MINUTES		
FIBER	PRONOUNCED	MODERATE	MINIMAL
Polyester			
Acrylic			
Cotton			

3. What generalizations can you make about the crease recovery of fabrics made from synthetic fibers? Natural fibers?

ASSIGNMENT 2–7   **EVALUATE THE WRINKLE RECOVERY OF SELECTED FIBERS**

1. Perform the following experiment.
   a. Gather the following materials:
      two 5″ squares of greige cotton
      two 5″ squares of greige polyester
   b. Hold one square of cotton inside your tightly closed fist for 1 minute.
   c. Place the wrinkled fabric on a flat surface, but do not smooth it.
   d. Compare it to the untreated cotton sample.
   e. Allow the wrinkled fabric to relax for 10 minutes and compare it to the untreated sample.
   f. Repeat steps b through e with the polyester samples.
   g. Use your observations to answer the following questions:
      Which fabric was more wrinkled immediately after wrinkling?
      Which fabric had better recovery after 10 minutes?
      Which fabric is more resilient?

ASSIGNMENT 2–8   **COMPARE THE SPECIFIC GRAVITIES OF SELECTED FIBERS**

1. Define the term *specific gravity*.
2. What is the specific gravity of water?
3. Perform the following experiment.
   a. Gather the following materials:
      1″ square sample of greige olefin fabric
      1″ square sample of greige glass fabric
      250 ml beakers or 8-oz glasses

detergent

water

spoon or pick

    b. Fill the beaker or glass ¾ full with water.

    c. Add 1 or 2 drops of detergent.

    d. Put both samples in water, stir gently, and observe

4. Use your observations to answer the following questions:

    Which fabric sank?

    Which fabric floated?

    Which fiber has the higher specific gravity?

ASSIGNMENT 2–9

DETERMINE THE RELATIVE STRENGTHS OF SELECTED FIBERS

1. Perform the following experiment to compare the strengths of regular tenacity filament rayon, filament nylon, and filament glass fibers.

    a. Cut one 6″ sample of each fiber. Make sure the samples have about the same number of fibers and are about the same size.

    b. Tightly grasp the ends of one sample and pull until the sample breaks or until it becomes evident it will not break.

    c. Repeat for each sample.

    d. Describe the relative strength of each sample using these phrases in the following table: resists breaking, moderately resistant to breaking, or breaks readily.

FIBER	RELATIVE STRENGTH
Filament rayon (regular tenacity)	
Filament nylon	
Filament glass	

ASSIGNMENT 2–10

DETERMINE ABSORBENCY OF SELECTED FIBERS

1. Define the term *absorbency*.

2. Define the term *wicking*.

3. Perform the following experiment.

a. Gather the following materials:
   one 8″ square of greige rayon
   one 8″ square of greige nylon
   one 6″ embroidery hoop
   eyedropper
   stopwatch
b. Mount the rayon sample in the embroidery hoop. Be sure to smooth all wrinkles.
c. Holding the eyedropper 1″ above the sample, allow one drop of water to fall on the sample.
d. Start the stopwatch and record in the following table the time required for the water to be absorbed (the point when the drop can no longer be seen on the surface of the sample).
e. Repeat step c in two additional places on the sample.
f. Repeat steps b through e with the nylon sample.

FIBER	ABSORBENCY TEST WETTING TIMES			
	1ST TEST	2ND TEST	3RD TEST	4TH TEST
Rayon				
Nylon				

4. Which sample indicated poor absorbency?
5. Which sample indicated good absorbency?
6. Did you observe any wicking? If so, which sample?

ASSIGNMENT 2–11   EXAMINE THE EFFECT OF HEAT ON SELECTED FIBERS

1. Gather the following materials:
   one 1½″ × 3″ sample of each of the following greige fabrics:
      cotton, rayon, wool, and nylon
   hand iron (dry, no steam)
   ironing board, sleeve board, or padded surface
   aluminum foil
2. Set the iron at the lowest temperature and preheat for 5 minutes.
3. Fold a sheet of aluminum foil in half, placing the fabric samples inside. The samples should not touch, but they should be close enough for the iron to cover all samples at once.

4. Press the samples for 1 minute.
5. Observe the results.
6. Increase the temperature to the next temperature setting and pre-heat for 5 minutes.
7. Repeat steps 3 and 4.
8. Continue increasing the temperature of the iron until each sample is visibly affected.
9. In the following table, record the temperature at which the fabric was affected and describe what happened to each fabric.

FIBER	TEMPERATURE	EFFECT OF HEAT
Cotton		
Rayon		
Wool		
Nylon		

ASSIGNMENT 2-12　　**EVALUATE THE THERMOPLASTICITY OF SELECTED FIBERS**

1. Define the term *thermoplasticity*.
2. Perform the following experiment.
   a. Gather the following materials:
      one 4″ square of each of the following greige fabrics: cotton, wool, polyester, and nylon
      hand iron (dry, no steam)
      ironing board, sleeve board, or padded surface
      aluminum foil
      warm water
      detergent
      paper towel
   b. Fold each sample in half and place it inside a folded sheet of aluminum foil.
   c. Iron each fabric for 30 seconds using a temperature that is slightly higher than the safe ironing temperature indicated for the fabric on the iron.
   d. Wash each sample in warm, soapy water for 30 seconds.
   e. Rinse in clear, warm water.

f. Place the fabric samples flat on the paper towel and allow to dry. Do not squeeze or pat the samples.

g. Evaluate the degree to which the fabrics held the ironed crease and indicate with a check mark which fibers are thermoplastic. The fibers that held the creases are thermoplastic.

FIBER	THERMOPLASTIC	NOT THERMOPLASTIC
Cotton		
Wool		
Polyester		
Nylon		

Because the following seven assignments involve lighted candles or chemicals, proper laboratory safety procedures must be followed. You *must:*

Wear safety goggles.

Tie back long hair.

Wear old clothes, a lab coat, or an apron.

Keep your work area neat and free of clutter.

Work carefully and slowly.

Do not leave your experiment unattended.

The Safety Rules outlined in the Instructor's Guide that accompanies this book should be reviewed for a more complete discussion of appropriate safety procedures.

ASSIGNMENT 2–13   **DETERMINE THE EFFECT OF A WEAK ORGANIC ACID AT ROOM TEMPERATURE ON SELECTED FIBERS**

1. Gather the following materials:

1″ squares of the following greige fabrics: cotton, polyester, rayon, wool, and silk

vinegar

pick (use of the pick is described in the Appendix)

five watch glasses

2. Place each specimen in a watch glass and cover with full-strength vinegar. Use the pick to submerge the samples.

3. Observe immediately, and again after 5 minutes, 10 minutes, and 15 minutes. Record changes after each observation.
4. After 20 minutes remove the specimens from the vinegar and rinse them thoroughly.
5. Pull on each specimen to see if it has weakened.
6. Examine the specimens for any effect from the acid. Strength? Color? Hand? Record your observations in the following table.

FIBER	IMMEDIATE EFFECT	AFTER 5 MIN.	10 MIN.	15 MIN.	20 MIN.
Cotton					
Polyester					
Rayon					
Wool					
Silk					

ASSIGNMENT 2–14   **EVALUATE THE EFFECT OF ALKALIS AT ROOM TEMPERATURE ON SELECTED FIBERS**

1. Perform the following experiment.
   a. Gather the following materials:
      1″ squares of the following greige fabrics:
         cotton, polyester, rayon, wool, and silk
      sodium hydroxide or potassium hydroxide 5% solution
      pick
      five watch glasses
   b. Place each test specimen in a watch glass.
   c. Cover with sodium hydroxide or potassium hydroxide solution. Use the pick to submerge the samples.
   d. Observe immediately, and again after 5 minutes, 10 minutes, and 15 minutes.
   e. Record changes after each observation in the following table.
   f. After 20 minutes, remove the specimens from the alkali and rinse them thoroughly.
   g. Pull on each specimen to see if it has weakened.

h. Examine the specimens for any effect from the alkali. Strength? Color? Hand?

i. Record your observations in the following table.

FIBER	IMMEDIATE EFFECT	AFTER			
		5 MIN.	10 MIN.	15 MIN.	20 MIN.
Cotton					
Polyester					
Rayon					
Wool					
Silk					

ASSIGNMENT 2–15 **DETERMINE THE EFFECT OF HOT ALKALI ON SELECTED FIBERS**

1. Perform the following experiment.
   a. Gather the following materials:
      $4'' \times 4''$ samples of the following greige fabrics:
         wool, silk, and cotton
      hot plate
      three enamel pots
      sodium hydroxide or potassium hydroxide, 5% solution
      tongs
   b. Place each specimen in an enamel pot.
   c. Cover the specimen with sodium hydroxide or potassium hydroxide.
   d. Bring the solutions to a boil.
   e. Observe each specimen as soon as the solution boils.
   f. Note any change in the specimens and record your observations in the following table.
   g. Continue boiling the solution for 5 minutes. Observe and record the results in the following table.
   h. If specimen does not dissolve, remove it from the solution with tongs and rinse it thoroughly. *Be careful not to spill any solution on your hands or clothing. Rinse hands and/or clothing immediately if any spills should occur.*

    i. Pull on the specimen to see if it has weakened.

    j. Examine the specimens for any effect from the alkali. Stretch? Color? Hand?

    k. Record your observations in the following table.

FIBER	UPON BOILING	AFTER 5 MIN.
Cotton		
Wool		
Silk		

2. Heavy-duty laundry detergents contain alkaline substances to improve their cleaning effectiveness. What effect would these substances have on:

Wool?

Cotton?

Silk?

ASSIGNMENT 2–16   **ESTABLISH THE EFFECT OF CHLORINE BLEACH AT ROOM TEMPERATURE ON SELECTED FIBERS**

1. Perform the following experiment.

    a. Gather the following materials:

        2″ squares of the following greige fabrics:

            cotton, polyester, rayon, wool, silk, and nylon

        commercial liquid chlorine bleach

        pick

        water

        six 250 ml beakers or 8-oz glasses

    b. In each of the six beakers, dilute 25 ml of bleach with 125 ml of water.

    c. Place each test specimen in a beaker.

    d. Label each beaker with the fabric it contains.

    e. Cover each sample with bleach solution. Use the pick to submerge the samples.

f. Observe immediately, and again after 5 minutes, 10 minutes, and 15 minutes.

g. Record changes after each observation in the following table.

h. After 20 minutes, remove the specimens from the bleach solutions and rinse them thoroughly.

i. Pull on each specimen to see if it has weakened.

j. Examine the specimens for any effect from the bleach. Strength? Color? Hand?

k. Record your observations in the following table.

FIBER	IMMEDIATE EFFECT	AFTER 5 MIN.	10 MIN.	15 MIN.	20 MIN.
Cotton					
Polyester					
Rayon					
Wool					
Silk					
Nylon					

ASSIGNMENT 2–17

EVALUATE THE EFFECT OF WARM CHLORINE BLEACH ON SELECTED FIBERS

1. Perform the following experiment.
    a. Gather the following materials:
        4″ × 4″ samples of the following greige fabrics:
            cotton, polyester, rayon, wool, silk, and nylon
        hot plate
        enamel pot
        commercial liquid chlorine bleach
        water
        tongs
    b. Label each sample with a ballpoint pen (e.g., *c* for cotton).
    c. Prepare a solution of 50 ml of commercial liquid bleach in 250 ml of water.

d. Place each specimen in the enamel pot.

e. Cover each sample with the bleach solution.

f. Place the pot over heat, and heat to warm. Maintain the heat for 20 minutes.

g. After 20 minutes, remove the specimens from the bleach. Rinse the samples well and dry.

h. Examine the specimens for any effect from the bleach. Strength? Color? Hand?

i. Record your observations in the following table.

FIBER	COLOR	STRENGTH	OTHER SIGNS OF DAMAGE
Cotton			
Polyester			
Rayon			
Wool			
Silk			
Nylon			

2. Wool and silk should not be exposed to chlorine bleach. Why?

ASSIGNMENT 2–18   **DETERMINE THE EFFECTS OF ACETONE ON SELECTED FIBERS**

1. Perform the following experiment.

a. Gather the following materials:
   1″ samples of the following greige fabrics: cotton and acetate
   two watch glasses
   pick
   acetone (nail polish remover)

b. Place each sample in a watch glass.

c. Cover with acetone. Use the pick to submerge the samples.

d. Observe immediately and record any changes in the following table.

e. Observe after 5 minutes. Record any changes in the following table.

f. If the samples have not dissolved, rinse them thoroughly.

g. Pull on the fabrics to see if they weakened.

h. Examine the specimens for any effect from the bleach. Strength? Color? Hand?

i. Record your observations in the following table.

FIBER	IMMEDIATE	AFTER 5 MIN.
Cotton		
Acetate		

ASSIGNMENT 2–19   **DISCOVER THE BURNING CHARACTERISTICS OF SELECTED FIBERS**

1. Perform the following experiment.

a. Gather the following materials:
   3″ × 1″ samples of the following greige fabrics: nylon, cotton, acrylic, glass, wool, rayon, and polyester
   matches
   candle
   aluminum pie plate
   protected counter surface

b. Light a candle and affix it to a pie plate with a little melted wax.

c. Move a fabric sample close to, but not into, the flame.

d. Record the appearance of the fabric in the following table. Does it melt? Shrink from the flame? Does it show no change?

e. Move the fabric into the flame and record what happens. Does the fabric burn? Melt? Show no change?

f. Remove the fabric from the flame very carefully and slowly.

g. Record whether the yarns continue to burn outside the flame. Be sure the yarns were ignited before determining this.

h. If the fabric is still burning, blow out the flame. Smell the smoke. Record the odor.

i. Record the appearance of the residue in the following table.

FIBER	NEAR THE FLAME	IN THE FLAME	OUT OF THE FLAME	ODOR OF SMOKE	RESIDUE
Cotton					
Rayon					
Wool					
Nylon					
Acrylic					
Polyester					
Glass					

Natural Protein Fibers

OBJECTIVES

The student will be able to:

1. Recognize and classify protein fibers
2. Discuss the properties common to protein fibers
3. Differentiate between silk, wool, specialty hair fibers, and fur fibers
4. Recommend appropriate end uses for silk, wool, specialty hair fibers, and fur fibers
5. List care procedures for silk, wool, specialty hair fibers, and fur fibers
6. Appreciate the importance of protein fibers in the marketplace

Textile Industry Terminology

Bombyx mori—Cultivated silkworm

Carbonization—Using sulfuric acid to destroy cellulosic materials such as leaves and twigs that may be on fleece

Duoppioni silk—Silk produced when two silkworms spin a cocoon together. The resulting strand of silk has a thick/thin appearance

Filature—Factory where silk is reeled

Fulling—Controlled shrinkage of wool to produce a more compact fabric

Garnetting—Mechanically shredding wool yarns or fabric to a fibrous state; resulting fiber is weakened and of lower quality

Lamb's wool—First shearing from a sheep less than 7 months old; wool is fine and soft

Melton—A compact wool fabric with the appearance of felt

Momme—Unit of weight for silk fabrics; also spelled "mommie." Higher momme numbers indicate heavier fabrics

New wool or **virgin wool**—Previously used wool

Pure silk or **degummed silk**—Silk after the sericin has been removed. Degumming reduces the weight of silk 20 to 30 percent

Raw silk or **silk-in-the-gum**—Silk before the sericin is removed

Recycled wool—Wool yarns and fabrics that have been shredded to a fibrous state and reused

Scroop—The rustle of silk as it rubs against itself

Sericulture—The scientific production of silk

Shattered silk—Weighted silk that is disintegrating

Silk noil or **waste silk**—Short fibers from broken cocoons and the outside fibers of the cocoon. Silk noil is of lower quality and is less lustrous than filament silk. It is used to make spun silk

Spun silk—Silk yarn made from short fibers. Spun silk feels more like cotton than filament silk. *See* **silk noil**

Thrown silk—Reeled silk filament from four or more cocoons that are combined to make yarn

Tussah silk—A variety of wild silk that is coarser and less lustrous than the silk produced by cultivated silkworms

Weighted silk—Metallic salts may be added to improve the body and drape of degummed silk. Weighted silks deteriorate more quickly than unweighted silks

Introduction

The predominant protein fibers are silk, wool, and specialty hair fibers and fur fibers. Silk, the product of the silkworm, contains the protein fibroin. Wool, specialty hair fibers, and fur fibers contain keratin, the same protein found in human hair. Most specialty hair fibers come from camels and goats. Fur fibers come from rabbits and other fur-bearing animals. Because these fibers have similar chemical structures, they have some common characteristics:

- lower specific gravity than cellulosics (cotton, flax, ramie)
- good resiliency
- good absorbency
- damaged by alkalis and chlorine bleach
- damaged by dry heat
- burn slowly and self-extinguish when the flame is removed

Silk

Silk is the only natural fiber that occurs in filament form. The silkworm is actually a caterpillar. It spins a cocoon to protect itself while it changes from a worm to a moth. Each silkworm spins, or extrudes, two silk strands that are held together by **sericin**, a gummy protein substance. Around 2600 B.C. the Chinese discovered that unwinding the cocoon would produce a fiber

Because the cost of production is high, silk is produced in countries where the cost of labor is low. China is the major producer and exporter of silk fiber. Other fiber producers are Thailand, India, and Japan. Italy, France, and England are important producers of finished silk fabrics. The United States produces no silk and must import all that it consumes.

PRODUCTION OF CULTIVATED AND WILD SILKS

The finest quality silk, **cultivated silk**, is produced by cultivated silkworms in a controlled environment. See Table 3–1 for basic steps in the production process. Figures 3–1A and B show the silkworm in production.

Long silk fibers are higher quality and more costly than short fibers. To obtain the longest silk fiber possible, the pupa, which is the moth developing inside the cocoon, is exposed to dry heat, which kills it. If the moth were permitted to break through its cocoon, the silk fibers would be shorter and less valuable. At this stage select silkworms are allowed to escape the pupae to provide eggs for the next crop of

TABLE 3–1   BASIC STEPS IN SILK PRODUCTION

1. The silk moth lays 400 to 600 eggs.

2. The eggs hatch into caterpillars.

3. Each caterpillar spins a cocoon.

4. The developing pupa is subjected to dry heat, which kills it. Wild silk moths and cultivated moths to be used as breeding stock are allowed to break through their cocoons naturally.

5. The cycle begins again.

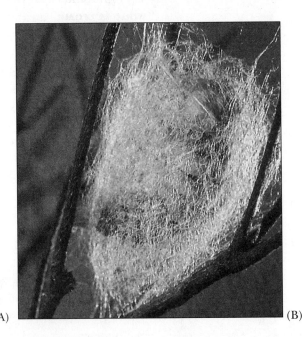

(A)   (B)

FIGURE 3–1

Stages in silk production: (A) Silkworm on a bed of mulberry leaves and (B) Silkworm beginning to spin its cocoon. (Courtesy of the International Silk Association.)

worms. The unbroken cocoons are softened in hot water so their silk can be unwound in one long strand or filament in a process called **reeling**. A silk filament may range from 300 to 1000 yards long. Short silk fibers from the broken cocoons and the outside fibers of the cocoon are used for spun silk yarns, which feel like cotton yarns.

Wild silkworms produce **wild silk**, which is coarser and less lustrous than the silk produced by cultivated silkworms. Wild silk must be spun into staple yarns, because the caterpillars break through their cocoons and shorten the silk fibers. **Tussah silk** is a common variety of wild silk.

SELECTED PROPERTIES OF SILK

Silk, whether wild or cultivated, has certain physical, mechanical, and chemical properties that make it a unique fiber.

PHYSICAL PROPERTIES OF SILK. Silk is the thinnest natural fiber. A triangular cross section gives silk fiber its traditional luster. Cultivated silk is more lustrous than wild varieties like tussah silk and comes in off-white to cream. Cultivated silk can be bleached white, unlike wild silk. Wild silk is normally brown, but it may be yellow, orange, or green.

The surface contour of silk is smooth and rodlike with some striations. Wild silk is more irregular and coarser than cultivated silk. As a result, fabrics made of wild silk have greater stiffness and texture than fabrics made of cultivated silk.

MECHANICAL PROPERTIES OF SILK. Although silk is one of the strongest natural fibers, it loses up to 20 percent of its strength when wet. Silk has only moderate abrasion resistance and abrades easily, but it is lightweight and has good dimensional stability. Because silk is only moderately resilient, it tends to wrinkle more than other protein fibers.

CHEMICAL PROPERTIES OF SILK. Because silk has good absorbency, it is comfortable to wear and fairly easy to dye; it also wicks well. Silk is a poor conductor of heat, so heavy fabrics are warm, though sheer fabrics are cool. Silk turns yellow and degrades when exposed to alkaline detergents and chlorine bleach, and it is damaged by perspiration and by some chemicals in antiperspirants. When exposed to an open flame silk burns, but it self-extinguishes when the flame is removed.

END USES OF SILK

Silk is a luxury fiber known for its beautiful drape, hand, and luster. It is costly because it is labor intensive to produce. Silk's primary end uses are in the apparel and home furnishings markets. In apparel, silk is the fiber of choice for expensive dresses, blouses, lingerie, scarves, and men's ties. Silk long underwear and socks are gaining popularity due to the fiber's absorbency and wicking.

In the home, silk and silk blends are used for luxury upholstery fabrics and draperies. Other uses include wall hangings and wall coverings. Overall, however, silk's performance as a home furnishings fiber is poor. It has poor abrasion resistance and is damaged by sunlight.

CARE OF SILK

The high cost of silk demands careful attention to care instructions. Dyes, finishes, yarn formation, and garment construction impact care procedures. Frequently dyes or finishes require that silk be dry cleaned. Although dry cleaning is usually recommended, silk fiber is washable.

Washable silks must be washed gently in mild detergents. Chlorine bleach yellows silk, but nonchlorine bleaches can be used. Silk may water spot, that is, discolor from contact with water droplets. Silks stiffened by the return of some of the sericin are more likely to water spot. Silk garments should be ironed with a dry iron and pressing cloth and kept out of sunlight and away from perspiration to avoid damage. Insects, especially carpet beetles, attack silk. Clean silk products before storage and protect historical pieces from light and air.

TRADE NAMES OF SILK

Silk is a natural fiber and has no trade names.

Wool

The history of humankind is intertwined with the history of wool. During the Stone Age, animal hides were used for warmth. Early civi-

FIGURE 3–2

Merino sheep. (Courtesy of The Wool Bureau, Inc.)

lizations made felt from the wool of sheep, llamas, and alpacas. Wool dominated textiles until the Industrial Revolution, when cotton became the more important fiber.

Approximately 200 breeds of sheep produce wool fiber. Merino sheep produce the finest and most valuable wool (see Figure 3–2). Rombouillet and Debouilet breeds also yield high-quality wool fiber. Australia dominates worldwide wool production at 32 percent. Eastern Europe and New Zealand are other major wool producers.

PRODUCTION OF WOOL

In the first step of wool production, shearers use power shears to remove fleece from live sheep in the spring. A Merino ewe may produce 15 pounds of fleece; a Merino ram may produce 20 pounds. Wool is also removed from sheep slaughtered for meat. This wool, which is treated chemically to aid in its removal, is called **pulled wool** and is generally considered to be of lower quality than wool from live animals. Researchers are experimenting with a growth hormone which allows wool to be pulled from live sheep.

After removal the fleece is graded and sorted. Grading classifies the wool according to the length and fineness of the fiber. Sorting separates the fleece into sections of different qualities. The highest-quality wool comes from the sides, shoulders, and back of the sheep. The poorest quality comes from the lower legs. Fleece at this stage (whether pulled or sheared) is called **raw wool** or **grease wool**.

The raw wool is cleaned or scoured in a warm alkaline solution to remove oil, dirt, leaves, and twigs. The oil, or **lanolin**, is a valuable natural by-product of this process. It is recovered for use in soaps, cosmetics, and creams.

SELECTED PROPERTIES OF WOOL

Wool has characteristic physical, mechanical, and chemical properties.

PHYSICAL PROPERTIES OF WOOL.

The color of wool ranges from white to cream, beige, tan, and black. Peroxide bleach may be used to whiten wool.

The fiber length of wool generally varies from 1 inch to 15 inches. The fiber has three parts: the medulla, the cortex, and the cuticle (see Figure 3–3). The cortex is the main part of the fiber, and the medulla is the core. Some finer wools may not have medullas. The cuticle or epidermis is the outer layer. It is composed of overlapping scales (see Figure 3–4). This overlapping scale structure contributes to wool's felting ability. Felt is discussed more fully in Chapter 12.

The natural crimp of wool fiber is a very favorable property. It contributes to the resilience and elasticity of the fiber and makes spinning the fiber into yarn easier. It also contributes to the bulk and warmth of the spun yarn. Crimped yarns trap air, which warms and acts as an insulator.

The luster of wool varies with the breed of sheep, the section of the fleece, and the environmental conditions under which the sheep was raised. In general, wool has low luster.

MECHANICAL PROPERTIES OF WOOL.

In general, wool fibers have moderate abrasion resistance but low strength. Moisture decreases the strength of wool. The abrasion resistance of wool apparel and home furnishings depends on the structure of the yarn and fabric.

FIGURE 3–3

A cross section of the wool fiber under magnification shows three distinct parts of wool's physical structure: the cuticle or epidermis—the outer layer composed of scales; the cortex—composing 90 percent of the fiber mass; and the medulla—the central, honeycomb-like core containing air spaces (and absent in fine wool). (Courtesy of the American Wool Council, Division of American Sheep Industry Association, Inc.)

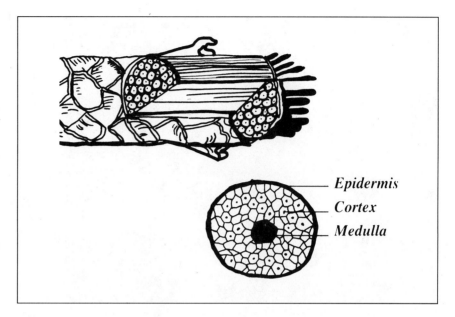

Epidermis
Cortex
Medulla

Close, evenly woven fabrics made with tightly twisted yarns provide the best service. The good elongation, elastic recovery, and flexibility of wool fibers contribute to its durability. Wool carpeting is made with coarser, more resilient fibers to be more durable. However, the scaly structure of the wool fiber causes wool to entangle and form pills.

Wool is known for its excellent resilience. Dry wool resists wrinkling. If wrinkled, it returns to its original shape easily. A damp or wet wool garment wrinkles badly, and the wrinkles must be removed carefully.

Wool has medium density, making it a relatively lightweight fiber. Therefore, less wool is required to make an equally warm garment or blanket of cotton, which is a denser fiber.

The dimensional stability of wool is poor. As a result, dry cleaning is usually recommended for wool products. Wool shrinks progressively and continues to shrink with each washing. The moisture and agitation of laundering cause the fabric to shrink and felt. Because the overlapping scales of the wool fiber prevent the fibers from slipping over one another easily, as the fibers move closer they cannot return to their original positions. Wool can be treated chemically to reduce shrinkage and felting.

(A)

FIGURE 3–4

*Photomicrographs in
(A) cross–sectional and
(B) longitudinal views of wool.
(Courtesy of the American
Wool Council, Division of
American Sheep Industry
Association, Inc.)*

(B)

CHEMICAL PROPERTIES OF WOOL. Wool is generally a very absorbent fiber, but it absorbs moisture slowly because its scaly structure resists moisture. Wool does not wick, again due to its scaly structure. However, wool is hygroscopic and can hold moisture and not feel wet. Because it is absorbent, wool is comfortable to wear and dyes well.

Wool is weakened by alkalis, which are found in "heavy-duty" laundry detergents. Chlorine bleaches also damage wool. Acids, unless highly concentrated, do not damage wool, however.

Dry heat, such as that produced when ironing fabric with a dry iron, causes the wool to become brittle and weak. Although the electrical conductivity of wool is low, the fiber does not normally generate static electricity because it absorbs moisture readily. In dry climates, or in centrally heated homes, wool may build static electrical charges.

Wool is generally considered to be flame resistant. When exposed to an open flame, it burns slowly and self-extinguishes when the flame is removed.

END USES OF WOOL

Although synthetic fibers, which are inexpensive and easy to care for, have commanded much of the market for wool, wool remains the premier fiber for both men's and women's tailored suits. Wool suits maintain their shape, drape well, and are durable. Blends of wool and synthetic fibers provide the benefits of both fibers.

The wool fiber is ideal for use in sweaters and other cold-weather garments. The natural crimp of wool allows the fiber to be spun into bulky yarns which trap air and provide insulation. Wool also has applications in home furnishings. It can be used in carpeting, upholstery fabrics, blankets, and sometimes draperies.

There are also several disadvantages to using wool in apparel and home furnishings, including:

1. poor dimensional stability and felting;
2. susceptibility to moths and carpet beetles; and
3. allergic reactions in people with sensitive skin.

These advantages can be overcome with special finishes or chemical treatments.

CARE OF WOOL

Because wool has a natural tendency to shrink and felt and is susceptible to insect damage, it requires special care. Care recommendations include:

1. Dry cleaning is suggested for wool fabrics unless they have been treated to allow washing.
2. If washing wool, lukewarm water; mild, nonalkaine detergent; and gentle agitation are suggested. Chlorine bleach should not be used because it yellows wool.
3. Garments should be air dried flat. Automatic drying encourages shrinkage and felting.
4. A press cloth and steam iron are recommended for pressing.
5. Wool should be protected from attack by insects such as moths and carpet beetles. All wool articles should be cleaned before storage. Special finishes provide mothproofing. A dry cleaner can apply some of these finishes. Due to their toxicity, mothballs should be used very carefully.

TRADE NAMES OF WOOL

Wool is a natural fiber and has no trade names. The Wool Bureau is a trade organization that produces educational materials and publicizes the fiber. Woolmark® and Woolblend® symbols are logos the Wool Bureau developed to promote wool use. Woolmark® indicates that the product is 100 percent wool; Woolblend® indicates that the product is at least 60 percent wool. (See Figure 3–5.)

FIGURE 3–5

(A) Woolmark® and
(B) Woolblend® symbols.
(Courtesy of The Wool
Bureau, Inc.)

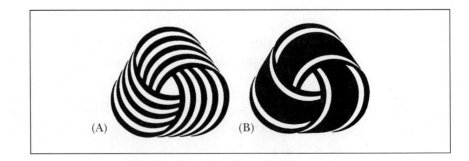

(A)   (B)

Specialty Hair Fibers

Specialty hair fibers are synonymous with luxury and high-status apparel because their beauty and cost limit their use to expensive garments. Specialty hair fibers are frequently blended with other fibers to reduce cost. The Mohair Council of America promotes mohair use (see Figure 3–6). Table 3–2 summarizes the major specialty hair fibers.

Most specialty hair fibers come from animals in the goat or camel families (see Figure 3–7).

FIGURE 3–6

Logo for the Mohair Council of America. (Courtesy of the Mohair Council of America.)

FIGURE 3–7

Angora goats. (Courtesy of the Mohair Council of America.)

TABLE 3-2 SUMMARY OF THE MAJOR SPECIALTY HAIR FIBERS

Specialty Hair Fiber	Source	Characteristics
Alpaca	Alpaca (South American branch of the camel family)	Noted for its luster, fineness, softness, and durability
Cashmere	Kashmir goat (Kashmir, China, Tibet, Mongolia)	Extremely fine fiber, drapes well, outstanding softness
Camel hair	Two-humped Bactrian camel (Central Asia)	Weak fiber, usually used in its natural tan color
Guanaco	Guanaco (South America)	Similar to alpaca
Llama	Llama (Andes Mountains)	Similar to alpaca
Huarizo	Llama sire and alpaca dam	Similar to llama
Misti	Alpaca sire and llama dam	Similar to llama
Mohair	Angora goat (South Africa, United States, Turkey)	Especially good for novelty loop yarns, very good abrasion resistance, slippery, smooth hand
Qiviut	Domesticated musk ox (Alaska)	Provides exceptional warmth
Vicuña	Vicuña (South American camel family)	Weak fiber with smooth hand and high luster; softest, finest, and most expensive textile fiber

The physical, mechanical, and chemical properties of specialty hair fibers are very similar to those of wool, although specialty hair fibers are generally smoother, finer, and longer than wool fibers and their scales are less pronounced. The care of specialty hair fibers is also similar to that of wool. Specialty hair fibers are natural and have no trade names.

Fur Fibers

Fur-bearing animals such as fox, mink, beaver, and rabbit provide fiber that is soft and usually textured. The angora rabbit is raised in France and the United States. It is known for its long, fine, silky fiber, which is lustrous, soft, and durable. **Fur fibers** are natural and have no trade names.

LABORATORY ASSIGNMENTS

ASSIGNMENT 3–1   **LOCATE SILK FIBER AND FABRIC SAMPLES**

Attach a fiber and greige fabric sample of silk in your swatch book. (Your instructor will provide or you will purchase a swatch kit. Your instructor will show you how to mount with glue, staples, or tape.)

ASSIGNMENT 3–2   **LIST THE ADVANTAGES AND DISADVANTAGES OF SILK**

Complete the following chart:

ADVANTAGES	DISADVANTAGES

ASSIGNMENT 3–3   CREATE A COLLAGE OF END USES FOR SILK

Use magazines, catalogs, trade papers, newspapers, and so on, to create a collage of current end uses for silk. Include apparel, home furnishings, and/or any other application of silk.

ASSIGNMENT 3–4   LOCATE WOOL FIBER AND FABRIC SAMPLES

Attach a fiber and greige fabric sample of wool in your swatch book. (Your instructor will provide or you will purchase a swatch kit. Your instructor will show you how to mount with glue, staples, or tape.)

ASSIGNMENT 3–5   LIST THE ADVANTAGES AND DISADVANTAGES OF WOOL

Complete the following chart:

ADVANTAGES	DISADVANTAGES

ASSIGNMENT 3–6 **CREATE A COLLAGE OF END USES FOR WOOL**

Use magazines, catalogs, trade papers, newspapers, and so on, to create a collage of current end uses for wool. Include apparel, home furnishings, and/or any other application of wool.

ASSIGNMENT 3–7 **LOCATE SPECIALTY HAIR FIBERS AND FUR FIBERS AND FABRIC SAMPLES**

Attach a fiber and greige fabric samples of specialty hair fibers and fur fibers in your swatch book. (Your instructor will provide or you will purchase a swatch kit. Your instructor will show you how to mount samples with glue, staples, or tape.)

ASSIGNMENT 3–8 **LIST THE ADVANTAGES AND DISADVANTAGES OF SPECIALTY HAIR AND FUR FIBERS**

Complete the following chart:

ADVANTAGES	DISADVANTAGES

ASSIGNMENT 3–9   **CREATE A COLLAGE OF END USES FOR SPECIALTY HAIR FIBERS AND FUR FIBERS**

Use magazines, catalogs, trade papers, newspapers, and so on, to create a collage of current end uses for specialty hair fibers and fur fibers. Include apparel, home furnishings, and/or any application of specialty hair fibers.

Natural Cellulosic Fibers

OBJECTIVES

The student will be able to:

1. Recognize and classify natural cellulosic fibers
2. Discuss common properties of natural cellulosic fibers
3. Differentiate between cotton, flax, ramie, and minor cellulosic fibers
4. Recommend appropriate end uses for cotton, flax, ramie, and minor natural cellulosic fibers
5. List care procedures for cotton, flax, ramie, and minor natural cellulosic fibers
6. Appreciate the importance of natural cellulosic fibers in the marketplace

Textile Industry Terminology

Byssinosis—Serious lung disease caused by constantly inhaling cotton fibers, commonly known as "brown lung"

Fox Fibre®—Naturally colored cotton fiber grown organically by Natural Cotton Colors, Inc.

Intermediate-staple cotton—Fiber that is $^{13}/_{16}''$ to $1\frac{1}{4}''$ long. Upland is an intermediate-length cotton fiber

Long-staple cotton—Fiber that is $1\frac{1}{2}''$ to $2\frac{1}{2}''$ long. Sea Island Egyptian and Pima or American Egyptian are long-staple cotton fibers

Short-staple cotton—Fiber that is $^{3}/_{8}''$ to $^{3}/_{4}''$ long

Transgenic cotton—Cotton genetically engineered to repel insects

Introduction

Cellulosic fibers are sometimes called "vegetable fibers" because they come from plants. All plants are fibrous, but only a few produce fiber appropriate for textile use. Natural cellulosic fibers are classified according to the plant part from which they come: the seed, stem, or leaf. Cotton is the most important seed fiber. Flax and ramie are important stem fibers. Stem fibers are also known as bast fibers.

Common properties of natural cellulosic fibers are:

- good absorbency
- poor resilience
- good conductor of electricity
- flammable
- damaged by strong mineral acids but not alkalis
- attacked by mildew
- may be damaged by silverfish, especially if starched heavily

Cotton

Cotton is the most widely used fiber. Almost one-half of total world fiber demand is for cotton. As is the case with most fibers, fashion trends affect demand. When styles change, demand changes. When natural fibers are in style, the demand for cotton increases.

Most authorities agree that cotton was first cultivated in the area of India and Pakistan, probably before 3000 B.C. Current major producers of cotton are China and the United States. The warm climate of the southern United States is ideal for cultivating cotton.

PRODUCTION OF COTTON

Cotton is planted in the spring. About 6 months later the cotton boll is ready to be picked (see Figure 4–1). In the United States most cotton production is mechanized. In other parts of the world much of the labor is done by hand.

After picking, the cotton is ginned to remove seeds. Short cotton **linters**, pieces of waste cotton lint, are attached to the seeds. Linters are too short to be spun into yarn but are used to make rayon and acetate. Cottonseeds are used to make cottonseed oil and fertilizer.

The quality of cotton is determined by the cotton fiber's spinnability. A fiber's spinnability depends on fiber length, diameter, and crimp. Longer, thinner fibers with greater crimp are easier to spin. The highest-grade cotton species are **American Egyptian** and **Sea Island**. **Pima cotton** is a variety of American Egyptian cotton.

SELECTED PROPERTIES OF COTTON

Cotton has certain physical, mechanical, and chemical properties that make it one of the most widely used fibers.

FIGURE 4–1

Cotton boll. (Courtesy of the National Cotton Council of America.)

PHYSICAL PROPERTIES OF COTTON. The cotton fiber is characterized by convulsions or natural twists. Under a microscope cotton resembles twisted ribbon. The cross section of the fiber shows a central canal known as a **lumen** (see Figure 4–2).

Cotton fiber is usually creamy white or yellowish. It ranges from ½″ to 2½″ long. The higher-quality cotton fibers are 1⅛″ long or longer and are called "long-staple fibers" or "extra-long staple." American Egyptian and Sea Island cottons are long-staple fibers.

The luster of cotton is relatively low, but the fiber can be treated to increase its luster as well as its strength. This treatment, called mercerization, is discussed under the mechanical properties of cotton (see following).

MECHANICAL PROPERTIES OF COTTON. In general, cotton is a moderately strong fiber with moderate abrasion resistance. Although it is not as strong as flax, it is stronger than rayon. The strength of cotton increases 10 to 20 percent when the fiber is wet. As just mentioned, cotton

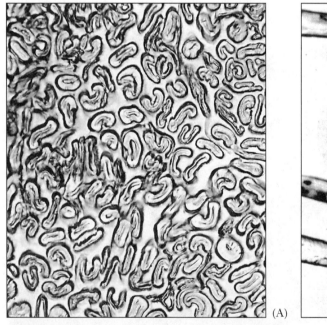 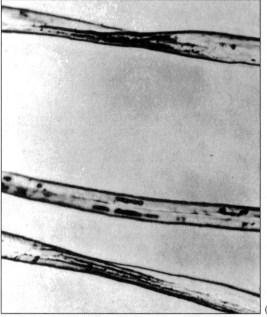

(A)   (B)

FIGURE 4–2

Photomicrographs in (A) cross–sectional and (B) longitudinal views of cotton. (Courtesy of DuPont, Wilmington, DE.)

can be mercerized to improve its luster and strength. During **mercerization** the cotton yarn or fabric is treated with controlled solutions of sodium hydroxide. A resin-finish, in contrast, weakens cotton. Unless the fiber is treated with a resin finish, however, it wrinkles easily in laundering and use because its resiliency is poor. Cotton can be blended with resilient fibers like polyester to create fabrics with improved wrinkle resistance. The elastic recovery of cotton is also poor.

Although the cotton fiber is dimensionally stable, cotton fabrics are not dimensionally stable because they are stretched during production. Cotton fabrics should be preshrunk to reduce relaxation shrinkage during washing and drying. Some cotton products, such as fitted sheets, can be stretched back to their former size. This is not possible with items such as tablecloths or flat sheets, since equal force is not exerted in all directions during use. Likewise, some cotton garments, such as jeans, can be stretched back to former widths, but the length cannot be restored because there is no force pulling in that direction.

CHEMICAL PROPERTIES OF COTTON. Because cotton is a very absorbent fiber, it is a comfortable fiber to wear in hot, humid weather. However, it dries slowly and may feel damp or wet against the skin. Cotton has poor wicking ability. Mercerization improves the absorbency of cotton, as does treatment with liquid ammonia. Both processes also improve the dyeability of cotton.

Concentrated mineral acids, like sulfuric acid, and chlorine bleach, if not used properly, destroy cotton. In contrast, strong alkalis, like sodium hydroxide, do not harm cotton and in fact improve cotton's absorbency, luster, and strength during mercerization.

Cotton is damaged by exposure to dry heat (300° F or higher). It scorches or burns at extremely high ironing temperatures. Cotton is also flammable and burns when exposed to an open flame. It continues to burn when the flame is removed, producing grey ash. The odor is like that caused by burning paper.

Because cotton conducts electricity, it does not build static electricity.

END USES OF COTTON

Cotton is used extensively in apparel and home furnishings. The list of its end uses in apparel is enormous, primarily due to its comfort, dyeability, and washability. In general, cotton is used when a casual appearance is appropriate. Blends of cotton with synthetic fibers, especially polyester, are commonly used when a wrinkle-free appearance is important. The cotton provides comfort and a pleasant appearance while the polyester provides good resilience. Special wrinkle-resistant finishes can also be used on cotton to improve resilience.

Cotton is also a very important home furnishings textile. Towels and sheets are commonly made from cotton, again because the fiber is absorbent, dyeable, and washable. Other household uses for cotton include curtains, draperies, upholstery fabrics, slipcovers, bedspreads, and table linens.

Specialized applications of cotton include medical and sanitary supplies, book bindings, bagging, luggage, and handbags.

CARE OF COTTON

Caring for cotton is relatively easy. It can be machine washed with strong detergents and controlled bleaching. Hot water can be used on white cotton, but it may fade colored cottons. Automatic drying is usually appropriate. Shrinkage may be a problem if cotton fabrics have not been preshrunk appropriately.

Special care must be taken when cotton is blended with other fibers, when special finishes or dyes have been used, or when decorations such as screen printing or transfer printing have been applied. Product labels provide appropriate care instructions.

Cotton furnishings, such as drapery, should be dry cleaned due to the fabric's tendency to shrink when washed. Cotton only moderately resists sunlight degradation, so draperies should be lined.

Because cotton is susceptible to mildew, it must be stored clean and dry. Because it is damaged by acid, special acid-free tissue paper and boxes should be used to protect valuable cotton articles. Silverfish attack starched cotton. Moths and carpet beetles do not.

TRADE NAMES OF COTTON

Cotton is a natural fiber and has no trade names. The National Cotton Council promotes cotton use through educational programs and publicity. Its Cotton®seal indicates products are made of 100 percent cotton. The Natural Blend® seal indicates products contain at least 60 percent cotton. (See Figure 4–3.)

FIGURE 4–3

Natural Blend® seal. (Courtesy of Cotton Incorporated.)

Bast Fibers— Flax and Ramie

The major bast, or stem, fibers are flax and ramie. Bast fiber production is time and labor intensive. Due to their high costs, both flax and ramie are generally considered luxury fibers.

FLAX

Flax, one of the oldest fibers, was first used in basket weaving. A small piece of woven linen (see Chapter 10) from southeastern Turkey has been dated by the radiocarbon method to 7000 B.C. Technically, **linen** is the fabric made from flax fiber, but both the fabric and fiber are commonly called linen. Linen was used widely in Europe until the invention of power spinning. Cotton then became more commonly used because it was easier to spin into yarn and more suited to power spinning. The historical importance of linen is reflected in current use of terms like *bed linens*, *table linens*, and *household linens* for products likely to be made from fibers other than flax. Today, most flax is produced in western Europe.

SELECTED PROPERTIES OF FLAX. Flax has certain physical, mechanical, and chemical properties that make it a luxury fiber.

Physical Properties of Flax. Flax fiber ranges in color from off-white to tan. Fiber length varies from 2″ to 36″. Length averages from 6″ to

20″. Microscopic views reveal that flax has a central canal, or lumen, similar to that of cotton. Longitudinally, however, flax resembles bamboo. The horizontal markings in the latter are called nodes or joints (see Figure 4–4). Because flax fiber is straight and smooth, it has natural luster.

Mechanical Properties of Flax.   Flax is one of the strongest natural fibers and is stronger wet than dry. It is stronger than cotton, but it is also more brittle and less flexible. Therefore, it is harder to spin into yarn. Flax is similar to cotton in weight. Linen has good abrasion resistance but tends to abrade where folded, so care must be taken when storing linen articles.

Linen's dimensional stability is good but, like cotton, it is subject to tension during production and may therefore exhibit relaxation shrinkage. Preshrinking linen fabric is recommended.

Because linen has very poor resilience, it wrinkles dramatically unless treated with special crease-resistant finishes. Its elastic recovery is also poor.

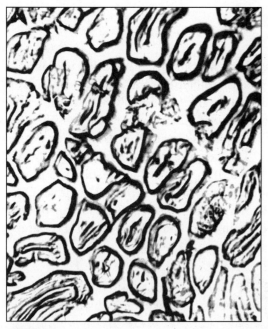 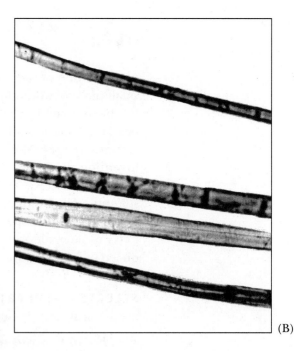

(A)   (B)

FIGURE 4–4

Photomicrographs in (A) cross–sectional and (B) longitudinal views of flax. (Courtesy of DuPont, Wilmington, DE.)

Chemical Properties of Flax.   The absorbency of flax is like that of cotton, but because it has superior wicking ability, it is more comfortable to wear in warm, humid conditions. Flax also dries more quickly than cotton.

Chemically flax reacts like cotton. Acids deteriorate flax, but alkalis do not. Flax is not harmed by dry-cleaning solvents.

Although linen can withstand higher ironing temperatures than cotton, linen and cottons have similar flammabilities. Like cotton, linen burns when exposed to an open flame and continues to burn when the flame is removed. Its odor is like that of burning paper.

Flax conducts electricity and does not build static electricity.

END USES OF FLAX.   Flax is a luxury fiber used for apparel and home furnishings. In apparel linen is an especially popular fabric for summer clothing. Applying wrinkle-resistant finishes or blending flax with synthetic fibers helps minimize its wrinkling. In the home, linen is used for tablecloths, napkins, place mats, upholstery fabrics, slip-covers, draperies, and wall coverings. Additional end uses are luggage and handbags.

CARE OF FLAX.   Linen fabric may be dry cleaned or machine washed with strong detergents. Controlled use of chlorine bleach will not harm the fabric, but it may cause color loss in dyed linen. Dry cleaning is often recommended to minimize shrinkage and improve color retention. High ironing and drying temperatures can be used. Dry cleaning is recommended for furnishings made of linen. Linen resists sunlight better than cotton.

Linen is susceptible to mildew if stored in damp areas. Silverfish may attack starched linens.

TRADE NAMES OF FLAX.   Flax is a natural fiber and has no trade names. The Western Europe Linen Symbol of Quality identifies products made of 100 percent European flax (see Figure 4–5).

RAMIE

Ramie, or **China grass**, is a bast or stem cellulosic fiber. It is grown in hot, humid regions. The main producers of ramie are the Philippines,

FIGURE 4–5

Western Europe linen symbol of quality. (Courtesy of MASTERS OF LINEN/USA.)

China, and Brazil. Much of the processing of ramie has been modernized so it can be produced at a lower cost than flax. Recent advances in ramie production are proprietary and therefore not available to the public.

SELECTED PROPERTIES OF RAMIE.   There are certain physical, mechanical, and chemical properties that characterize ramie.

Physical Properties of Ramie.   The properties and appearance of ramie are very similar to those of flax, except color. Ramie is pure white.

Mechanical Properties of Ramie.   The mechanical properties of ramie and flax are alike except that ramie is slightly heavier and less flexible. Ramie's stiff, brittle quality makes it difficult to spin. As a result, it is frequently blended with other fibers, especially cotton, to improve its spinnability. Ramie's resiliency is also poor. Applying wrinkle-resistant finishes or blending with synthetic fibers is recommended to improve resilience.

Chemical Properties of Ramie.   Ramie and flax are similar chemically.

END USES OF RAMIE.   Ramie has not achieved the popularity of cotton or linen, but it is an important natural cellulosic fiber and its use is expected to increase. It is frequently blended with cotton, linen, wool, polyester, and other synthetic fibers.

Summer-weight apparel and sweaters are frequent end uses for ramie. In the home ramie is used in table linens and window treatments. The industrial end uses for ramie include auto upholstery, erosion-control ground covers, and belting for machinery.

CARE OF RAMIE.   Ramie may be machine washed or dry cleaned. Unless it is treated with a wrinkle-resistant finish or is blended with resilient fibers, it needs ironing. Special dyes, blended fibers, and decoration may require special cleaning care.

Ramie only moderately resists sunlight, so window treatments should be lined. Ramie resists both insects and mildew.

TABLE 4–1   MINOR NATURAL CELLULOSIC FIBERS

Fiber	Source	End Use(s)
Seed		
Coir	Coconut	Brushes, ropes, mats
Kapok	Kapok tree	Filling for life preservers, household furnishings (has been replaced by foam)
Bast		
Hemp	Hemp plant	Twine, ropes
Jute	Jute	Burlap, bagging, cordage
Kenaf	Kenaf plant	Twine, cordage
Leaf		
Pina	Pineapple	Pina cloth, mats, bags, table linens
Sisal	Sisal plant	Cordage, wall coverings, rope, twine, brushes, rugs
Abaca	Abaca plant	Ropes, cordage, floor mats, table linens
Henequen	Henequen plant	Rope, twine, brushes

TRADE NAMES OF RAMIE. Ramie is a natural fiber and has no trade names.

Other Natural Cellulosic Fibers

Many other natural cellulosic fibers have limited commercial production and distribution. Table 4–1 outlines some of these fibers and their end uses. Many of these fibers have been replaced by synthetic fibers, especially in high-strength applications or where resistance to rotting and mildew is important. Natural cellulosic fibers are natural and have no trade names.

LABORATORY ASSIGNMENTS

ASSIGNMENT 4–1   LOCATE COTTON FIBER AND FABRIC SAMPLES

Attach a fiber and greige fabric sample of cotton in your swatch book. (You will purchase or your instructor will provide you with a swatch kit. Your instructor will show you how to mount the samples.)

ASSIGNMENT 4–2   LIST THE ADVANTAGES AND DISADVANTAGES OF COTTON

List the advantages and disadvantages of cotton in the following chart:

ADVANTAGES	DISADVANTAGES

ASSIGNMENT 4–3   **CREATE A COLLAGE OF END USES FOR COTTON**

Use magazines, catalogs, trade papers, newspapers, and so on, to create a collage of current end uses for cotton. Include apparel, home furnishings, and any other applications.

ASSIGNMENT 4–4   **LOCATE FLAX FIBER AND LINEN FABRIC SAMPLES**

Attach samples of flax fiber and greige linen in your swatch book. (You will purchase or your instructor will provide you with a swatch kit. Your instructor will show you how to mount the samples.)

ASSIGNMENT 4–5   **LIST THE ADVANTAGES AND DISADVANTAGES OF FLAX/LINEN**

List the advantages and disadvantages of flax/linen in the following chart:

ADVANTAGES	DISADVANTAGES

ASSIGNMENT 4–6   **CREATE A COLLAGE OF END USES FOR FLAX/LINEN**

Use magazines, catalogs, trade papers, newspapers, and so on, to create a collage of current end uses for linen. Include apparel, home furnishings, and/or any other applications.

ASSIGNMENT 4–7   **LOCATE RAMIE FIBER AND FABRIC SAMPLES**

Attach fiber and greige fabric sample of ramie in your swatch book. (You will purchase or your instructor will provide a swatch kit. Your instructor will show you how to mount the samples.)

ASSIGNMENT 4–8   **LIST THE ADVANTAGES AND DISADVANTAGES OF RAMIE**

List the advantages and disadvantages of ramie in the following chart:

ADVANTAGES	DISADVANTAGES

ASSIGNMENT 4-9 **CREATE A COLLAGE OF END USES FOR RAMIE**

Use magazines, catalogs, trade papers, newspapers, and so on, to create a collage of current end uses for ramie. Include apparel, home furnishings, and/or any other applications.

Production of Manufactured Fibers

OBJECTIVES

The student will be able to:

1. Explain why manufactured fibers dominate the textile industry
2. List the three main categories of manufactured fibers
3. Describe the processes of manufacturing fibers
4. List and discuss the purposes of specialized fiber formations and common manufactured fiber modifications

Introduction

Over 70 percent of the textiles consumed in the United States are manufactured fibers. Several characteristics of manufactured fibers contribute to their dominance of the industry:

1. Quantities of manufactured fibers can be controlled easily because the supply does not depend on nature.
2. The properties of manufactured fibers can be tailored to the needs and desires of the consumer.

3. Blending manufactured fibers and natural fibers allows the consumer to enjoy the benefits of both types. In a polyester/cotton blend, for example, the cotton provides comfort and pleasant hand while the polyester adds good resilience and durability.

CATEGORIES OF MANUFACTURED FIBERS

There are three main categories of manufactured fibers: manufactured cellulosics, synthetics, and inorganic fibers. Manufactured cellulosics, which are derived from cellulose (wood pulp and cotton linters), cannot be used as textiles in original form. They must be chemically processed to be used as textiles. Many synthetics are created from petrochemicals. These fibers are synthesized chemically and do not occur naturally. The **inorganic fibers**, (glass, metal, asbestos, and ceramic) do not contain carbon and must be processed for textile application.

Organic compounds contain carbon. The carbon atom can join with itself and many other atoms to form molecules. In the manufactured-fiber field, science has engineered long-chain molecules, or **polymers**, using these carbon atoms. Polymers can be modified to meet specific end uses. The Textile Fiber Products Identification Act classifies manufactured fibers by their chemical structures (see Figure 5–1).

Formation of Manufactured Fibers

The process of making a manufactured fiber is called **spinning**. Spinning requires the fiber-forming substance (or polymer) to be melted or dissolved in a solvent. The resulting liquid spinning solution is called **dope**. The dope is extruded, or forced, through a **spinneret**.

The spinneret looks like a showerhead with numerous holes (see Figure 5–2). Each hole creates one filament. The filaments are hardened as they emerge from the spinneret. There are several techniques for hardening the filaments. The most widely used methods are melt spinning, dry spinning, and wet spinning.

In **melt spinning**, the polymer is melted and forced through a spinneret. Upon extrusion, cool air solidifies the melted polymer into filaments (see Figure 5–3A). Melt-spun fibers include nylon, olefin, polyester, saran, and glass.

Extract from Federal Trade Commission Rules and Regulations under the Textile Fiber Products Identification Act

Pursuant to the provisions of Section 7(c) of the Act, the following generic names for manufactured fibers, together with their respective definitions, are hereby established:

(a) **acrylic** — a manufactured fiber in which the fiber-forming substance is any long chain synthetic polymer composed of at least 85% by weight of acrylonitrile units ($-CH_2-CH-$).
$$\underset{CN}{|}$$

(b) **modacrylic** — a manufactured fiber in which the fiber-forming substance is any long chain synthetic polymer composed of less than 85% but at least 35% by weight of acrylonitrile units ($-CH_2-CH-$), except fibers qualifying under
$$\underset{CN}{|}$$
subparagraph (2) of paragraph (j) of this section and fibers qualifying under paragraph (q) of this section.

(c) **polyester** — a manufactured fiber in which the fiber-forming substance is any long chain synthetic polymer composed of at least 85% by weight of an ester of a dihydric alcohol and terephthalic acid ($p-HOOC-C_6H_4-COOH$).

(d) **rayon** — a manufactured fiber composed of regenerated cellulose, as well as manufactured fibers composed of regenerated cellulose in which substituents have replaced not more than 15% of the hydrogens of the hydroxyl groups.

(e) **acetate** — a manufactured fiber in which the fiber-forming substance is cellulose acetate. Where not less than 92% of the hydroxyl groups are acetylated, the term triacetate may be used as a generic description of the fiber.

(f) **saran** — a manufactured fiber in which the fiber-forming substance is any long chain synthetic polymer composed of at least 80% by weight of vinylidene chloride units ($-CH_2-CCl_2-$).

(g) **azlon** — a manufactured fiber in which the fiber-forming substance is composed of any regenerated naturally occurring proteins.

(h) **nytril** — a manufactured fiber containing at least 85% of a long chain polymer of vinylidene dinitrile ($-CH_2-C(CN)_2-$) where the vinylidene dinitrile content is no less than every other unit in the polymer chain.

(i) **nylon** — a manufactured fiber in which the fiber-forming substance is any long chain synthetic polyamide having recurring amide groups
$$\begin{array}{c} (-C-NH-) \\ \parallel \\ O \end{array}$$
as an integral part of the polymer chain.

(j) **rubber** — a manufactured fiber in which the fiber-forming substance is comprised of natural or synthetic rubber, including the following categories:

(1) a manufactured fiber in which the fiber-forming substance is a hydrocarbon such as natural rubber, polyisoprene, polybutadiene, copolymers of dienes and hydrocarbons, or amorphous (non-crystalline) polyolefins.

(2) a manufactured fiber in which the fiber-forming substance is a copolymer of acrylonitrile and a diene (such as butadiene) composed of not more than 50% but at least 10% by weight of acrylonitrile units ($-CH_2-CH-$). The term "lastrile" may be
$$\underset{CN}{|}$$
used as a generic description for fibers falling within this category.

(3) a manufactured fiber in which the fiber-forming substance is a polychloroprene or a copolymer of chloroprene in which at least 35% by weight of the fiber-forming substance is composed of chloroprene units ($-CH_2-C=CH-CH_2-$).
$$\underset{Cl}{|}$$

(k) **spandex** — a manufactured fiber in which the fiber-forming substance is a long chain synthetic polymer comprised of at least 85% of a segmented polyurethane.

(l) **vinal** — a manufactured fiber in which the fiber-forming substance is any long chain synthetic polymer composed of at least 50% by weight of vinyl alcohol units ($-CH_2-CHOH-$), and in which the total of the vinyl alcohol units and any one or more of the various acetal units is at least 85% by weight of the fiber.

(m) **olefin** — a manufactured fiber in which the fiber-forming substance is any long chain synthetic polymer composed of at least 85% by weight of ethylene, propylene, or other olefin units, except amorphous (non-crystalline) polyolefins qualifying under category (1) of Paragraph (j) of Rule 7.

(n) **vinyon** — a manufactured fiber in which the fiber-forming substance is any long chain synthetic polymer composed of at least 85% by weight of vinyl chloride units ($-CH_2-CHCl-$).

(o) **metallic** — a manufactured fiber composed of metal, plastic-coated metal, metal-coated plastic, or a core completely covered by metal.

(p) **glass** — a manufactured fiber in which the fiber-forming substance is glass.

(q) **anidex** — a manufactured fiber in which the fiber-forming substance is any long chain synthetic polymer composed of at least 50 percent by weight of one or more esters of a monohydric alcohol and acrylic acid, $CH_2=CH-COOH$.

FIGURE 5–1

Extract from the Textile Fiber Products Identification Act. (Courtesy of the FTC.)

FIGURE 5–2

Spinning nylon fiber.
(Courtesy of Hagley Museum
and Library.)

DRY SPINNING

In **dry spinning**, the polymer is dissolved in a solvent and then extruded into an atmosphere of warm, dry air. The warm air evaporates the solvent and hardens the filaments (see Figure 5–3B). The solvent can be recycled and reused. Acetate, some acrylics, modacrylic, and vinyon are dry spun.

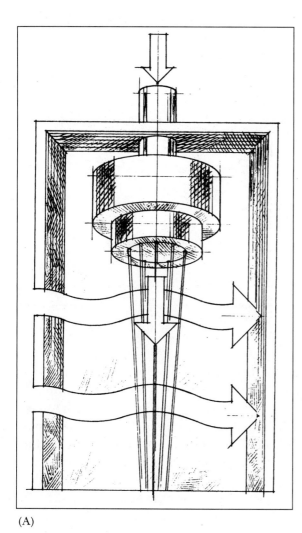

(A)

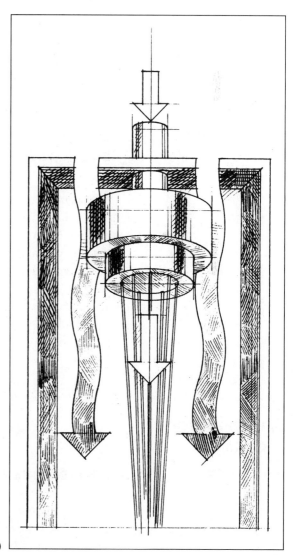

(B)

FIGURE 5–3

(A) Melt spinning and
(B) dry spinning.
(Courtesy of the American
Fiber Manufacturers
Association, Inc.)

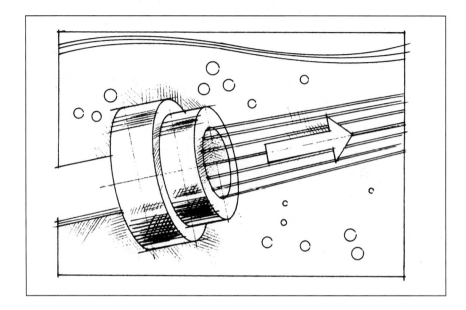

FIGURE 5–3

(C) Wet spinning.
(Courtesy of the American
Fiber Manufacturers
Association, Inc.)

WET SPINNING

Wet spinning involves dissolving the polymer in a solvent and then extruding it into a chemical bath which hardens the polymer into filaments (see Figure 5–3C). Acrylic and viscose rayon fibers are wet spun.

Other special-use methods include gel spinning and emulsion spinning. **Gel spinning** is a hybrid of wet and dry spinning and is used to create solvent-spun manufactured cellulosics. **Emulsion spinning** is a complex process that is used for insoluble polymers with high melting points. The polymer is dispersed in a carrier, extruded, and then heated to form the fiber.

Specialized Fiber Formation

There are several different kinds of manufactured fibers.

HETEROGENEOUS FIBERS

Heterogeneous fibers are created using two or more different types of polymer. Heterogeneous fibers are classified as biocomponent or multicomponent fibers and matrix or biconstituent fibers.

BICOMPONENT OR MULTICOMPONENT FIBERS. In **bicomponent** or **multicomponent fibers**, two or more polymers combine to form one fiber. The polymers may be variations of the same generic fiber, such as nylon 6 and nylon 6,6, or they may come from different generic fibers. If the polymers are from different generic fibers, such as spandex and nylon, the resulting combined fiber is **bicomponent-bigeneric**. In these cases, the unique characteristics of each fiber blend into one.

The two forms of bicomponent fibers are **bilateral** and **sheath core**. Two different polymers feed into the spinneret.

Bilateral fibers offer the important benefit of **crimp**. If one of the polymers shrinks more than the other when exposed to heat, the resulting fiber crimps. Crimped fibers have improved hand and increased cover, loft, and elasticity. Cross-dyed effects are another benefit of bicomponent fibers. See Chapter 13 for a discussion of cross dyeing.

MATRIX OR BICONSISTUENT FIBERS. **Matrix** or **biconstituent fibers** are created using two generically different fibers. In the production process fine short lengths of one fiber are embedded in another.

HOLLOW FIBERS

As their name suggests, hollow fibers have one or more open spaces in their centers (see Figure 5–4). These fibers can be formed by injecting air into the fiber as it is being formed, by the shape of the spinneret holes, or by adding gas-producing compounds to the spinning solution. New production techniques have been developed, but manufacturers have not made details available to the public. Because they are lightweight and trap air, hollow fibers are often used to make the insulation for cold-weather clothing. Examples include Hollofil® and Thermax® by DuPont, and Polarguard HV® by Hoechst Celanese.

MICROFIBERS

Microfibers, or **microdenier fibers**, can be produced by carefully controlled melt spinning. Other methods involve techniques similar to those used to produce bilateral bicomponent and matrix fibers. In the bilateral method two incompatible polymers are extruded and then separated. Alternating segments of two incompatible polymers can also be extruded

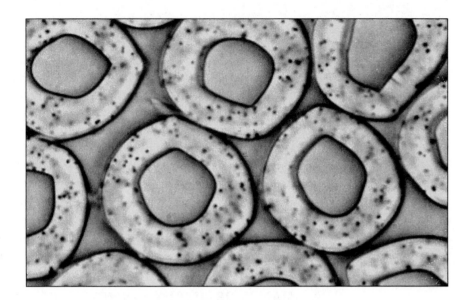

FIGURE 5–4

Cross section of single hole polyester. (Courtesy of DuPont, Wilmington, DE.)

and then separated. In the matrix fiber method the polymer for the microfiber is embedded in another polymer, which is later dissolved.

Microfibers have application in both apparel and industry. Microfibers are used in apparel because they are soft and have excellent drape. They are also used for filters, surgical masks, and ski jacket insulation.

FIBRILLATED FIBERS

Fibrillated fibers are coarse fibers often used for bagging and twine. The first step in creating fibrillated fibers is extruding a sheet of polymer. Next is drawing or stretching the sheet, which causes the sheet to break into interconnected fibers. This process, called fibrillation, is also a method of forming yarns and is discussed in Chapter 9.

Manufactured Fiber Modifications

After a fiber has been formed it may be subjected to various modifications which are dictated by the projected end use of the fiber. Common modifications include drawing, heat setting, texturing, and cutting.

DRAWING

Drawing can be done immediately after the fiber is formed or later in processing. Drawing stretches the fiber and increases its strength. It also makes the fiber thinner.

HEAT SETTING

Heat setting uses heat and pressure to permanently change the shape and improve the dimensional stability of thermoplastic fibers. Fabrics of thermoplastic fibers are also heat set to create permanent pleats and creases.

TEXTURING

The comfort and appearance of manufactured yarns is improved through texturing processes. **Texturing** may be done to produce:

1. Bulkier yarns, which are used in open-weave fabrics and bulky fabrics for warmth. Textured filament yarns have a bulkier hand which is similar to that of staple yarns.
2. Opaque yarns, which provide better cover.
3. Yarns with elastomeric qualities for use in sportswear and hosiery.

Texturing may be done simultaneously to drawing, or it may be done later. During texturing, the fiber or yarn is twisted, heated, cooled, and then untwisted. The moldable nature of synthetic fibers allows the fiber to retain a permanently textured shape. Yarn texturing is discussed in Chapter 9.

CUTTING

Manufactured fibers can be used as filaments, or they can be cut into staple lengths. When producing filament yarns the manufacturer extrudes all the fibers for a yarn at one time. If the yarn is to have twenty fibers, then the spinneret will have twenty holes and twenty fibers will be produced together.

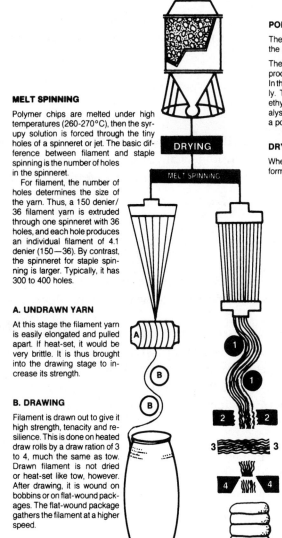

MELT SPINNING

Polymer chips are melted under high temperatures (260-270°C), then the syrupy solution is forced through the tiny holes of a spinneret or jet. The basic difference between filament and staple spinning is the number of holes in the spinneret.

For filament, the number of holes determines the size of the yarn. Thus, a 150 denier/ 36 filament yarn is extruded through one spinneret with 36 holes, and each hole produces an individual filament of 4.1 denier (150—36). By contrast, the spinneret for staple spinning is larger. Typically, it has 300 to 400 holes.

A. UNDRAWN YARN

At this stage the filament yarn is easily elongated and pulled apart. If heat-set, it would be very brittle. It is thus brought into the drawing stage to increase its strength.

B. DRAWING

Filament is drawn out to give it high strength, tenacity and resilience. This is done on heated draw rolls by a draw ration of 3 to 4, much the same as tow. Drawn filament is not dried or heat-set like tow, however. After drawing, it is wound on bobbins or on flat-wound packages. The flat-wound package gathers the filament at a higher speed.

FILAMENT YARN

STAPLE FIBER

POLYMERIZATION

The raw material used to form a man-made fiber is known as the polymer and the chemical process of manufacturing the polymer is called polymerization.

There are two polymerization processes: batch and continuous. In the batch process, the polymer is made up in batches, then sent into the spinning process. In the continuous process, polymer is made continuously and spun continuously. To make the polyester polymer, dimethyl terephthalate is reacted with ethylene glycol at a temperature range of 150 - 210°C, in the presence of a catalyst. A monomer (dihydroxydiethyl terephthalate) is created and transferred to a polymerization autoclave, where the temperature is raised to about 280°C.

DRYING

When the desired viscosity is reached, the polymer is extruded, cooled and formed into chips. All moisture must be removed to prevent irregularities.

1. DRAWING TOW

After the molten tow is quickly cooled or quenched, it is dropped or loosely coiled into "sub-tow" cans like rope. Many sub-tows are creeled up or gathered in a parallel run, then drawn on heated tension rollers which actually elongate the tow by a draw ratio of 3-4 times (typically 3.6 times). Drawing the tow increases its strength three fold, since random molecules are all drawn into a parallel formation, also increasing resilience.

2. CRIMPING

The tow comes into compression boxes, forcing the fiber to buckle back on itself like an accordian, 9-15 crimps per inch. Crimping holds the fiber together, giving it coherence during the yarn spinning stage. Crimping is the mechanical equivalent of what nature does to cotton.

3. DRYING/HEAT SETTING

The crimped tow is dried at 100-150°F to set the crimp. Some of the crimp is lost in yarn spinning later on, which is why fiber companies try to achieve a balance of properties during the drawing and crimping stage by applying finish to hold fibers together and to overcome static.

4. CUTTING

The crimped and heat-set tow is cut into lengths, determined by eventual end-use. Fiber companies generally cut the tow into lengths of 1½ inches (for blending with combed cotton), 1¼ inches (carded cotton) and 2 inches (rayon) under the cotton system. An outside contractor will cut tow into longer lengths of 3 to 6 inches on the Pacific Converter for worsted processing, thence bales.

FIGURE 5–5

The spinning process for polyester

Filaments to be cut are extruded using spinnerets with multiple holes so the fiber can be produced more economically. After spinning the filament fibers are cut to staple length. Multistrand filament yarn to be processed into staple is called **tow**. See Chapter 9 for additional information on staple yarn formation.

Figure 5–5 summarizes the formation of melt spun polyester from polymerization to filament yarn and staple fiber.

ADDITIONAL TREATMENTS

Many additional treatments can be applied to manufactured fibers during spinning. Additives such as dyes, pigments, delusterants, and whiteners can be added to the polymer before extrusion. The fiber can also receive sunlight resistance, fire resistance, and static control treatments. These treatments are discussed more fully in chapters 13 and 14.

LABORATORY ASSIGNMENTS

ASSIGNMENT 5–1　　**EXPERIMENT WITH MELT SPINNING**

1. Gather the materials:
   6″ × 6″ sample of greige nylon fabric
   tweezers
   matches
   candle
   aluminum pie plate
2. Light the candle and allow a few drops of wax to collect in the bottom of the pie plate. Stick the candle in the melted wax.
3. Hold one end of the fabric in the flame until a generous amount of the fabric has melted.
4. Grasp some of the melted fabric with the tweezers and draw out a fiber.
5. Note your observations.

ASSIGNMENT 5–2 **EXPERIMENT WITH DRAWING**

1. Cut 2″ × 10″ strips from a polyethylene bag.
2. Hold the ends of the polyethylene strip and stretch it slowly until part of the strip begins to narrow.
3. Compare the narrow section to an unstretched section of plastic.
4. Note your observations. Is the narrow section stronger than the unstretched plastic?

ASSIGNMENT 5–3 **EXPERIMENT WITH TEXTURING**

1. Gather the following materials:
   100% polyester yarn or sewing thread, 12″
   100% cotton yarn or sewing thread, 12″
   aluminum foil
   2 straight pins, small nails, or straightened paper clips
   household or laboratory oven or an iron
   detergent
   250 ml beakers or 8-oz glasses
   warm water
2. Preheat the over to 300° F, or preheat the iron at the steam setting.
3. Wind the polyester yarn or thread around a pin, nail, or paper clip.
4. Repeat Step 3 with the cotton thread or yarn.
5. If using an oven, place the coiled yarns or threads on a sheet of aluminum foil and place them in the oven for 20 minutes. If using an iron, wrap the yarns or threads around a paper clip and place them inside a folded sheet of aluminum foil. Press the foil at steam setting for 30 seconds.
6. Remove the yarns or threads from oven and allow them to cool. With the iron, allow to cool.
7. Unwind the yarns or threads and complete the following activities:
   a. Describe the appearance of each yarn or thread.
   b. Stretch both yarns or threads to their original lengths. Hold them fully extended for 30 seconds and release. Describe the results.
   c. Place both yarns in warm, soapy water for about 30 seconds. Agitate the yarns to simulate laundering. Rinse and dry the yarns by blotting them with a towel. Describe the results.
   d. Explain why the polyester and the cotton behaved in the manner described.

Manufactured Cellulosic Fibers

OBJECTIVES

The student will be able to:

1. Recognize and classify manufactured cellulosic fibers
2. Discuss the properties of manufactured cellulosic fibers and differentiate between rayon, lyocell, acetate, and triacetate
3. Recommend appropriate end uses for rayon, lyocell, acetate, and triacetate
4. List proper care procedures for rayon, lyocell, acetate, and triacetate
5. Appreciate the importance of rayon, lyocel, acetate, and triacetate in the marketplace

Introduction

There are two categories of manufactured cellulosics: regenerated cellulosic fibers and derivative cellulosic fibers. Both are made from wood pulp and cotton linters that cannot be used as fibers in their natural form, but need to be chemically processed into a solution which is then extruded through a spinneret. Regenerated cellulosics, such as rayon, are pure cellulose fibers and have many of the same properties as natural cellulosic fibers such as cotton. Acetate and triacetate are derivative cellulosics. They are chemically changed during production so the resulting fibers are not cellulose but are derivatives of cellulose known as esters. Their properties are quite different from those of natural cellulosic fibers.

Lyocell, the newest regenerated cellulosic fiber, has improved aesthetics and performance. The fiber is the result of 10 years of research and development by Courtaulds Fibers, Inc.

Regenerated Cellulosic Fibers

In 1891, Counte Hilaire de Chardonnet established a factory in Besancon, France, to produce rayon from mulberry trees. De Chardonnet chose mulberry trees because silkworms eat their leaves. The first rayon was called **"artificial silk"** and marked the beginning of the manufactured fiber industry.

The FTC formally established the name *rayon* in 1924. Early rayon was a bright, lustrous fiber used to make velvet, tweed, challis, crepe, and silk- and linen-like fabrics. The method for processing **viscose rayon** was developed by Cross, Bevan, and Beadle in England in 1892. In 1910 the American Viscose Company started producing viscose rayon. Chardonnet's process was discontinued in 1949 when it became outdated. Currently viscose rayon is the only type of rayon produced in the United States.

Originally rayon was very inexpensive to produce. Recent environmental protection regulations that require companies to meet strict air and water pollution standards have dramatically increased production costs. Higher production costs have contributed to increased rayon prices. Prices for viscose rayon now compare to those for cotton.

Since the beginning of rayon production, research and development has continued to create new varieties of the fiber. Varieties of rayon include:

1. Viscose
2. Cuperammonium
3. High-wet-modulus (HWM) (high-performance [HP] or polynosic)

Most rayon is marketed without a trade name to indicate its variety, so it is important to discuss some general properties of the rayon fiber. Because rayon is a cellulosic fiber, its properties closely resemble those of cotton. Rayon is an absorbent fiber, which means it is comfortable to wear and dyes well. Its dimensional stability and wet strength are lower than those of cotton, and it wrinkles badly unless given a wrinkle-resistant finish. Rayon does not pill.

TRADE NAMES OF RAYON

Table 6–1 lists the trade names for rayon.

VISCOSE RAYON

Viscose rayon is wet spun.

SELECTED PROPERTIES OF VISCOSE RAYON.   There are certain physical, mechanical, and chemical properties that characterize viscose rayon.

Physical Properties of Viscose Rayon.   Viscose rayon is a white, lustrous fiber with an irregular cross section. Titanium dioxide may be used to reduce its luster. The irregular cross section of viscose rayon is caused by uneven shrinkage of the fiber during spinning. This irregular cross section in turn causes the fiber to have longitudinal striations (see Figure 6–1). Viscose rayon has a comfortable hand, similar to that of cotton.

Mechanical Properties of Viscose Rayon.   Viscose rayon is a medium-weight fiber, like cotton or linen. It is not as strong as cotton, however,

TABLE 6–1 SELECT MANUFACTURER/TRADE NAMES FOR RAYON	
Manufacturer	**Trade Name(s)**
Courtaulds Fibers, Inc. Axis, AL	Fibro, Tencel
North American Rayon Elizabethton, TN	Beaugrip
Lenzing Fibers Corp. Charlotte, NC	

(A)

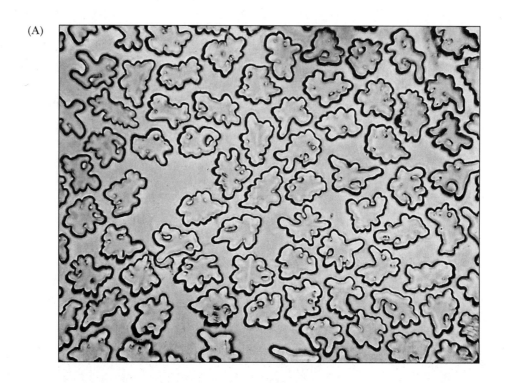

(B)

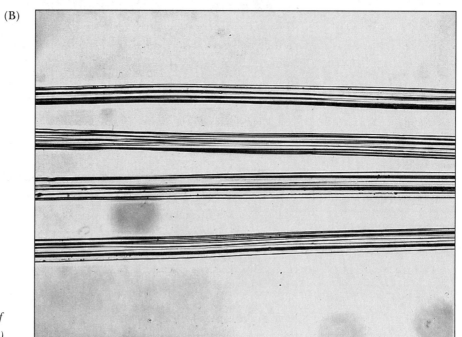

FIGURE 6–1

*Photomicrographs in
(A) cross–sectional and
(B) longitudinal views of
viscose rayon. (Courtesy of
DuPont, Wilmington, DE.)*

and it abrades more easily. It is weaker when wet than when dry. Viscose rayon is not dimensionally stable, and it tends to shrink progressively in laundering. Resin treatments can be applied to improve its stability. It has poor elastic recovery and poor resiliency. The fiber is flexible, however, and rayon fabrics are known for their beautiful drape.

Chemical Properties of Viscose Rayon. Viscose rayon is a very absorbent fiber, which means it is comfortable to wear and dyes readily in rich, vibrant colors. While the ironing temperature for rayon is lower than that for cotton, rayon burns like cotton. It catches fire readily when exposed to an open flame and continues to burn when the flame is removed. It produces a smell like burning paper.

Because rayon conducts electricity, static electricity does not build on its surface. Both acids and alkalis degrade rayon.

END USES OF VISCOSE RAYON. The end uses for rayon are extensive. The fiber's characteristics can be controlled during production, so it can be made to resemble wool, silk, cotton, or linen. Because it can also be engineered to complement other fibers, it is frequently used in blends. Most rayon fabrics are woven.

In apparel, rayon has wide application. It has been used for dresses, shirts, suits, lingerie, and sportswear. Its home furnishings applications include blankets, tablecloths, bedspreads, slipcovers, upholstery fabrics, curtains, and draperies.

Nonwoven rayon fabric is widely used in medical and sanitary products where absorbency is important.

CARE OF VISCOSE RAYON. In general, dry cleaning is recommended for viscose rayon. Shrinkage and low wet strength are problems in laundering this fiber. While automatic drying may increase shrinkage, special finishes may reduce shrinkage. Chlorine bleach may damage viscose rayon, but non-chlorine bleaches are safe. Care labels should be followed. Sunlight degrades rayon faster than cotton, so window treatments should be lined. Both silverfish and mold damage rayon.

CUPERAMMONIUM RAYON

Cuperammonium rayon is no longer produced in the United States due to the high cost of conforming to environmental pollution standards.

Cuperammonium rayon is sometimes called Bemberg® rayon because it was manufactured by Bemberg Industries until they ceased production in 1975. Cuperammonium rayon is still produced in East Germany, Italy, and Japan.

Cuperammonium rayon, while quite similar to viscose rayon, is silkier in feel and appearance. It is wet spun and can be drawn into very fine fibers. Its cross section is round, and its longitudinal appearance is smooth with either very fine or no striations. This fiber is particularly suited to lightweight summer clothing. It has special medical application in making artificial kidneys.

HIGH-WET-MODULUS RAYON

High-Wet-Modulus **(HWM) rayon** is stronger, more resilient, and more dimensionally stable than viscose rayon, but less absorbent. HWM rayon, which is sometimes referred to as **high-performance (HP)** or **polynosic rayon**, resembles cotton more than it does viscose rayon. **HWM** means that it resists deformation when wet.

The cross section of HWM rayon is round. HWM rayon is appropriate for the same end uses as cotton and may be washed or dry cleaned.

LYOCELL

In April 1996, the FTC gave the newest regenerated cellulosic fiber the generic name of lyocell. It is produced by Courtaulds Fibers, Inc. under the trade name of TENCEL®. TENCEL® is a solvent spun fiber. To create solvent-spun rayon, the fiber is spun into a weak solvent bath. Solvent spinning allows the chemicals in the bath to be recovered and recycled and makes it easier for the manufacturer to meet pollution-control regulations. This process is more expensive than traditional spinning methods, however.

TENCEL®, a solvent-spun rayon fiber, it produced by Courtaulds Fibers, Inc., Axis, AL. TENCEL® is more like cotton than either regular viscose rayon or HWM rayon. TENCEL® is also stronger than regular viscose rayon or HWM rayon and it has better dimensional stability and resiliency. The fiber is round and smooth with no striations.

End uses for TENCEL® include both apparel and home furnishings. Because of its high cost, however, it has limited nonwoven application.

TENCEL® can be washed or dry cleaned. Please note that TENCEL® is a regenerated cellulosic fiber which is being marketed under its trade name.

Derivative Cellulosic Fibers

As mentioned earlier, the derivative cellulosic fibers are cellulose acetate and triacetate. Because each is processed differently, each has different characteristics.

CELLULOSE ACETATE

Cellulose acetate, which is commonly referred to as "acetate," was developed during World War I as a coating for airplane wings. After the war, it was developed into a fiber. Its production in the United States began in 1924. The fibers are dry spun.

SELECTED PROPERTIES OF CELLULOSE ACETATE. There are certain physical, mechanical, and chemical properties that characterize cellulose acetate.

Physical Properties of Cellulose Acetate. Cellulose acetate is a white fiber with longitudinal striations and an irregular cross section that resembles popcorn. Although it is lustrous, it may be delustered. It has a smooth hand.

Mechanical Properties of Cellulose Acetate. Cellulose acetate is a very weak fiber made weaker when wet. It is lighter than rayon or cotton and has poor abrasion resistance, poor elasticity, and poor resilience. It is not dimensionally stable and shrinks during laundering, but it does not pill. Acetate fabrics can be treated to prevent shrinkage. Fabrics made from acetate are flexible and drape well.

Chemical Properties of Cellulose Acetate. Cellulose acetate has moderate absorbency and builds static electricity. It is not as comfortable to wear as cotton, linen, or rayon. Cellulose acetate melts at temperatures over 275° F and forms a hard bead when exposed to an open flame. However, acetate is thermoplastic and can be heat set with attractive surface designs like moiré.

Although cellulose acetate has good resistance to weak acids and alkalis, it is dissolved by acetone. Acetate is particularly susceptible to fume or gas fading. Atmospheric gases may change the color of acetate fabrics. Blues and grays turn pink or purple, for example. Greens turn brown. Solution dyeing, which is discussed in Chapter 13, eliminates this problem.

END USES OF CELLULOSE ACETATE.   Cellulose acetate is used for both apparel and home furnishings, but it should not be used when durability is important because it is a weak fiber that abrades easily. Its end uses include dresses, robes, lingerie, and window treatments. Fabrics commonly made from acetate include brocade, satin, and taffeta. Acetate is also used for cigarette filters.

CARE OF CELLULOSE ACETATE.   Dry cleaning is recommended for acetate fabrics, although they may be carefully laundered by hand. Nonchlorine bleaches may be used with care, but, as just mentioned, the fiber cannot be exposed to acetone, because acetone dissolves acetate. Sunlight also degrades acetate, so window treatments should be lined. Mildew grows on acetate and silverfish attack starched acetate.

TRADE NAMES OF CELLULOSE ACETATE.   Table 6–2 lists the trade names for acetate.

CELLULOSE TRIACETATE

Although environmental regulations forced U. S. production of cellulose triacetate to end in 1986, it is still produced overseas by Hoechst Celanese, New York, NY, and imported to the United States. It is commonly called triacetate.

TABLE 6-2 MANUFACTURER/TRADE NAMES FOR ACETATE	
Manufacturer	**Trade Name(s)**
Eastman Chemical Co. Kingsport, TN	Chromspun Estron
Hoechst Celanese New York, NY	Celebrate!

SELECTED PROPERTIES OF CELLULOSE TRIACETATE.   Cellulose triacetate, while similar to cellulose acetate physically and chemically, differs from it mechanically.

Physical Properties of Cellulose Triacetate.   Cellulose triacetate and cellulose acetate have similar physical properties. See Figure 6–2 for photomicrographs of triacetate in cross-sectional and longitudinal views.

(A)

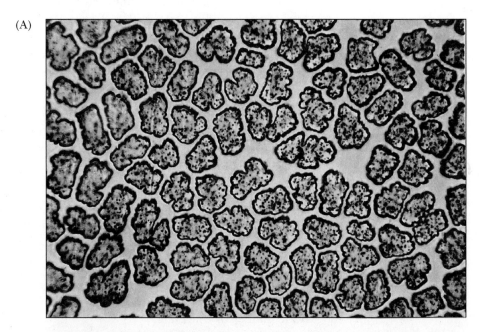

(B)

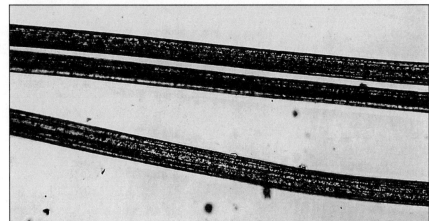

FIGURE 6–2

Photomicrographs in (A) cross–sectional and (B) longitudinal views of triacetate. (Courtesy of DuPont, Wilmington, DE.)

Mechanical Properties of Cellulose Triacetate. While they have similar physical properties, cellulose triacetate and cellulose acetate differ in several mechanical properties. Triacetate has better resiliency, dimensional stability, and elasticity than acetate.

Chemical Properties of Cellulose Triacetate. Chemically cellulose triacetate and cellulose acetate are similar, with some exceptions. First, cellulose triacetate is less absorbent than acetate. Next, triacetate is often given a special heat-setting treatment to render it less heat sensitive. Creases and pleats are therefore more permanent in triacetate than acetate because higher temperatures can be used with the former. Finally, the chemical reactivity of triacetate is similar to that of acetate, except that triacetone is much less sensitive to acetone.

END USES OF CELLULOSE TRIACETATE. Cellulose triacetate is primarily used when pleat and crease retention is important, such as in pleated skirts and dresses. Other end uses for cellulose triacetate include bedspreads, comforters, and draperies.

CARE OF CELLULOSE TRIACETATE. Triacetate fabrics may be washed by machine or by hand, and they may also be dry cleaned. Nonchlorine bleaches may be used. Triacetate moderately resists sunlight, so window treatments may need lining.

TRADE NAMES OF CELLULOSE TRIACETATE. Table 6–3 lists the trade names for triacetate.

TABLE 6–3 MANUFACTURER/TRADE NAME FOR TRIACETATE	
Manufacturer	**Trade Names**
Hoechst Celanese New York, NY	Arnel

LABORATORY ASSIGNMENTS

ASSIGNMENT 6-1

LOCATE REGENERATED CELLULOSIC FIBER AND FABRIC SAMPLES

Attach a fiber and greige fabric sample of regenerated cellulosic in your swatch book. (Your instructor will provide or you will purchase a swatch kit. Your instructor will show you how to mount the samples.)

ASSIGNMENT 6-2

LIST THE ADVANTAGES AND DISADVANTAGES OF REGENERATED CELLULOSIC FIBERS

Complete the following charts for viscose rayon, HWM rayon, and lyocell:

VISCOSE RAYON	
ADVANTAGES	DISADVANTAGES

HWM RAYON	
ADVANTAGES	**DISADVANTAGES**

LYOCELL	
ADVANTAGES	**DISADVANTAGES**

ASSIGNMENT 6-3 **CREATE A COLLAGE OF END USES FOR REGENERATED CELLULOSIC**

Use magazines, catalogs, trade papers, newspapers, and so on, to create a collage of current end uses for regenerated cellulosics. Include apparel, home furnishings, and/or any other applications.

ASSIGNMENT 6-4 **LOCATE ACETATE AND TRIACETATE FIBER AND FABRIC SAMPLES**

Attach fiber and greige fabric samples of acetate and triacetate in your swatch book. (Your instructor will provide or you will purchase a swatch kit. Your instructor will show you how to mount the samples.)

ASSIGNMENT 6-5 **LIST THE ADVANTAGES AND DISADVANTAGES OF ACETATE AND TRIACETATE**

Complete the following charts for acetate and triacetate:

ACETATE	
ADVANTAGES	**DISADVANTAGES**

TRIACETATE	
ADVANTAGES	DISADVANTAGES

ASSIGNMENT 6-6 **CREATE A COLLAGE OF END USES FOR ACETATE AND TRIACETATE**

Use magazines, catalogs, trade papers, newspapers, and so on, to create a collage of current end uses for acetate and triacetate. Include apparel, home furnishings, and/or any other applications.

Primary Synthetic Fibers

OBJECTIVES

The student will be able to:

1. Discuss the properties, care procedures, and end uses common to synthetic fibers
2. List and identify the characteristics of the major synthetic fibers
3. Recommend appropriate end uses for major synthetic fibers
4. Appreciate the importance of synthetic fibers in the textiles industry

Introduction

The first synthetic fiber, nylon, was introduced in 1939 by DuPont. The fiber, which was sheer as silk but much stronger, revolutionized the hosiery industry (see Figure 7–1). Since their introduction, chemically synthesized fibers, also called "noncellulosic manufactured fibers" or "chemical fibers," have become prominent in the textile industry.

As technology has improved, synthetic fibers have been engineered increasingly to meet specific consumer needs. Synthetics are no longer considered substitutes for natural fibers, but instead are

FIGURE 7–1

Post-war reappearance of consumer nylon—hosiery buyer trying on stockings on curb. (Courtesy of Hagley Museum and Library.)

often preferred for their own outstanding characteristics in many apparel, furnishings, and industrial applications.

In general, synthetic fibers have similar properties which are inherent to the nature of their composition. Synthetics can be modified by changing spinning solutions, spinning methods, yarn and fabric formations, and finishes. Most synthetics are melt spun.

Properties Common to Synthetic Fibers

Synthetic fibers have certain physical, mechanical, and chemical properties in common.

PHYSICAL PROPERTIES COMMON TO SYNTHETIC FIBERS

Most synthetic fibers are white unless they are solution or dope dyed. **Solution dyeing** is the process of adding color to the polymer before extrusion. It requires the manufacturer to make a color decision very early in the production process. As a result, it is difficult to respond to quickly changing fashion trends. An advantage of solution dyeing is that it is colorfast. Solution dyeing is discussed more fully in Chapter 13.

Synthetic fibers are spun as filaments but may be cut to staple length. The shape of the holes in the spinneret determines the cross section of synthetic fibers. These various shapes include round, oval, dog bone, flat, triangular, "U," tri- and multilobal, serrated, and hollow. The shape of the cross section in turn determines the fiber's longitudinal appearance and luster. In general, synthetic fibers have luster. They may be chemically delustered with titanium dioxide or other finishing processes. Finishes are discussed in Chapter 14. Flat, round, and trilobal fibers have increased luster. Pentalobal fibers have more subdued luster, and fibers with greater than five lobes have decreased luster.

The surface of synthetic fibers affects their hand (how the fibers or fabrics feel). Round fibers tend to feel soft and smooth while dog-bone and flat fibers have a harsher hand.

The diameter of synthetic fibers, which is also determined by the holes in the spinneret, can be modified to meet specific needs. High-denier fibers are used in industry and carpeting; very fine, microdenier fibers are used in apparel and medical supplies.

Various texturing processes can be used to improve the stretch, cover, absorption, insulation, hand, and wrinkle resistance of filament fibers. Textured filament yarns include bulky, loopy, stretch, and crimped types. Textured filament yarns have qualities similar to staple yarns but are cheaper to produce. To improve spinnability, filament fibers are crimped before being cut to staple length. Textured filament yarns are discussed in Chapter 9.

MECHANICAL PROPERTIES COMMON TO SYNTHETIC FIBERS

The abrasion resistance of most synthetic fibers is good to excellent. Acrylics exhibit the poorest abrasion resistance. The tenacity of most synthetic fibers is also good to excellent, but their pilling propensity is high. Pills tend to form on the surface of fabrics made from strong fibers because the fiber ends become entangled by abrasion from wear or laundering and hold the pills to the fabric surface. Weak fibers, in contrast, allow the loose ends to fall off.

The resilience of synthetic fibers is excellent. They provide consumers with easy-care apparel and home furnishings that stay wrinkle free throughout use.

Synthetic fibers in general have low specific gravity. Most are lightweight.

CHEMICAL PROPERTIES COMMON TO SYNTHETIC FIBERS

Synthetic fibers tend not to be very absorbent and to be sensitive to heat.

ABSORBENCY OF SYNTHETIC FIBERS. In general, synthetic fibers have poor absorbency. The positive aspects of poor absorbency are that fabrics:

1. usually dry quickly;
2. resist waterborne stains; and
3. are dimensionally stable in water.

The negative aspects of poor absorbency are:

1. Fibers are more difficult to dye.
2. Fabrics are uncomfortable in warm, humid conditions.
3. "Static cling" is likely to develop due to the fiber's low electrical conductivity. Dry, cold weather or centrally heated buildings increase the fiber's static potential. Factory-applied antistatic finishes and fabric softeners may help solve the problem. Carbon and metal fibers are also used to control static electricity. Carbon and metal fibers are discussed in Chapter 8.
4. Fabrics have increased pilling propensity. The low electrical conductivity of low-absorbency fibers contributes to pilling because lint pills are attracted to the fabric's surface. Lint pills form when the fabrics pick up fibers from other fabrics.
5. Fibers are **oleophilic**, which means they have an affinity for oil. Fibers with low moisture absorbency tend to hold oilborne stains.

Because these fibers also do not wet out, or become thoroughly wet, during laundering, pretreatment of oily stains is necessary.

Most synthetics exhibit poor wicking. One exception, olefin, has good wicking. Research and modification continues to improve the comfort of synthetics. Microdenier synthetic fibers have shown improved moisture transfer through modification. Microdenier fibers are more comfortable to wear because they have improved wicking.

CHEMICAL RESISTANCE OF SYNTHETIC FIBERS.   In general, synthetic fibers have good resistance to most chemicals. They are especially useful in industry when chemical resistance is essential. Home and commercial cleaning products are safe to use on most synthetic fibers, although dyes or finishes may be affected by these chemicals.

HEAT SENSITIVITY OF SYNTHETIC FIBERS.   Most synthetic fibers are heat sensitive. Some fibers are more sensitive than others. Heat-sensitive fibers need special care during manufacturing; washing, drying, ironing, and dry cleaning. As with absorbency, heat sensitivity has both positive and negative aspects. The positive aspects of heat sensitivity are:

1. Fibers and yarns can be textured to increase bulk and stretch, and to improve hand.
2. Fibers, yarns, and fabrics can be stabilized to reduce shrinkage.
3. Furlike fabric can be made.
4. Creases and pleats can be set permanently.
5. Fabrics can be glazed or embossed permanently.

Glazing is a shiny, lustrous finish. Glazing and embossing are discussed in Chapter 14. The negative aspects of heat sensitivity are:

1. Excessive heat can cause shrinkage and holes.
2. Undesirable glazing may occur when the fabric is pressed.
3. Special care may be needed during manufacturing. Dyeing, finishing, and other production processes may need to be modified.
4. Special care may be necessary in home and professional cleaning. Washing, drying, and ironing temperatures must be monitored carefully.
5. Altering garments made from heat-sensitive fabrics may be difficult. Seam lines and creases can be impossible to remove.

6. Garment patterns may need to be adjusted because it is difficult to shrink out the fullness of darts, sleeves, and so on.

With some important exceptions, like aramid, synthetic fibers melt when exposed to open flame, usually self-extinguish when removed from the flame, form hard beads, and produce a chemical odor. Aramid fibers do not burn but carbonizie. Nomex® carbonizes at 700° F, and Kevlar® at 900° F.

CARE OF SYNTHETIC FIBERS

Due to their common properties, some general care procedures can be recommended for synthetic fibers. In general, synthetics are easy to care for and are used frequently in wash-and-wear garments. Machine laundering and line or machine drying are normal care procedures for these fibers. Typically, strong laundry detergents and bleaches can be used because synthetics are chemically resistant. Oil-borne stains need pretreatment for best removal, however. Extreme care is needed when ironing or pressing most synthetics because they are heat sensitive. Melted fibers, undesirable glazing, and holes may result from excessive heat. Frequently, synthetics need no ironing. However, the heat sensitivity of synthetics requires they be removed promptly from automatic dryers. If they are allowed to cool in a wrinkled state, garments made of synthetic fibers will retain those wrinkles. Rewashing and drying or ironing may remove the wrinkles. Synthetics may usually be dry cleaned.

With the predominance of blends in the marketplace, the consumer must follow all care label instructions. Each fiber in the blend must be cared for appropriately. Dyes, pigments, decorative designs, and finishes may also require special care.

Storing synthetic textiles is relatively easy because most are not subject to attack by such things as moths, mildew, silverfish, or carpet beetles.

END USES OF SYNTHETIC FIBERS

Synthetic fibers have many uses in apparel, furnishings, and industry. Budget-conscious shoppers are drawn to synthetics because they are easy to care for, durable, and priced modestly. Manufacturers and designers have responded by mass producing basic, practical apparel and furnishings for the low-end market. Because they are so popular for low-cost textile products, synthetics have acquired a negative image for high fashion goods. Synthetic fibers producers are trying to establish synthetics as fashionable alternatives to natural fibers in high-end textiles.

Acrylic

DuPont developed acrylilc fiber during the 1940s and began producing Orlon® in 1950. Acrilan® by Monsanto followed Orlon® in 1952, and Creslan® by American Cyanamid followed in 1958. DuPont ceased Orlon® production in 1991, and in 1992 American Cyanamid spun off its fiber division, Cytec Industries.

There are many varieties of acrylic, including bicomponent acrylic fibers with exceptional resilience, elasticity, and bulk. Acrylic may be dry or wet spun.

SELECTED PROPERTIES OF ACRYLIC

There are certain physical, mechanical, and chemical properties that characterize acrylic.

PHYSICAL PROPERTIES OF ACRYLIC. As with all manufactured fibers, the spinning process determines acrylic's cross section, surface contour, and diameter. Wet-spun acrylics are round or bean shaped. Dry-spun acrylics are dog-bone shaped. Bean and round shapes have greater resilience, while dog-bone shapes have increased softness and luster.

Acrylic fibers may have striations and they may be smooth or twisted. Most acrylic is crimped. The fiber is available as staple or tow. Acrylic fiber, when it is textured and spun, is known for its wool-like qualities. It is soft, pleasant, and provides good cover. Some filament acrylic is imported into the United States.

MECHANICAL PROPERTIES OF ACRYLIC. Acrylic has moderate tenacity and moderate abrasion resistance. It is similar to wool or cotton in durability, so it is not as durable as nylon, olefin, or polyester. Pilling is a major problem with acrylic. Some low-pilling varieties have been developed, and special finishes can be used to reduce the pilling tendency. In general, acrylic's resiliency, elastic recovery, and dimensional stability are considered moderate. There are many types of acrylic, and dimensional stability can vary among the types. Specially crimped acrylics may need automatic drying after washing to restore the fibers' original shape. The specific gravity of acrylic is low.

CHEMICAL PROPERTIES OF ACRYLIC. Acrylic has poor absorbency but good wicking, especially in microdenier. Chemically, acrylic resists acids except nitric acid, which will dissolve it. It moderately resists alkalis but is degraded by sodium hydroxide. Strong lanudry detergents and most bleaches, except chlorine bleach, are safe to use, although dry-cleaning solvents may cause some stiffening. Because the electrical conductivity of acrylic is very low, static cling is a problem unless appropriate finishes are applied or fabric softeners are used.

Acrylic is sensitive to heat, so crimp, pleats, and creases can be heat set. However, high temperatures may discolor the fiber, and steam may cause shrinkage. Acrylic fibers burn and melt when exposed to open flame. They continue to burn when the flame is removed, form black beads, and produce a chemical odor.

END USES OF ACRYLIC

Acrylics are frequently used as lightweight, nonallergenic wool substitutes. The fiber's resilience, bulk, cover, and insulating qualities are very similar to those of wool. Acrylic offers easy care and a pleasant hand, free of the itchiness of wool. End uses for acrylic in apparel include sweaters, socks, blankets, and fleece or high-pile fabrics. Acrylic is also used to create fur substitutes.

End uses for acrylics in furnishings include upholstery fabrics and carpet. Because acrylic resists the sun, draperies and outdoor items such as awnings, tarpaulins, tents, and outdoor furniture are other appropriate end uses.

Acrylic is an important craft yarn for such items as hand-knit or crocheted sweaters, vests, and afghans. It is also used for weaving and other crafts.

TRADE NAMES OF ACRYLIC

Table 7–1 lists selected acrylic trade names.

TABLE 7–1 SELECT MANUFACTURER/TRADE NAMES FOR ACRYLIC	
Manufacturer	**Trade Name(s)**
Cytec Industries, Inc. West Paterson, NJ	Creslan MicroSupreme
Monsanto Fibers Strategic Business Group New York, NY	Acrilan, Bi-loft, Pil-Trol, Sayelle

CARE OF ACRYLIC

As mentioned earlier, acrylic is an easy-care fiber which may be machine washed and dried. Strong detergents and nonchlorine bleach may be used, but dry-cleaning solvents may cause stiffening. Lower drying temperatures are recommended. Because there are several varieties of acrylic, it is important to follow the care-label instructioins. Steam may shrink acrylics, so steam cleaning carpets, upholstery fabrics, and draperies is not recommended. Dry extraction is recommended for furnishings. Storing acrylics is easy. Mildew and insects do not harm acrylics, and the fiber has good to excellent resistance to sunlight.

Modacrylic

Modacrylic, a modified acrylic, was first produced in the United States in 1947. Monsanto is the only current American producer of the fiber. Modacrylic may be dry spun or wet spun. Only tow or staple fiber is available. The properties of modacrylic are very similar to those of acrylic.

SELECTED PROPERTIES OF MODACRYLIC

There are certain physical, mechanical, and chemical properties that characterize modacrylic.

PHYSICAL PROPERTIES OF MODACRYLIC. The modacrylic fiber is creamy white with dog-bone or an irregular cross section (see Figure 7–2). The fiber surface may appear grainy or striated. The fiber, which is available in varying lengths, diameters, and amounts of crimp, has a soft and warm hand. Modacrylic can be spun into fine, hairlike fibers.

MECHANICAL PROPERTIES OF MODACRYLIC. While both the strength and abrasion resistance of modacrylic are moderate, its pilling propensity is high. Its resilience and elastic recovery are good. Its dimensional stability is moderate. The fiber is heat sensitive and may shrink at high automatic-dryer temperatures. Its specific gravity is like that of wool.

CHEMICAL PROPERTIES OF MODACRYLIC. The absorbency and electrical conductivity of modacrylic are low. Modacrylic has good

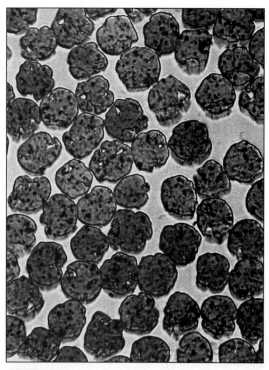 

(A)   (B)

FIGURE 7–2

Photomicrographs in (A) cross–sectional and (B) longitudinal views of modacrylic. (Courtesy of the Fibers Unit of Monsanto Company.)

resistance to acids and moderate resistance to alkalis. The fiber is fire retardant; it is difficult to ignite in open flame but if ignited burns slowly. It self-extinguishes when the flame is removed; leaves a hard, black bead; and burns with a chemical odor. The fiber is very sensitive to heat. It shrinks at 250° F and stiffens at 300° F. As a result, high automatic-dryer temperatures can damage modacrylic textile products.

END USES OF MODACRYLIC

Most end uses of modacrylic take advantage of the fiber's hairlike structure or its flame retardancy. Manufacturers also take advantage of the fiber's shrink potential to create fleece and simulated fur fabrics with both long and short fibers. Modacrylic is used for wigs, hairpieces, and paint-roller covers. Modacrylic's flame-retardant characteristics suit it to children's pajamas, robes, and some work clothes.

Other end uses of modacrylic include wall coverings, industrial filters, window treatments, and blankets and upholstery fabrics for the home and for airplanes. Specialized varieties of modacrylic are used for awnings and boat covers.

TRADE NAMES OF MODACRYLIC

Table 7–2 lists the trade names for modacrylic.

CARE OF MODACRYLIC

Due to its heat sensitivity, modacrylic needs special care. Only "no" or "low-heat" dryer temperatures and low ironing temperatures can be

TABLE 7–2 SELECT MANUFACTURER/TRADE NAMES FOR MODACRYLIC	
Manufacturer	**Trade Name(s)**
Monsanto Fibers Strategic Business Group New York, NY	SEF plus

used with this fiber. Heavy-duty laundry detergents are safe to use, but chlorine bleach may cause discoloration. The care instructions for pile and furlike garments should be followed carefully. Brushing and pressing may cause damage, and steam cleaning may cause shrinkage. Mildew and insects do not attack modacrylic. The fiber's resistance to sunlight is excellent.

Nylon

During the 1930s, Dr. Wallace H. Carothers directed a team of DuPont research scientists working with polymers. Together they created nylon 6,6. At about the same time, German scientists created nylon 6, which is a variation of nylon 6,6. The numbers refer to the number of carbon atoms in the starting material. Most of the nylon made in the United States is nylon 6,6. In Europe nylon 6 is more common. The properties of nylon 6,6 and nylon 6 are very similar.

Nylon is the second most-used manufactured fiber in the United States after polyester. Another generic name for nylon is polyamide. Nylon is melt spun.

SELECTED PROPERTIES OF NYLON

There are certain physical, mechanical, and chemical properties that characterize nylon.

PHYSICAL PROPERTIES OF NYLON.   Regular nylon is a transparent fiber which resembles a glass rod when viewed under a microscope (see Figure 7–3). It is usually spun with a round cross section. Some nylons, however, are spun with trilobal or square cross sections. Nylon is produced in multifilament and monofilament forms, as staple and tow, and in many deniers. It may be dull, semidull, or lustrous, and the fiber may be textured. Nylon's hand is smooth, but the hand may be altered through fiber modifications.

MECHANICAL PROPERTIES OF NYLON.   The abrasion resistance of nylon is outstanding and its strength is excellent. It is an extremely durable fiber, but pilling may be a problem. Nylon is lightweight, its

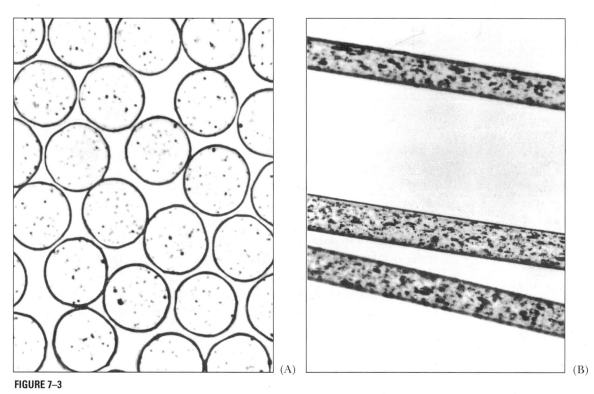

FIGURE 7–3

Photomicrographs in (A) cross–sectional and (B) longitudinal views of nylon 6,6. (Courtesy of DuPont, Wilmington, DE.)

resiliency is good, and its elasticity is high. Nylon's flexibility depends on its denier. High-denier fibers tend to be stiff and therefore have poor drape. In general, nylon has good drape. Fabric structure also impacts nylon's drape. In general, although nylon has good dimensional stability, it may shrink under high temperatures.

CHEMICAL PROPERTIES OF NYLON. Nylon has better absorbency than most synthetic fibers, but it is still considered hydrophobic and it is uncomfortable in warm, humid weather. Nylon made into open fabric structures is more comfortable. Although nylon is chemically resistant, strong acids will dissolve it.

Permanent pleats and creases can be heat set into nylon, but high ironing temperatures (445° F may cause undesirable glazing. The fiber burns and melts in open flame and usually self-extinguishes after removal from the flame. It leaves a hard bead and produces a celerylike odor. Nylon does not conduct electricity well and builds static electricity.

END USES OF NYLON

The primary end uses for nylon take advantage of the fiber's three outstanding properties: strength, abrasion resistance, and elastic recovery. As a result, nylon dominates the markets for women's hosiery and carpeting.

Because there are many varieties of nylon and the fiber can be modified to meet consumer demands, it has an exceptionally large number of end uses in apparel, furnishings, and industry. Nylon is often used in apparel items such as lingerie and active sportswear.

The major use of nylon in furnishings is carpeting. Nylon carpeting is durable, maintains its original appearance, and is easy to clean. However, nylon is weakened by sunlight. Unless it has been modified to resist sunilght, nylon should not be used for window treatments or other applications requiring long-term sun exposure.

Tire cord is an important industrial end use for nylon. Automotive end uses include upholstery fabrics, carpet, clutch pads, and break linings. Belts, ropes, and parachute fabric are only a few of nylon's many other industrial end uses.

TRADE NAMES OF NYLON

Selected trade names of nylon are listed in Table 7–3.

TABLE 7–3 SELECT MANUFACTURER/TRADE NAMES FOR NYLON	
Manufacturer	**Trade Name**
Allied Signal Fibers Petersburg, VA	Anso Anso IV Caprolan Hydrofil
BASF Corporation Charlotte, NC	Crepeset Zeftron
DuPont Wilmington, DE	Antron Cordura Supplex

CARE OF NYLON

Nylon was the first of the easy-care fibers. Machine washing and drying are usually recommended, but only at low temperatures because high temperatures can cause permanent wrinkles and shrinkage. High ironing temperatures may cause glazing.

Heavy-duty laundry detergents may be used on nylon, but chlorine bleach may cause yellowing. During washing white nylon has a tendency to scavenge colors, which means it picks up colors from other fabrics in the wash. To guard against this, white nylon articles should be washed only with other white clothes. Static electricity is also a problem. Bicomponent fiber modifications, fabric softeners, or antistatic sprays may be used to help eliminate this problem. Dry extraction is recommended for furnishings. Mildew and insects do not attack nylon so storage is not a problem.

Olefin

Early research on olefin fibers was conducted in Germany and Italy. In the United States commercial production of olefin began in 1960. Olefin is a relatively inexpensive fiber, and its use in apparel, furnishings, and industry is increasing.

There are two categories of olefin: **polypropylene** and **polyethylene**. Polypropylene is used more extensively, but use of polyethylene as a high technology fiber is growing. Olefin may be fibrillated mechanically or melt spun.

SELECTED PROPERTIES OF OLEFIN

There are certain physical, mechanical, and chemical properties that characterize olefin.

PHYSICAL PROPERTIES OF OLEFIN.
Olefin fibers are usually round, but their cross sections can be modified by changing shape of the hole in the spinneret (see Figure 7–4).

MECHANICAL PROPERTIES OF OLEFIN.
Olefin has excellent abrasion resistance and high strength, and its elastic recovery is excellent. A

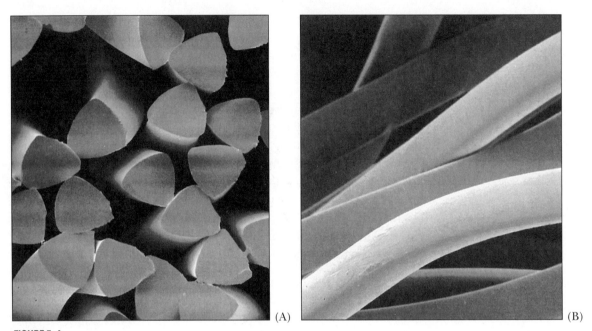

(A) (B)

FIGURE 7–4

Photomicrographs in (A) cross–sectional and (B) longitudinal views of olefin. (Courtesy of Amoco Fabrics and Fibers Company.)

special-application olefin with exceptional strength is also available. Although the fiber's dimensional stability is excellent, it will shrink if exposed to temperatures over 250° F. Its resilience is average.

Olefin's flexibility is determined by fiber production processes, yarn, fabric formations, and finishes. Good drape is achieved with fine-denier fibers.

The low specific gravity of olefin is one of its most positive characteristics, and it is extremely lightweight. Olefin is especially useful when durability, low cost, and low density are necessary.

CHEMICAL PROPERTIES OF OLEFIN. Olefin has extremely poor absorbency but good wicking. Due to its poor absorbency, solution or dope dyeing is the best method to impart color to olefin fibers.

Olefin resists acids and alkalis but is damaged by some dry-cleaning solvents. It is also heat sensitive, melting at 320-350° F. It melts and burns in open flame, but usually self-extinguishes when the flame is removed. It produces sooty smoke, a hard bead, and a chemical odor.

Due to its poor absorbency, olefin has poor electrical conductivity and therefore builds static electricity. Bicomponent fiber modifications and antistatic finishes can be used to eliminate this problem.

END USES OF OLEFIN

Olefin is used in apparel, furnishings, and industry. Its uses are expanding and take advantage of its durability, low specific gravity, and low cost.

Apparel end uses of olefin include underwear, socks, and active sportswear. The wicking ability of olefin contributes comfort to these pieces. Olefin is also blended with other synthetic fibers.

In furnishings olefin is used extensively in carpeting. It is often used for indoor/outdoor carpeting, but light stabilizers are needed to control its degradation from intense sunlight. Olefin is also used in upholstery fabrics, slipcovers, and draperies.

Geotextiles are an important end use for olefin. Applications include roadbed support fabrics and soil-erosion-control fabrics. Other industrial uses include protective garments, ropes, filters, bagging, and car and boat interiors. Olefins are also used in the construction industry.

TRADE NAMES OF OLEFIN

Table 7–4 lists trade names for olefin.

TABLE 7–4	SELECT MANUFACTURER/TRADE NAMES FOR OLEFIN
Manufacturer	**Trade Name(s)**
Allied Signal Fibers Petersburg, VA	Spectra
Amoco Fabrics & Fibers Co. Atlanta, GA	Essera Alpha
Hercules, Inc. Oxford, GA	Herculon (polypropylene) Nouvelle (polypropylene)

CARE OF OLEFIN

Olefin is easy to care for. Due to its low absorbency, it resists most stains. Waterborne stains can be wiped off, but oilborne stains are difficult to remove and need pretreatment. Home laundering at low temperatures and line drying are recommended. Ironing is usually not necessary. If ironing is desired, only low temperatures should be used. Dry cleaning is not usually recommended because olefin is damaged by some dry-cleaning fluids. The dry extraction method of cleaning is recommended for furnishings.

Olefin has excellent resistance to mold, mildew, and insects, so storage is not a problem. Intense sunlight should be avoided unless light stabilizers have been added to the fiber to control light degradation.

Polyester

DuPont introduced polyester in the United States in 1951 under the trade name Dacron®. Polyester is the most widely used synthetic fiber. It is versatile, easily modified to meet consumer preferences, and can be blended with many other fibers. In blends, polyester's positive characteristics complement the positive characteristics of the other fibers. Research has produced many varieties of polyester with outstanding properties. Polyester is melt spun.

PROPERTIES OF POLYESTER

There are certain physical, mechanical, and chemical properties that characterize polyester.

PHYSICAL PROPERTIES OF POLYESTER. In general, polyester, a white fiber, is available in many different cross sections: round, tri- and multilobal, oval, and hollow (see Figure 7–5). Tri- and multilobal fibers have longitudinal striations. Polyester is produced with varying amounts of crimp and comes in bright, medium, or dull luster and in filament, staple, and tow. The hand of polyester can be modified to meet consumer requirements.

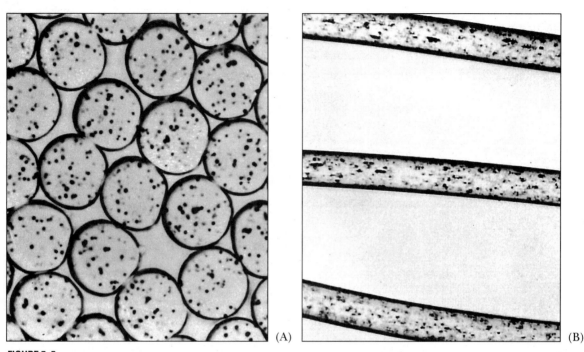

FIGURE 7–5

Photomicrographs in (A) cross–sectional and (B) longitudinal views of Dacron® polyester. (Courtesy of DuPont, Wilmington, DE.)

MECHANICAL PROPERTIES OF POLYESTER. Polyester has excellent abrasion resistance and strength but its pilling may be a problem. Low-pilling varieties of polyester have been developed. Heat-set polyester has excellent dimensional stability. Shrinkage may occur if fabrics have not been heat set.

The excellent resilience of polyester is one of the main reasons it is used in blends. Polyester also has good elasticity. The flexibility of polyester depends on denier, yarn and fabric formations, and finishes. Polyester is a medium-weight fiber.

CHEMICAL PROPERTIES OF POLYESTER. Polyester has low absorbency and average wicking ability. Soil-release finishes, which are discussed in Chapter 14, improve the wicking ability of polyester.

In general, polyester is chemically resistant. It is not harmed by acids, bleaches, or dry-cleaning solvents. Although it may be damaged by strong alkalis, it is not harmed by heavy-duty laundry detergents. Polyester does not conduct electricity, so static electricity is a problem.

Because polyester is heat sensitive, creases and pleats can be permanently set in it. Heat setting also improves polyester's wrinkle resistance and dimensional stability. The fiber melts at 480-490° F, so warm, but not hot, ironing temperatures should be used. Polyester burns slowly and melts in open flame. Usually it self-extinguishes when the flame is removed. It produces black smoke, a hard bead, and a sweet odor.

END USES OF POLYESTER

Polyester's importance as a textile fiber cannot be overemphasized. It is used in apparel, furnishings, and industry. It is used alone or in blends. It is used in knits, wovens, and nonwovens. It is blended predominantly with cotton, but also with wool, silk, rayon, flax, ramie, acetate, and acrylic.

Polyester is used in all types of apparel: underwear, casual and formal wear, uniforms, and outerwear. It is also used extensively in furnishings: sheets and bedding, curtains, table linens, and upholstery fabrics. Polyester fiberfill is a low-cost alternative to down. Polyester is used in pillows, comforters, sleeping bags, and quilted fabric.

Industrial end uses of polyester include tire cord, ropes, sails, and filters.

TRADE NAMES OF POLYESTER

Selected trade names for polyester appear in Table 7–5.

TABLE 7–5 SELECT MANUFACTURER/TRADE NAMES FOR POLYESTER	
Manufacturer	**Trade Name(s)**
AlliedSignal Fibers Petersburg, VA	A.C.E. Compet
DuPont Wilmington, DE	Dacron, Hollofil, Micromattique
Hoechst Celanese New York, NY	E.S.P. Trevira
Wellman, Inc. New York, NY	Fortrel Fortrel Ecospun

CARE OF POLYESTER

In general, polyester can be washed or dry cleaned. Warm water, heavy-duty laundry detergents, and moderate dryer temperatures are recommended. Oily stains, however, require pretreatment, and garments must be removed from the dryer promptly to avoid wrinkles. Moderate ironing temperatures are recommended. All bleaches may be used.

Care labels for polyester must be followed. While polyester is easy to care for, the fibers it is blended with may require special care. Dyes, pigments, decorative designs, and finishes may also require special treatment.

Polyester tends to develop odors caused by the buildup of bacteria and soil in its fabric. Bleach, hot wash water, and special odor-reducing detergents are effective in removing the odor.

Dry extraction cleaning is recommended for furnishings.

Mildew and insects do not attack polyester, and it resists sunlight.

Spandex and Other Elastomeric Fibers

Spandex, or synthetic rubber, is a manufactured elastic fiber. It was introduced by DuPont in 1958. Elastic fibers, also referred to as "elastomeric fibers," also include natural rubber and anidex. Anidex is not produced in the United States. In July 1996, the FTC granted Teijin Limited, a Japanese manufacturer, a new generic classification for its elastomeric fiber, Rexe®. Rexe® is similar to spandex, but chemically different enough to merit its own generic designation. The new generic name has not been determined.

Spandex and natural rubber have many common properties, but spandex is generally considered superior. Spandex is melt spun or solvent spun.

SELECTED PROPERTIES OF SPANDEX

There are cetain physical, mechanical, and chemical properties that characterize spandex.

PHYSICAL PROPERTIES OF SPANDEX. The shape of the cross section of spandex can be round, peanut shell, or dog done. The fiber's longitudinal appearance may be smooth or striated. Spandex is usually white or gray and delustered. The denier of spandex ranges from 20 to 4300. Natural rubber cannot be produced in as fine a denier as spandex. Spandex is available as monofilament or multifilament.

MECHANICAL PROPERTIES OF SPANDEX.   In general, both spandex and natural rubber have poor abrasion resistance and poor tenacity when compared to nonelastic fibers. Spandex is about twice as strong as natural rubber.

Elasticity is the most important property for both spandex and natural rubber. Both have excellent elastic recovery. Spandex can be stretched from 400 to 700 percent of its original length before it breaks. Natural rubber breaks at 500 percent. The elastic recovery for spandex is 99 percent, for natural rubber, it is 97 percent.

The specific gravity of spandex is low. In general, it is heavier than natural rubber but has better strength and can be produced in finer denier. As a result, garments with spandex fibers are lighter and more comfortable than those with natural rubber. Both spandex and natural rubber have good resiliency and dimensional stability.

CHEMICAL PROPERTIES OF SPANDEX.   Spandex has poor absorbency, but it can be dyed. Natural rubber will not accept dye. Spandex resists chemicals much more than natural rubber. Perspiration, body oils, and suntan oil degrade natural rubber but not spandex. Strong concentrations of chlorine bleach degrade and yellow spandex, however. Chlorine concentrations in swimming pools are not high enough to damage spandex. Dry-cleaning solvents and dilute acids and alkalis do not harm spandex.

Spandex is thermoplastic and melts at 446° F. In open flame it burns and melts and continues to burn when the flame is removed. It produces a soft ash and a chemical odor.

END USES OF SPANDEX

Elastomeric fibers are used to add power stretch or comfort stretch to textile products. **Power stretch** provides holding power and elasticity.

Garments with power stretch are foundation garments, swimsuits, and surgical support hose. **Comfort stretch** adds only elasticity and is found in lingerie, stretch lace, leggings, dancewear, fitted sheets, and slipcovers. Athletic apparel and hosiery may have comfort or power stretch.

TRADE NAMES OF SPANDEX

Trade names of spandex are listed in Table 7–6.

Spandex is used as a bare filament, a covered yarn, or a core spun yarn. An elastomeric **covered yarn** has a spandex core which is wrapped with a yarn of another fiber. Elastomeric **core-spun yarn** has a spandex core and is covered with a sheath of staple fiber.

CARE OF SPANDEX

Spandex may be machine washed or dry cleaned, while natural rubber must be washed with care. Moderate dryer and ironing temperatures (below 300° F) are recommended for spandex. Natural rubber should be line dried. Natural rubber deteriorates with age. Spandex retains its appearance longer but also deteriorates with age. Spandex fibers that have aged or been subjected to extreme stretching may break and work themselves to the surface of a garment, and unsightly white or gray fibers appear on the fabric. This effect, sometimes called **"grin-through,"** cannot be reversed.

TABLE 7-6 SELECT MANUFACTURER/TRADE NAMES FOR SPANDEX	
Manufacturer	**Trade Name**
Globe Manufacturing Co. Fall River, MA	Glospan
DuPont Wilmington, DE	Lycra

LABORATORY ASSIGNMENTS

ASSIGNMENT 7–1   **LOCATE ACRYLIC FIBER AND FABRIC SAMPLES**

Attach a fiber and greige fabric sample of acrylic in your swatch book. (Your instructor will provide or you will purchase a swatch kit. Your instructor will show you how to mount the samples.)

ASSIGNMENT 7–2   **LIST THE ADVANTAGES AND DISADVANTAGES OF ACRYLIC**

List the advantages and disadvantages of acrylic on the following chart:

ADVANTAGES	DISADVANTAGES

ASSIGNMENT 7–3   **CREATE A COLLAGE OF END USES FOR ACRYLIC**

Use magazines, catalogs, trade papers, newspapers, and so on, to create a collage of current end uses for acrylic. Include apparel, home furnishings, and/or any other applications.

ASSIGNMENT 7–4   **LOCATE MODACRYLIC FIBER AND FABRIC SAMPLE**

Attach a fiber and a greige fabric sample of modacrylic in your swatch book. (Your instructor will provide or you will purchase a swatch kit. Your instructor will show you how to mount the samples.)

ASSIGNMENT 7–5   **LIST THE ADVANTAGES AND DISADVANTAGES OF MODACRYLIC**

List the advantages and disadvantages of modacrylic on the following chart:

ADVANTAGES	DISADVANTAGES

ASSIGNMENT 7–6   **CREATE A COLLAGE OF END USES FOR MODACRYLIC**

Use magazines, catalogs, trade papers, newspapers, and so on, to create a collage of current end uses for modacrylic. Include apparel, home furnishings, and/or any other applications.

ASSIGNMENT 7–7   **LOCATE NYLON FIBER AND FABRIC SAMPLES**

Attach a fiber and a greige fabric sample of nylon in your swatch book. (Your instructor will provide or you will purchase a swatch kit. Your instructor will show you how to mount the samples.)

ASSIGNMENT 7–8   **LIST THE ADVANTAGES AND DISADVANTAGES OF NYLON**

List the advantages and disadvantages of nylon on the following chart:

ADVANTAGES	DISADVANTAGES

ASSIGNMENT 7–9   **CREATE A COLLAGE OF END USES FOR NYLON**

Use magazines, catalogs, trade papers, newspapers, and so on, to create a college of current end uses for nylon. Include apparel, home furnishings, and/or any other applications.

ASSIGNMENT 7–10   **LOCATE OLEFIN FIBER AND FABRIC SAMPLES**

Attach a fiber and a greige fabric sample of olefin in your swatch book. (Your instructor will provide or you will purchase a swatch kit. Your instructor will show you how to mount the samples.)

ASSIGNMENT 7–11   **LIST THE ADVANTAGES AND DISADVANTAGES OF OLEFIN**

List the advantages and disadvantages of olefin on the following chart:

ADVANTAGES	DISADVANTAGES

ASSIGNMENT 7–12   **CREATE A COLLAGE OF END USES FOR OLEFIN**

Use magazines, catalogs, trade papers, newspapers, and so on, to create a collage of current end uses for olefin. Include apparel, home furnishings, and/or any other applications.

ASSIGNMENT 7–13   **LOCATE POLYESTER FIBER AND FABRIC SAMPLES**

Attach a fiber and a greige fabric sample of polyester in your swatch book. (Your instructor will provide or you will purchase a swatch kit. Your instructor will show you how to mount the samples.)

ASSIGNMENT 7–14   **LIST THE ADVANTAGES AND DISADVANTAGES OF POLYESTER**

List the advantages and disadvantages of polyester on the following chart:

ADVANTAGES	DISADVANTAGES

ASSIGNMENT 7–15   **CREATE A COLLAGE OF END USES FOR POLYESTER**

Use magazines, catalogs, trade papers, newspapers, and so on, to create a collage of current end uses for polyester. Include apparel, home furnishings, and/or any other applications.

ASSIGNMENT 7–16   **LOCATE SPANDEX FIBER AND FABRIC SAMPLES**

Attach a fiber and a greige fabric sample of spandex in your swatch book. (Your instructor will provide or you will purchase a swatch kit. Your instructor will show you how to mount the samples.)

ASSIGNMENT 7–17   **LIST THE ADVANTAGES AND DISADVANTAGES OF SPANDEX**

List the advantages and disadvantages of spandex on the following chart:

ADVANTAGES	DISADVANTAGES

ASSIGNMENT 7–18   **CREATE A COLLAGE OF END USES FOR SPANDEX**

Use magazines, catalogs, trade papers, newspapers, and so on, to create a collage of current end uses for spandex. Include apparel, home furnishings, and/or any other applications.

Special-Application Fibers

OBJECTIVES

The student will be able to:

1. Recognize and classify special application fibers
2. Discuss the properties of special application fibers
3. Recommend appropriate end uses for special application fibers
4. Appreciate the importance of special application fibers

Introduction

The fibers discussed in this chapter, the special-application fibers, have specific applications or limited use in the textile industry. Some are no longer produced in the United States but are examples of important technological developments. Some special-application fibers provide important benefits. Glass curtains do not burn, for example. These fibers represent significant ways in which the textile industry continues to develop and improve products that meet the needs of its consumers, both private and industrial.

Anidex

Anidex is a lightweight elastomeric fiber which was produced by Rohm and Haas from 1970 to 1975 for use in swimwear and skiwear. It is no longer produced in the United States.

Aramid

DuPont introduced fibers under the trade name Nomex® nylon in 1963. Aramids are used primarily in industry for their strength and flame-resistant characteristics. Previously classified with nylon, in 1974, the FTC created a generic category for aramid fibers.

Aramid fibers are usually produced in a round or dog-bone shape (see Figure 8–1). Regular-tenacity aramid fibers have exceptional strength. High-tenacity aramids have excellent impact and abrasion resistance and good dimensional stability but a higher specific gravity than nylon. Aramid fibers have poor absorbency and poor electrical

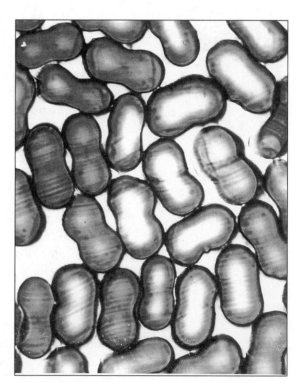

FIGURE 8–1

Photomicrograph of the cross section of aramid. (Courtesy of DuPont, Wilmington, DE.)

TABLE 8–1 SELECT MANUFACTURER/TRADE NAMES FOR ARAMID	
Manufacturer	**Trade Names**
DuPont	Kevlar
Wilmington, DE	Nomex

conductivity. They resist most chemicals but are degraded by hot concentrated acids and alkalis. They are also difficult to dye. Some dyes can increase flammability. They do not melt, have very low flammability, and decompose at temperatures above 700° F.

The two most common trade names for aramid are Kevlar® and Nomex®. Both are produced by DuPont. Kevlar® is five times stronger than steel and is used primarily in strength applications where low weight is desirable. It has excellent impact resistance and is used in bullet-resistant garments, automobile tires, and sporting equipment. Nomex® is used when flame resistance is important. Examples include apparel for firefighters and race-car drivers. Other end uses for aramid fibers are ropes, cables, electrical insulation, and military clothing.

Cleaning aramid fibers is not typically a concern because they are used primarily in industrial applications, as mentioned earlier. A major disadvantage of aramid fibers is their poor resistance to sunlight. Therefore, appropriate accommodations for their use and storage must be made.

Table 8–1 lists the trade names for aramid.

Azlon

Azlon is the generic name for regenerated protein fibers made from milk, peanut, corn, and soybean proteins. The United States, Britain, Italy, and Japan have developed protein fibers. Research continues, but at this time no regenerated protein fibers are produced in the United States. Japan has developed a fiber made of milk protein and acrylic under the trade Chinon® which it exports to the United States. It resembles silk and is used in blouses, scarves, and ties and as filters to purify medicine.

Carbon

Carbon fibers are especially important in industry because they are often used in the same applications as glass or aramid and as substitutes for asbestos. Graphite is a special type of carbon fiber. The characteristics of carbon fibers include:

- high strength
- lightweight
- do not melt or ignite
- excellent resistance to solvents and hot concentrated acids and alkalis
- degraded by chlorine bleach

Carbon fibers are used in the construction industry to reinforce buildings and bridges; in sporting goods such as bicycles, golf clubs, and skis; and in medicine to replace bone. Carbon is also blended with other fibers to create epitropic fibers, which conduct electricity. Such fibers are used in static-resistant carpeting.

Table 8–2 lists the trade names for carbon fibers.

TABLE 8–2 SELECT MANUFACTURER/TRADE NAMES FOR CARBON FIBERS	
Manufacturer	**Trade Name**
Akzo Nobel Fortafil Fibers, Inc. Knoxville, TN	Fortafil
Amoco Performance Products, Inc. Alpharetta, GA	Thornel

Fluorocarbon

Fluorocarbon fibers are sometimes referred to as polytetrafluoroethylene (PTFE) fibers. They have no generic classification and have not been defined by the FTC. In general, PTFE fibers are:

- abrasion resistant
- nonabsorbent
- chemically resistant (PTFE fibers have the best chemical resistance of any fiber)
- heat resistant

TABLE 8–3 SELECT MANUFACTURER/TRADE NAME FOR FLUOROCARBON FIBERS	
Manufacturer	**Trade Name**
DuPont Wilmington, DE	Teflon
W.L. Gore & Assoc., Inc. Elkton, MD	GORE-TEX

Teflon®, which most consumers recognize as a nonstick coating for cookware, is a fluorocarbon. It can be produced as a thin film with many microscopic holes. PTFE is used to make GORE-TEX® fabrics, which are popular for outdoor-sports apparel. A layer of PTFE is laminated to the back of a piece of outerwear fabric to provide the benefit of waterproofing while allowing perspiration to evaporate, thereby keeping the wearer comfortable. Refer to Chapter 12 for additional discussion of GORE-TEX®.

Other end uses for PTFE include gaskets, filters, bearings, and protective clothing.

Table 8–3 lists the trade names for flurocarbon fibers.

Glass

The Owens-Corning Fiberglas Corporation first produced glass fiber in 1936. Glass fibers have almost no application in apparel and limited application in furnishings, but they are extremely useful in industry. Glass fibers have the following properties:

- Exceptional strength but very poor abrasion resistance. The fibers are very brittle and break when bent or creased. These broken fibers are very irritating to the skin.
- High specific gravity.
- Completely nonabsorbent, requiring special dyeing procedures.
- Do not conduct heat or electricity.
- Completely noncombustible, but melt at 1350° F.
- Good resistance to organic solvents and acids; can be damaged by alkalis.

- Not attacked by mildew or insects.
- Not degraded by sunlight.
- Transmit light.

Most glass fibers are used in industry because they are effective thermal and electrical insulators. They are used as reinforcement in molded plastics for boats and airplanes (see Figure 8–2).

FIGURE 8–2

Fiber glass roving. (Courtesy of PPG Industries, Inc.)

TABLE 8–4 SELECT MANUFACTURER/TRADE NAMES FOR GLASS FIBERS	
Manufacturer	**Trade Name(s)**
Owens-Corning Fiberglas Corporation Toledo, OH	Fiberglas
PPG Industries, Inc. Pittsburgh, PA	LEX TEXO

Glass is also used when nonflamable draperies and curtains are needed. However, glass window treatments are very heavy and require special rods and additional support.

An important end use for glass fibers is in the fiber optics field. Fine filaments of glass can transmit beams of light over long distances.

Because glass fiber is very brittle, it must be cleaned very carefully. Glass is nonabsorbent, so it does not get dirty in the usual sense, but it does get dusty and dingy. Hand washing or vacuuming is recommended.

Table 8–4 lists the trade names for glass fibers.

Lastrile

Lastrile is an elastomeric fiber with properties similar to those of other elastic fibers. Lastrile fibers are not produced in the United States.

Metal

There are three methods to produce metallic fibers:

1. The fibers are drawn from a metal rod.
2. Thin sheets of metal are laminated between layers of acetate or polyester film and then cut into fine strips.
3. Aluminum is vaporized under high pressure, deposited on polyester film, then cut into fine strips.

Research into the use of stainless-steel fibers began in 1960. These fibers are frequently used in carpets to control static electricity because the metal conducts electrical charges and static does not build. Only a small amount, 1 to 3 percent, of metallic fiber is needed.

Metallic fibers have long been used to decorate clothing. Originally, thin strips of gold and silver were used. They were fragile and expensive, however, and silver threads tarnished. Now, aluminum, steel, iron, nickel, and cobalt-based superalloys are used.

In industry, metallic fibers are used not only to control static electricity but also to create tire cord, wiring, and cabling and to assist heart surgery.

In apparel and furnishings, metallic fibers add a decorative touch to swimwear, eveningwear, tablecloths, sweaters, and accessories.

Most metallic fibers can be washed or dry cleaned. Vaporized or laminated metallic fibers are heat sensitive, so only low ironing temperatures can be used. High heat melts the plastic film.

Memtec America Corporation of DeLand, Florida, produces metallic fibers under the trade name FIBERMET®.

Novoloid

Novoloid fibers have outstanding flame-resistant qualities. They do not melt or burn but carbonize at high temperatures. They have low strength, fair abrasion resistance, and good chemical resistance. Their primary uses are industrial. These fiber are no longer produced in the United States but are imported by American Kynol, Inc., under the trade name Kynol®.

Nytril

Nytril is no longer produced. It was a soft, resilient fiber used in pile fabrics and wool blends. It has been replaced by other synthetic fibers.

PBI

Hoechst Celanese began producing PBI in 1983. PBI stands for polybenzimidazole, which is its chemical name. The fiber has outstanding heat resistance and produces little or no smoke when exposed to

FIGURE 8–3

PBI® Gold is worn by most firefighters in the United States. PBI is identified by its gold color. It can be dyed black with some difficulty, but is most often seen in its natural gold color. (Courtesy of Hoechst Celanese PBI.)

open flame. It is used in protective apparel and in furnishings for aircraft and hospitals.

Saran

Saran is primarily used in industry and agriculture. In agriculture saran is used to provide shade for young plants. Some of its other end uses include webbing and upholstery for patio furniture, upholstery for public transit vehicles, and flame-resistant draperies.

Because saran is normally spun in very large denier, resulting fabrics tend to be stiff and have very poor drape. In general, saran is:

- strong
- heavier than most synthetics (high specific gravity)

- abrasion resistant
- resilient
- resistant to chemicals, mildew, insects, and sunlight
- slow burning in an open flame, self-extinguishing when the flame is removed
- nonabsorbent

Sulfar

Sulfar is a strong fiber with good chemical and heat resistance. Its applications include gas and liquid filters, papermaker felts, protective clothing, electrical insulation, and rubber reinforcement. Sulfar's generic classification was established in 1986.

Amoco Fabrics & Fibers Company, Atlanta, GA, produces sulfar under the trade name of Ryton®.

Vinal

Vinal fiber resists chemicals and biological attack. In the United States, vinal end uses are primarily industrial and include filters, brush bristles, and fishing nets. Overseas, it is also used for protective clothing. Vinal is no longer produced in the United States, but it is made in Japan and Germany.

Vinyon

Production of vinyon, a chemically resistant fiber with a low melting point (softens at 150° F to 170° F), began in the United States in 1939. The fiber's low melting point makes it unsuited to apparel but an especially appropriate bonding agent for rugs, papers, and nonwoven fabrics. It is also used to make tea bags.

Yarn Formation

OBJECTIVES

The student will be able to:

1. Outline procedures for forming filament and staple yarns
2. Compare and contrast the characteristics of combed and carded staple yarns and regular and textured filament yarns
3. Differentiate between single, ply, cord, and novelty yarns
4. Discuss the importance of yarn twist
5. Explain the reasons for blending
6. Discuss the yarn number systems
7. Relate the characteristics of yarns to the overall performance of apparel, furnishings, and industrial textiles
8. Suggest appropriate end uses for various kinds of yarns

Introduction

The American Society for Testing Materials (ASTM) defines a *yarn* as a continuous strand of textile fibers, filaments, or materials in a form that can be used to make fabric. Fiber properties can be enhanced or modified by the way the fibers are made into yarns. Some fibers need extensive processing to become yarns while others, such as monofilaments, need very little processing. The resulting yarns are used to make knitted or woven fabrics. Felt and nonwoven fabrics lack yarn structure and go directly from fiber to fabric. Nonwovens are discussed in Chapter 12.

FILAMENT VERSUS STAPLE YARNS

Yarns may take two basic forms: filament or long fibers and staple or short fibers. All natural fibers except silk begin as staple fibers and are made into spun yarns. Silk and all manufactured fibers are produced as filament fibers and are used to make filament yarns. All filament fibers may be cut to staple lengths and processed into spun yarns (see Figure 9–1). Twisting holds the fibers together.

INDUSTRY TERMINOLOGY

In the textiles industry, the term drawing has two definitions. It is the process of stretching manufactured filaments to increase strength, and it is the step in yarn formation which blends and combines several carded slivers into one drawn sliver. Spinning also has two industry definitions. It is the production of manufactured fibers, and it is the process of making yarn from staple fibers.

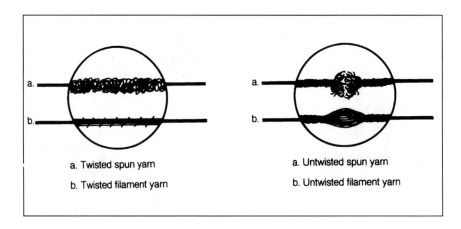

a. Twisted spun yarn

b. Twisted filament yarn

a. Untwisted spun yarn

b. Untwisted filament yarn

FIGURE 9–1

Filament and spun yarns

Filament Yarn Formation

There are several subcategories of filament yarns.

MONOFILAMENT AND MULTIFILAMENT YARNS

Manufactured fibers are extruded from the spinneret in filament form. Filament yarns may be monofilament or multifilament. A **monofilament yarn** is simply one fiber. Monofilament yarns usually are drawn, or stretched, to increase their strength. Monofilaments are used in women's hosiery, saran fabric webbing, fishing line, and industry.

Multifilament yarns are more common than monofilament yarns. To create a **multifilament yarn**, all fibers for one yarn, usually from 20 to 120, are extruded at once. The fibers are then drawn to increase their strength. Drawing may also be done later.

The resulting multifilament yarn is twisted to make it more cohesive. Twist is discussed in more detail later in this chapter. Silk filament yarns are reeled directly from the cocoons. After twisting, the multifilament yarn is wound onto a bobbin. From the bobbin the yarn is wound onto spools or cones. It is ready for use in weaving, knitting, or other textile applications, or it can be given treatments such as dye, finish, or texture. Filament yarns may be processed further by:

1. The fiber manufacturer.
2. Throwsters, who texture yarns.
3. Yarn converters, who add special finishes or dyes. Yarn converters may also serve as throwsters.

TEXTURED FILAMENT YARNS

The smooth, lustrous characteristics of regular, or conventional, filament yarns are appropriate for many used including lingerie, apparel linings, and evening clothing. However, many consumers prefer the feel of staple yarns. Filament yarns can be textured to produce a hand that resembles staple yarns. Textured filament yarns have many other positive characteristics, including:

- increased comfort
- warmth
- increased absorbency

- softer, bulkier hand
- decreased pilling (some yarns)
- added stretch (some yarns)

METHODS OF TEXTURING YARNS. Yarns may be textured to improve stretch or increase bulk. False twist, knife edge, or edge crimping are methods used to improve stretch. The processes for improving bulk are stuffer box, air jet, and knit-deknit. Table 9–1 summarizes the methods used to texture yarns. Figure 9–2 diagrams each process.

False Twist. In false twist, the yarn is twisted, heated, and then untwisted so it forms a helical coil. This method is used widely and produces yarn with excellent characteristics. It is used frequently to make yarns for fabrics resembling crepe (see Figure 9–2A).

Knife Edge or Edge Crimping. In the knife edge method, heated filaments are drawn over an edge, which flattens one side of the filaments and causes the yarn to curl. This process is similar to curling ribbon with a scissor blade (see Figure 9–2B).

Gear Crimping. A sawtooth crimp is created when yarn passes through the teeth of two heated gears in gear crimping. This method is seldom used because temperature and pressure must be carefully controlled to prevent yarn breakage (see Figure 9–2C).

Stuffer Box. In stuffer box, filament yarns are pushed into one end of a small heated box until they bend. They are then removed from the other end of the box in crimped form. This method produces a 200 to 300 percent increase in apparent volume. It is fast, inexpensive, and widely used (see Figure 9–2D).

TABLE 9–1   SUMMARY OF METHODS TO TEXTURE YARNS

I. Texturing for Stretch
   A. False Twist
   B. Knife Edge or Edge Crimping
   C. Gear Crimping

II. Texturing for Bulk
   A. Stuffer Box
   B. Air Jet
   C. Knit Deknit

African Weave

Kuna Indian Mola

Woven Fabric

Damask Silk

Gold Lamé

Guatemalan Woven

Indonesian Batik

Crushed Velvet

Gingham

Checkered Quilt

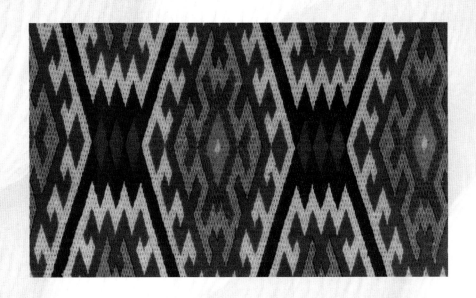

Embroidered Fabric

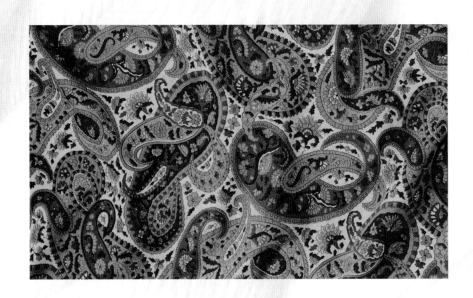

Paisley Print

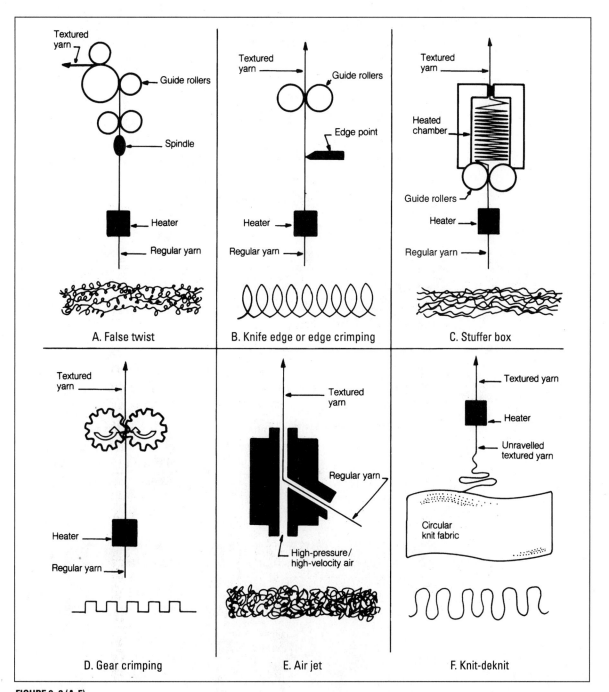

FIGURE 9–2 (A-F)

Methods of producing textured yarn.

Air Jet. High-velocity air or steam is used in the air jet method to distort some of the fibers in a yarn so they loop or cult (see Figure 9–2E). The volume of the yarn increases from 50 to 150 percent as a result. Because only some of the fibers are distorted, the loops remain even when the yarn is pulled taut. Stretch, however, is not improved.

Knit-Deknit. In the knit-deknit method, yarn is knitted into a thin tube, heat set, and unraveled. The unraveled yarn will retain the looped shape formed by the knitting (see Figure 9–2F).

CLASSIFYING FILAMENT YARNS

There are two major categories of filament yarn: regular or conventional and bulk (see Table 9–2). The ASTM has classified textured yarns as bulk yarns. **Bulk yarns** have greater covering power and apparent volume than similar conventional yarns. Filament bulk yarns are sometimes called **bulk-continuous-filament (BCF) yarns**. There are three types of bulk yarns:

1. bulky
2. crimped
3. textured

BULKY YARNS. **Bulky yarns** are created from fibers which, due to their inherent characteristics, cannot be packed closely together. The cross-sectional shape, natural crimp, and resilience of these fibers contribute to their bulk. Bulky yarns are used in sweaters, carpet, upholstery, and warm hosiery.

TABLE 9–2 CLASSIFICATION OF FILAMENT YARNS

I. Regular or Conventional

II. Bulk Yarns
A. Bulky Yarns
B. Crimped Yarns
C. Textured Yarns
1. Loopy yarns
2. High-bulk yarns
3. Stretch yarns

CRIMPED YARNS.   Crimped yarns are usually made of thermoplastic fibers, most commonly by the false-twist process. Crimped yarns may be used when stretch is needed or the yarn may be stabilized so it does not stretch.

TEXTURED YARNS.   Mechanical, chemical, and/or heat treatments are used to texture yarns. Spun as well as filament yarns may be textured. If thermoplastic yarns are textured, heat setting can make the new texture permanent. The ASTM has separated textured yarns into three categories:

1. textured
2. high-bulk
3. stretch

Loopy Yarns.   **Loopy yarns** can be identified by the irregularly spaced loops along their lengths. The loops are produced by air-jet texturing, a process any fiber can undergo.

High-Bulk Yarns.   **High-bulk yarns** are combinations of manufactured fibers, usually two variants of acrylic with different shrink potentials. When the yarn is exposed to steam or boiling water, the unstable fibers shring and crimp the shrink-resistant fibers. High-bulk yarns do not usually have much stretch. They have a soft, luxurious hand but tend to pill easily.

Stretch Yarns.   **Stretch yarns**, as defined by ASTM, have a high degree of elastic stretch and rapid recovery. The two methods used to create stretch yarns are false twist and knife edge or edge crimping. Stretch yarns created during the yarn formation process should not be confused with elastomeric yarns, in which elastic recovery is a property of the fiber.

Staple Yarn Formation

As has been discussed before, the process of creating a cohesive yarn from short fibers is called spinning. There are three major spinning systems:

1. cotton
2. worsted (originally used for longer wool fibers, but now also used for longer manufactured fibers)

3. woolen (originally used for shorter wool fibers, but now also used for shorter manufactured fibers)

Each system was designed to take advantage of the unique characteristics of the natural fiber for which it was named. Manufactured fibers may be processed on any of the three systems. More yarn is produced on the cotton system than the others. Figure 9–3 illustrates the basic steps in staple yarn formation.

THE COTTON SYSTEM

The **cotton system** is primarily used for cotton, silk noil, and short manufactured fibers. The four main steps in the cotton system are:

1. opening, cleaning, and blending
2. carding/combing
3. drawing
4. spinning or twisting

OPENING, CLEANING, AND BLENDING. In the first step of the cotton system, the cotton bales are opened and the fibers loosened. The bales contain sand, grit, leaves, and twigs from the fields. The cotton must be cleaned to remove dirt and vegetable matter. Cotton fiber from several different bales is blended to achieve more uniform yarns (see Figure 9–3A).

Modern textile mills, in compliance with Occupational Safety and Health Act (OSHA) requirements, have mechanized the opening and blending of cotton to protect workers from cotton dust. Breathing cotton dust appears to be related to byssinosis, a serious lung disease.

Although manufactured fibers do not need to be cleaned, the fibers may need to be loosened and separated, especially if they have been compressed for storage or shipping.

CARDING/COMBING. After the cotton bales are open, cleaned, and blended, the fibers are transported to a carding machine, which is set with many bent wires. During **carding**, these wires separate and partially align the fibers to form a thin web. This web is drawn through a funnel, which forms an untwisted strand of somewhat parallel fibers. This strand is called a **sliver** (see Figure 9–3B).

(A)

FIGURE 9–3

Cotton system of yarn formation. (A) opening the bales and (B) carding. (Courtesy of the National Cotton Council of America.)

(B)

Combing is the process of further aligning the fibers (see Figure 9–3C). A comblike device removes shorter fibers and makes the remaining fibers more parallel. This additional processing results in a combed yarn that is smoother, finer, and more expensive than carded yarn. **Percale** is an example of a fabric made from combed yarn. **Muslin** is a fabric made from carded yarn. Table 9–3 summarizes the difference between carded and combed yarns.

DRAWING.   In this step of the process, several slivers are combined and passed through a series of smooth drums which revolve at different speeds. The slivers are blended and elongated in this process, called drawing. Drawing increases yarn uniformity and adds a small amount of twist.

Carded sliver is drawn twice after carding. Combed sliver is drawn once after carding and twice after combing. The drawn sliver, either carded or combed, is then fed into a **roving frame** where the strands are further elongated and given a little more twist. At this point, the sliver becomes a **roving**. The sliver may be subjected to several roving operations (see Figure 9–3D).

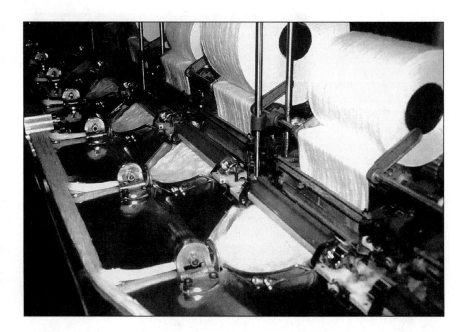

FIGURE 9–3

(C) combing

TABLE 9–3   CHARACTERISTICS OF CARDED AND COMBED YARNS

Carded Yarns

    Surface is fuzzier, bulkier, and has more fiber ends than that of combed yarns

    Diameter of the yarn is somewhat irregular

    Twist is medium to low

    Yarn is composed of fibers of varying lengths

    Increased pilling propensity

    May retain soil more easily

Combed Yarns

    Surface is smoother and has fewer fiber ends than that of carded yarns

    Diameter of the yarn is fairly even

    Twist may be medium to high

    Yarn is usually finer than carded yarn

    Yarn fibers are more uniform and longer than those of carded type

    Crisper hand

FIGURE 9–3

(D) drawing

SPINNING OR TWISTING. This step adds the twist necessary to make a yarn. The two spinning methods that dominate the industry are **open-end spinning** and **ring spinning** (see Figures 9-3E and F).

FIGURE 9–3

(E) open-end spinning

FIGURE 9–3

(F) ring spinning

In **ring spinning**, the roving is twisted and wound onto a bobbin in one operation, feeding through an eyelet and then through a traveler. As the traveler rotates around a stationary ring, the yarn winds onto a bobbin which is turning at a constant speed (see Figure 9–4).

Ring spinning produces finer and stronger yarns than other spinning systems. Ring-spun yarns are especially desirable for knits and polyester/cotton blends. Recent technological innovations have increased the speed and efficiency of ring spinning in response to increased demand for finer yarns. Ring spinning is expected to continue to be important in the industry.

Open-end or **break spinning** was developed as a high-speed alternative to ring spinning. It produces yarn at about four times the rate of ring spinning. In this process, no roving is formed. Instead, the sliver is

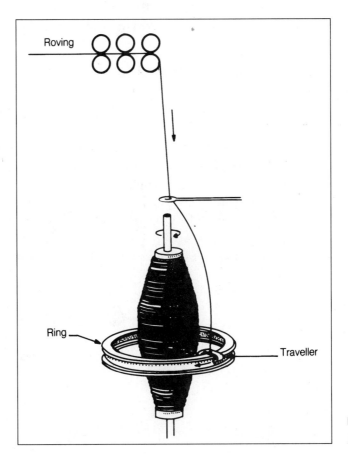

FIGURE 9–4

Ring spinning

broken up and fibers are fed into a rapidly turning roter where centrifugal force deposits them in a V-shaped groove. As yarn is pulled out, more fibers are added constantly.

Although faster, open-end spinning produces coarse and medium-size yarns which are about 20 percent weaker than ring-spun yarns. Open-end spinning is especially appropriate for toweling pile and muslin.

Tow-to-top spinning is a specialized process to create yarns directly from filament tow. Tow is a multifilament group to be cut to staple lengths. This multifilament group becomes sliver (or top) when the tow is cut into short lengths. Sometimes, instead of being cut, the strand is stretched until it breaks into short lengths. Because the broken fibers are already parallel, picking and carding are not necessary to create the sliver. Conventional spinning methods convert the sliver to yarn. (*Tow* has two industry definitions. It also refers to short linen fibers or linen yarns that are made of short fibers and used in fabric when a coarse texture is desired.)

OTHER YARN-SPINNING SYSTEMS

Other yarn-spinning methods include woolen and worsted yarns.

WOOLEN YARNS.   In the woolen system, after cleaning and blending, a small amount of oil is added to facilitate carding and spinning. The drawing step is eliminated. The woolen system produces **woolen yarns**, which are soft and bulky with fiber ends on their surface. The term *woolen* refers to a type of yarn. It does not mean a yarn is made of

FIGURE 9–5

(A) Woolen yarn and

(B) Worsted yarn

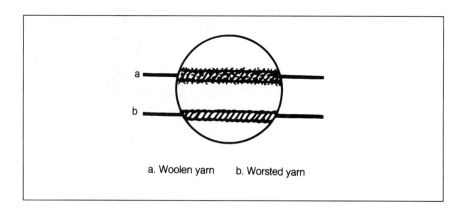

a. Woolen yarn   b. Worsted yarn

TABLE 9–4	CHARACTERISTICS OF CONVENTIONAL FILAMENT, STAPLE, AND TEXTURED FILAMENT YARNS

Conventional Filament Yarns
Yarn surface is smooth
Yarns may be less tightly twisted
Fibers are as long as the yarn
Yarn does not pull apart when untwisted
Fibers are parallel

Staple Yarns
Yarn surface is fuzzier
Yarns have higher twist
Fibers are shorter than the yarn
Yarn pulls apart when untwisted
Fibers may not be completely parallel

Textured Filament Yarns
Yarn surface is bulky, irregular
Yarn usually has low twist
Fibers are as long as the yarn
Yarn does not pull apart when untwisted
Fibers are not parallel

wool fibers. Woolens are weak and have poor abrasion resistance compared with other yarns. Shorter woolen fibers and manufactured staple fibers may be processed on this system.

WORSTED YARNS. Longer wool fibers and manufactured fibers are processed in the worsted system. After carding, the sliver is further processed for additional straightening. **Worsted yarns** are smoother, stronger, and twisted more tightly than woolen yarns. Figure 9–5 illustrates the difference between woolen and worsted yarns. Table 9–4 summarizes the characteristics of filament, staple, and textured yarns.

Types of Yarns

In addition to being classified as filament, textured filament, and staple, yarns may also be categorized as simple or novelty.

SIMPLE YARNS

Simple yarns are typically made into relatively flat, smooth fabrics. There are three types of simple yarns: single, ply, and cord.

SINGLE YARNS. A **single yarn**, if untwisted, will separate into individual fibers. Because single yarns are the least expensive to produce, most fabrics are made of singles.

PLY YARNS. **Ply yarns** are two or more single yarns twisted together. A two-ply yarn is two singles twisted together, a three-ply yarn is three singles twisted together, and so on. Ply yarns are stronger than singles and usually considered to be of higher quality. In apparel most plied yarns are two-ply. Sewing threads are ply yarns. It is important to use the terms *yarn* and **thread** correctly. Yarn is used to create fabric, thread is used to sew a garment.

CORD YARNS. **Cord** or **cable yarns** are two or more ply yarns twisted together. Cord yarns have little application in clothing or furnishings but are used in industry.

NOVELTY YARNS

Novelty yarns add textural interest and beauty to fabrics. They are sometimes called fancy or complex yarns. Most novelty yarns have three parts:

1. the base or core
2. the fancy or effect ply (which adds decorative or novelty appearance)
3. the binder (a single yarn that binds the fancy yarn to the core yarn)

Frequently novelty yarns abrade easily and/or are subject to snagging.

POPULAR TYPES OF NOVELTY YARNS.

Bouclé. **Bouclé yarns**, sometimes called loop or **curl yarns**, are ply yarns in which an effect yarn loops around the core yarn. The effect yarn is held in place by a binder. (See Figure 9–6A.)

FIGURE 9–6

(A) Bouclé yarn;

(B) Chenille yarn; (C) Flake,

flock, or seed yarn; (D) Knub,

spot, or knop yarn; (E) Slub

or thick-and-thin yarn;

(F) Spiral or corkscrew yarn

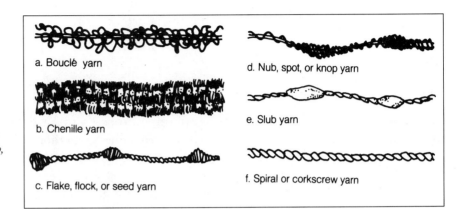

a. Bouclé yarn

b. Chenille yarn

c. Flake, flock, or seed yarn

d. Nub, spot, or knop yarn

e. Slub yarn

f. Spiral or corkscrew yarn

Chenille.   **Chenille yarns** are not traditional novelty yarns but are actually pieces of leno fabric which has been cut into strips. (See Figure 9–6B.) Leno fabric is discussed in Chapter 10.

Flake, flock, or seed.   A binder secures small tufts of fiber to the core yarn in **flake**, **flock spot,** and **seed yarns**. (See Figure 9–6C.)

Nub, knot, spot or knop.   In **nub**, **knot**, or **knop yarns**, the effect yarn is twisted around the core yarn several times to create bumps at regular intervals. A binder holds the bumps in place. (See Figure 9–6D.)

Ratiné.   **Ratiné yarns** are very similar to bouclé yarns except that the loops in the former are evenly spaced.

Slub or thick-and-thin.   **Slub** or **thick-and-thin** yarns are created by varying the amounts of twist in the yarn so some areas are thicker than others. (See Figure 9–6E.)

Snarl or spike.   In **snarl** or **spike yarns**, the effect yarn and core yarn are held at unequal tension during twisting so the effect yarn forms unclosed loops.

Spiral or corkscrew.   **Spiral** or **corkscrew yarns** are created when two piles, which differ in size, are twisted together. (See Figure 9–6F.)

OTHER YARN FORMATIONS

Several types of yarn do not fit the definitions of simple or fancy yarns. These include core-spun yarns, which are made by spinning a sheath of staple fibers around a filament core, and covered yarns, which are made by wrapping a core yarn with another yarn.

Importance of Twist

During the spinning process yarns are given varying amounts of twist. Twist holds the short fibers together and contributes to strength and fineness. Tightly twisted yarns are stronger and finer than comparable loosely twisted yarns. However, very tightly twisted yarns lose strength due to the shearing effect between the fibers.

Turns per inch (TPI) indicates the amount of twist in a yarn. In general, 2 to 12 TPI is considered **soft twist** for spun yarns and 20 to 30 TPI is considered **hard twist.** For filament yarns, soft twist is $\frac{1}{2}$ to 3 TPI, while hard twist may be as high as 40 to 80 TPI. Crepe yarns are examples of very high twist yarns.

Amount of twist affects performance. In general, high twist yarns provide added strength, more elasticity, and better abrasion resistance than low twist yarns. High-twist yarns also resist soil penetration. If they do become soiled, they are more difficult to clean. Low-twist yarns have better absorbency, a softer hand, and provide more warmth than high-twist yarns.

Yarns may have S or Z twist. If the spirals go from upper left to lower right, the yarn has **S twist**. If the spirals go from lower left to upper right, the yarn has **Z twist**. Traditionally, cotton and linen are produced with a Z twist and woolen and worsted yarns with an S twist.

Twist direction does not affect quality in single yarns. In a ply yarn, the ply can be given an S twist, while individual singles have a Z twist. This creates a more stable yarn. A yarn described at "two ply, S singles, Z" would have singles that are S twist and combined with a Z twist. Cords are made and described similarly. The letters "SZS" indicate that S singles are plied with a Z twist, and that the piles are combined with an S twist.

New Yarn Formation Methods

Technological advances have allowed fibers and yarns to be created directly from polymers, eliminating fiber and traditional yarn formation steps. Two of the newer processes currently being used are split film and slit film. Network yarns are still in the experimental stages.

SPLIT FILM

Split film yarns are created by drawing or stretching a polymer film. During drawing, the film is separated into a mass of fibers in a process called fibrillation. Sometimes these yarns are called fibrillated tape yarns. They are usually coarse and appropriate for use as twine, or they can be made into bagging, or ropes or used in industry.

SLIT FILM

Slit film yarns, or tape yarns, are created when films or thin sheets of polymer are extruded, cooled, and then slit into narrow tapes. The tapes may be stretched to improve strength. Lurex® is a slit film yarn with a metallic appearance. It is made when a thin sheet of aluminum is laminated between two layers of polymer film and then cut into strips. Sometimes a metallized polyester film is used in place of the aluminum sheet. Laminated fabrics are discussed more fully in Chapter 12. End uses for slit film yarns include carpet backing, bagging, and decorative yarns.

NETWORK YARNS

Network yarns are made by drawing a foamed polymer. As the foam is stretched it breaks into individual fibers which are attached to each other. These yarns are bulky but lack strength. Foams are discussed more fully in Chapter 12.

Research continues to develop innovative methods of yarn formation. Some other new methods include wrapped yarns, bonded sliver-spun yarns, integrated composite-spun yarns, and self-twist spun yarns.

Blending

Modern blended yarns have been available since the early 1950s when acrylic/cotton and polyester/cotton fabrics were introduced. Blending can be done during:

- Spinning of manufactured fibers.
- Yarn formation. Most blends are created at this time
- Weaving or knitting. Yarns of different fibers are combined during fabric production.

REASON FOR BLENDING

Three reasons **blends** are important in the textile industry are:

1. Aesthetics. Using luxury fibers like cashmere and mohair in blends adds interesting texture and improves hand and draping qualities.
2. Function. Blending synthetic fibers with natural fibers, like the popular polyester/cotton combination, creates fabrics with improved performance. Polyester provides strength and resilience and cotton provides wearing comfort and pleasant hand.
3. Reduced cost. Blending less expensive fibers with more expensive fibers reduces cost while maintaining acceptable levels of performance and aesthetics.

Yarn Size

In the textile industry it is necessary to distinguish yarns of various sizes. Because yarns are sold by weight, number systems have been developed to indicate yarn length as it compares to weight. The two main types of numbering systems are direct and indirect.

DIRECT SYSTEMS

In a direct system, smaller numbers indicate thinner yarns, and larger numbers indicate thicker yarns. **Denier, tex,** and **decitex** are direct systems for distinguishing filament yarns. Denier is the most commonly used direct method in the United States.

- *Denier* refers to the weight in grams of 9,000 meters of filament yarn.
- *Tex* refers to the weight in grams of 1,000 meters of filament yarn.
- *Decitex* refers to the weight in grams of 10,000 meters of filament yarn.

A yarn with a denier of 50 is twice as coarse as a yarn with a denier of 25.

INDIRECT SYSTEMS

In an indirect system, the larger the number the smaller the yarn. The yarn count systems, which are indirect, are used for spun yarns. There are four yarn count systems: **cotton count**, **woolen count**, **worsted count**, and **linen count** or **linen lea**. The cotton count is the predominant system. Spun yarns are traditionally sold in hanks. A **hank** is a skein of standardized length. The cotton system is based on the number of hanks (one hank equals 840 yards of yarn) in 1 pound. A yarn size of 3 indicates that there are 3 hanks or 2520 yards of yarn per pound. The other systems are also based on 1 pound, but the length of the hank differs as follows:

Woolen count – 1,600 yards per hank
Worsted count – 560 yards per hank
Linen count – 300 yards per hank

Metric yarn count indicates the number of 1000 meter hanks in one kilogram.

LABORATORY ASSIGNMENTS

ASSIGNMENT 9–1   **IDENTIFY SIMPLE YARN STRUCTURES**

1. Define the following terms.
   Single yarn
   Ply yarn
   Cord yarn
2. Gather the following materials:
   samples of single, ply, and cord yarns, and absorbent cotton
3. Mount the yarn samples.
4. Use the absorbent cotton to make samples of single, ply, and cord yarns.
5. Mount the samples. Your instructor will show you how.

ASSIGNMENT 9–2   **IDENTIFY STAPLE AND FILAMENT YARNS**

1. Gather the following materials:
   six samples of fabric (2½″ × 1½″ and/or yarn samples (3″ long).
   Samples should include some staple, some filament, and some textured filament yarns.
   linen tester
   pick

2. Unravel and untwist several yarns from the fabric and/or untwist the yarns.
3. Examine the fibers to determine their length and if they are parallel or somewhat randomly positioned.
4. Evaluate the yarn surface.
5. Determine whether each sample is staple, filament, or textured filament.
6. Mount and label each fabric or yarn sample.

ASSIGNMENT 9-3   **DETERMINE THE EFFECTS OF YARN TWIST**

1. Check the appropriate box in the following table:

	HIGH TWIST	LOW TWIST
Strength		
Elasticity		
Soil Release		
Absorbency		
Abrasion Resistance		
Warmth		

2. List two end uses for:
   High twist yarns
   Low twist yarns

ASSIGNMENT 9-4   **EVALUATE THE DIRECTION AND AMOUNT OF YARN TWIST**

1. Gather the following materials:
   four yarn samples (single, ply, and cord)
   linen tester
2. Unravel each yarn slowly and carefully.
3. Determine whether the sample is a single, ply, or cord yarn.

4. Use your linen tester to determine direction (S or Z) of each component.

5. Determine the amount of twist (TPI) of each sample.

6. Mount and label the samples by number and complete the following chart.

	YARN TYPE	DIRECTION	AMOUNT OF TWIST
Sample 1			
Sample 2			
Sample 3			
Sample 4			

ASSIGNMENT 9–5

IDENTIFY NOVELTY OR FANCY YARNS

1. Using teacher-supplied samples or purchased swatch kit samples, identify, mount, and briefly define each novelty yarn.
   Bouclé
   Chenille
   Corespun
   Flake, flock, seed
   Nub, knot, spot, knop
   Slub, thick-and-thin
   Snarl, spike
   Spiral, corkscrew
   Tape

2. List 3 examples of end uses for novelty yarns.

3. Suggest care methods for fabrics made from novelty yarns.

Chapter

10

Woven Fabrics and Their Properties

OBJECTIVES

The student will be able to:

1. Identify the parts of a loom and describe the steps of the weaving process
2. Distinguish between basic weaves and special weaves and their variations
3. Describe the characteristics of basic weaves and special weaves and their variations
4. Relate fiber, yarn, and fabric characteristics to the overall performance of apparel, furnishings, and industrial textiles

Introduction

There is evidence that weaving was done as far back as 9,000 years ago in the Middle East. Early weaving was also done in both North and South America. While the speed of weaving has increased dramatically in recent years, the basic process and patterns have remained the same.

169

While weaving is the most common method of forming fabric, it is only one of the many ways yarns and fibers can be processed into fabric. Fabric, also called cloth, material, piece goods, or goods, is formed when yarns and/or fibers are assembled into a cohesive structure. The most common of these fabric structures are wovens and knits. Fabrics can also be created from solutions and from fibers directly. Table 10–1 summarizes the ways fabric can be constructed.

FABRIC FACE AND BACK

It is important to determine the face (or front) and back (or reverse) of fabric because garments and other textile products should be constructed with only one side of the fabric showing. Usually the face of the fabric is identified easily because the print, finish, or weave is more pronounced on the front. The face, which is usually folded to the inside on a bolt of fabric, is generally on the outside of a garment. Table 10–2 summarized the characteristics of the face and back of fabric.

FABRIC TOP AND BOTTOM

Some fabrics are noticeably different when viewed from top and bottom. The difference usually cannot be seen when the fabric lies flat,

TABLE 10–1 WAYS TO CREATE FABRIC
Fabrics Made from Solutions
Films
Foams
Fabrics Made from Fibers
Felt
Nonwovens
Fabrics Made from Yarns
Wovens
Knits
Braids
Laces
Knotted fabrics
Stitch-through fabrics

TABLE 10-2   CHARACTERISTICS OF FABRIC FACE AND BACK
Fabric Face
1. Usually smoother and more lustrous
2. If printed, the print is usually clearer and brighter on the face
3. When aesthetic finishes (see Chapter 14) are applied, the finish is more pronounced on the face
4. In satin and twill weaves, the floats of the weave are on the face
5. In fancy weaves, the design may be clear on the front but not the back
Fabric Back
1. Knots and imperfections usually appear on the back
2. If printed, the print is less distinct and duller on the back
3. Tentering marks are usually more noticeable on the back (see Chapter 14 for discussion of tentering)

but it can be seen when the fabric is hung. Corduroy is an excellent example of this phenomenon. Corduroy has a darker, richer appearance when viewed in the "up" direction. Other fabrics with this characteristic are velvet, velveteen, fleece, fabrics with one-direction woven designs like damask or brocade, some plaids, some knits, fabrics with special finishes like napping or brushing, and fabrics with directional prints. It is essential to consider "up and down" when cutting garments, upholstery fabrics, slipcovers, and so on.

WARP AND FILLING YARNS

Warp yarns, also known as **ends,** traditionally run vertically in garments. For example, warp yarns run up and down the length of a sleeve or the leg of a pair of pants. Fabric swatches are customarily mounted with warp yarns vertical. Warp and **filling yarns** interlace at right angles to form woven fabric. The filling yarns, also known as **picks,** or **weft** yarns, run the width of the fabric, and traditionally run horizontally across garments.

Warp yarns, which run the length of a piece of fabric, are placed on the loom before weaving and must be strong enough to withstand the stress of weaving. Spun warp yarns are frequently treated with **sizing** or **slashing agents** like starches, resins, or gums to increase their strength. Filament warp yarns usually do not need to be treated.

In general, warp yarns are thinner and more tightly twisted than filling yarns. There are frequently more warp than filling yarns per square inch of fabric. If fabric is to have novelty yarns, the yarns will be used in the filling direction. Table 10–3 summarizes the characteristics of warp and filling yarns.

THREAD COUNT AND BALANCE

Thread count, or **fabric count**, is the number of yarns in 1 square inch of fabric. Thread count is often used to determine quality of a piece of fabric. In general, the more yarns per inch the higher the quality of fabric. Higher thread counts indicate more strength, better abrasion resistance, and improved hand.

Thread count is expressed numerically. Warp yarns are indicated first, then filling yarns. For example, "80 × 60 count" means there are 80 warp yarns per inch and 60 filling yarns per inch.

Balanced fabric has the same number of yarns in the warp and the filling. If a fabric is described as "80 square," it has 80 warp yarns and 80 filling yarns in 1 square inch. Another way to describe a balanced fabric is to give the total yarns in 1 square inch. Therefore, "80 square" fabric could also be referred to as having "160 thread count."

TABLE 10–3   CHARACTERISTICS OF WARP AND FILLING YARNS

Warp Yarns
1. Run parallel to the selvages (lengthwise edges of the fabric)
2. Usually thinner
3. Usually stronger
4. Usually have more twist
5. In an unbalanced weave, are usually greater in number
6. If both filament and staple yarns are used in one fabric, the filament are usually the warp yarns

Filling Yarns
1. Run perpendicular to the selvages (lengthwise edges of the fabric)
2. May be bulkier
3. May be weaker
4. May have less twist
5. In an unbalanced weave, are usually fewer in number
6. If both filament and staple yarns are used in one fabric, the staple are usually the filling yarns

Balanced fabrics tend to be more durable than unbalanced fabrics because they wear evenly in both the warp and filling directions. **Sheeting** is an example of a balanced weave. Unbalanced fabrics frequently have a distinctive rib. **Poplin** is an example of an unbalanced fabric with a rib.

FABRIC WEIGHT

Fabric weight is often used to indicate quality. Toweling is a fabric in which weight is very important. Higher-weight towels indicate more fiber and therefore better drying ability. Fabric weight may be expressed as:

1. ounces per square yard
2. linear yards per pound
3. ounces per linear yard

Cotton, cotton blends, and lightweight manufactured fiber fabrics are usually weighted in yards per pound. Woolens, worsteds, and similar fabrics are usually weighted in ounces per yard. See Table 10–4 for a comparison of fabric weights.

GRAIN

Grain refers to the relationship between the warp and filling yarns. If the warp yarns are perfectly perpendicular to the filling yarns, then the fabric is said to be **on grain** or **grain perfect**. It is important for a fabric to be on grain. If the warp and filling yarns are not aligned properly,

TABLE 10–4	COMPARISON OF FABRIC WEIGHTS	
Weight	**Fabric Weight**	**End Use(s)**
Light	less than 1 oz per square yard	gauze, mosquito netting, sheer curtains
Top	2 to 4 oz per square yard	blouses, shirts
Bottom	5 to 7 oz per square yard	slacks, skirts
Heavy	9 to 11 oz per square yard	work clothes
Very heavy	over 14 oz per square yard	heavyweight upholstery fabric

then the fabric is said to be **off grain**. Fabric may become off grain during weaving or during finishing processes. Off grain fabrics are considered to be of poorer quality because they do not hang or drape properly.

Fabric may also be skewed or bowed. In **skewed fabric** the filling yarns slant in a straight line. In **bowed fabric** the filling yarns curve.

The Weaving Process

The loom—in one of its many forms—is at the core of the weaving process.

THE LOOM

Weaving, interlacing warp and filling yarns, is done on a **loom**. Looms may be as simple as a hand model or as technologically advanced as an electronically controlled shuttleless type. See Figure 10–1 for a sketch of a simple loom and **shuttle**.

THE PROCESS

Before any weaving can be done, the warp yarns must be placed on the **warp beam**. Next the ends are threaded through the **heddles** and

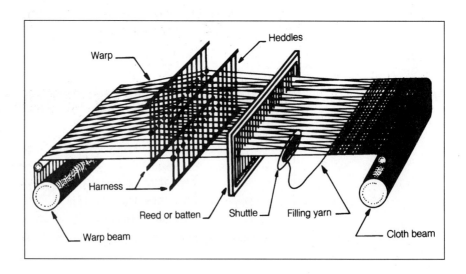

FIGURE 10–1

Parts of a simple loom and shuttle

TABLE 10-5 THE WEAVING PROCESS

1. Shedding—the raising and lowering of different warp yarns to create a space to insert the filling yarn.
2. Picking—using a shuttle to insert a filling yarn into the shed.
3. Beating—using the reed to beat the filling yarn into the completed cloth.
4. Letting off and taking up—releasing warp yarns from the warp beam and winding completed cloth onto the cloth beam.

the **reed** and are tied to the **cloth beam**. The heddles are attached to **harnesses**, which can be raised and lowered to create a **shed**. The shed is where the filling yarn is inserted. Each harness raises and lowers different warp yarns. The shuttle, a smooth, boat-shaped device, carries the filling yarn through the shed and holds small quills or pirns. The **quills** or **pirns** hold the filling yarn. The reed, which resembles a comb, beats the filling yarn into the completed cloth. The harnesses are then changed so another filling yarn can be inserted into a new shed. Table 10–5 summarizes the main steps in weaving.

CONVENTIONAL SHUTTLE LOOMS VERSUS SHUTTLELESS LOOMS

Two main types of looms are used in the textile industry today: conventional shuttle looms and shuttleless looms. **Conventional shuttle looms**, also called fly shuttle looms, are noisy and can only insert approximately 200 picks per minute. **Shuttleless looms** have the advantage of being quieter and operating at three times the speed of conventional looms. In shuttleless weaving, the filling yarn is measured and cut before it is inserted in the shed. The use of shuttleless looms is increasing in the United States. There are four types of shuttleless looms:

1. In **air-jet looms**, a jet of air propels the filling yarn across the shed. Air-jet looms are suitable for spun yarns. (See Figure 10–2.)
2. In **projectile looms**, a projectile, missile, or gripper carries the filling yarn across the shed. This loom is appropriate for very wide fabrics.
3. In **rapier looms**, a rapier (rod or tape) carries the filling across the shed. This loom is appropriate for cotton, woolen, and worsted yarns.

FIGURE 10–2

Air-jet loom. (Courtesy of Springs Industries.)

4. In **water-jet looms**, a jet of water carries the filling yarns across the shed. This loom is the fastest, but it is only appropriate for filament yarns, nonabsorbent yarns, and yarns with water-resistant sizing.

The most common shuttleless looms are the air jet and rapier.

OTHER MODERN LOOMS

Other modern looms include the multiphase loom, the circular loom, and the triaxial loom.

MULTIPHASE LOOM.   The **multiphase loom**, or multiple-shed loom, only forms sheds as the filling yarn is inserted so as many as 20 precut filling yarns may be inserted at the same time. Weaving speed is doubled.

CIRCULAR LOOM.   The **circular loom** weaves tubular fabric such as pillowcases and bagging.

TRIAXIAL LOOM.   The **triaxial loom** weaves three sets of yarns at 60° angles, creating fabric which is stable in all directions (see Figure 10–3). End uses for the fabric include baloons, sailcloth, and outerwear.

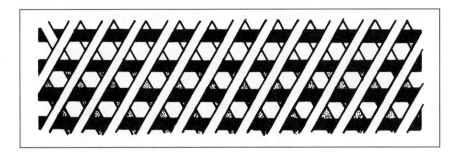

FIGURE 10–3

Triaxial weave

FIGURE 10–4

Selvages:

(A) Normal selvage;

(B) Fringed selvage;

(C) Tucked selvage;

(D) Leno selvage

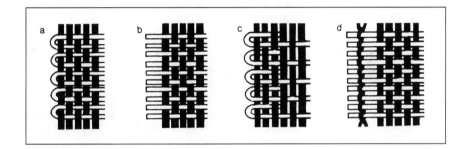

SELVAGES

Selvages run parallel to the warp yarns and form the lengthwise edges of the woven fabric. Different types of selvages are formed by different types of looms. The conventional shuttle loom creates a normal selvage because the filling is inserted in one long yarn. In shuttleless weaving, one or both edges are fringed. This fringe is usually reinforced by tucking the yarns in, adding a leno selvage, or hot melting the yarns if they are thermoplastic (see Figure 10–4).

Basic Weaves

Basic weaves include plain weave, twill weave, and satin weave.

PLAIN WEAVE

The **plain weave**, or **tabby weave**, is the simplest form of weaving. It is done by passing a filling yarn over and under one warp yarn at a time across the width of the fabric. The next filling yarn is inserted so the warp yarns that were under are now over. When diagrammed on graph paper or point paper, the plain weave looks like a checkerboard (see Figure 10–5).

CHARACTERISTICS OF PLAIN WEAVES. Plain weaves are the most commonly used and the most economical. The smooth surface of plain-weave fabrics is ideal for printed designs and surface manipulations like pleating and tucking. Plain weaves can be varied using novelty filling yarns. When compared to other weaves plain weaves tend to:

- wear well but have lower tearing strength
- ravel less
- wrinkle more
- be less absorbent

EXAMPLES OF PLAIN WEAVES. Many different fibers and yarns can be used to make plain-weave fabrics. Following are some of the most common balanced plain-weave fabrics.

Batiste is a semi-opaque, soft, plain-weave fabric made from cotton, linen, or cotton blends.
Calico is a percale fabric printed with small designs.
Challis, originally made of worsted wool, is a medium-weight, plain-weave fabric now made in fibers that resemble wool.

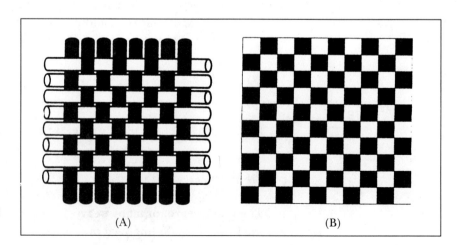

FIGURE 10–5

(A) Plain weave;

(B) Plain weave diagrammed

on point paper

(A)   (B)

Chambray, a medium-weight, plain-weave fabric, is made with white warp yarns and colored filling yarns from cotton or cotton blends.

Chintz, a percale fabric printed with stripes or a flowered design, is usually glazed.

Cretonne is a percale fabric with large floral designs.

Duck is a stiff, heavy, plain-weave fabric.

Gingham, a medium-weight, plain-weave fabric with a woven check or plaid, is made from cotton or cotton blends.

Muslin, the generic term for any balanced plain-weave fabric, is usually made from cotton in counts of 112, 128, and 140. *Muslin* also refers to medium-weight, plain-weave fabric that is white or unbleached. Muslin sheets are made from carded yarns.

Organdy is a sheer, crisp, lightweight cotton, plain-weave fabric.

Organza, a sheer, crisp, lightweight plain-weave fabric, is made from filament yarns.

Percale is a closely woven, medium-weight plain-weave fabric made from the carded yarns of cotton or cotton blends. Percale sheets are made from combed yarns, usually in thread counts from 180 to 200. Some percale thread counts go as high as 250.

Print cloth is any unfinished, medium-weight, balanced plain-weave fabric. It is usually made of cotton or cotton blends.

Voile is a lightweight plain-weave fabric with a two-ply warp. It is made from cotton, cotton blends, or manufactured fibers.

Other plain-weave balanced fabrics include buckram, burlap, butcher linen, cheesecloth, chiffon, crash, crinoline, canvas, gauze, georgette, homespun, longcloth, nainsook, and osnaburg.

PLAIN-WEAVE VARIATIONS.   The plain weave can be modified to create ribbed, basket weave, or seersucker fabric.

Ribbed Fabrics.   **Ribbed fabrics** are unbalanced and usually have noticeable lines on their surfaces. However, in some ribbed fabrics, such as broadcloth, these rib lines are almost invisible. Rib lines are created by using larger yarns or by grouping warp or filling yarns. When the rib occurs lengthwise on the fabric it is called a **cord.**

Ribbed fabrics tend to wear more quickly than balanced plain-weave fabrics because the rib is raised and thus exposed to more abrasion. Examples of ribbed fabric are bengaline, bedford cord, broadcloth, dimity, grosgrain, faille, ottoman, poplin, rep, shanting, and taffeta.

Basket-Weave Fabrics. **Basket-weave fabrics** are loosely woven with two or more filling yarns interlaced with two or more warp yarns (see Figure 10–6). Basket-weave fabrics tend to fray easily, snag, and stretch. Because they are not tightly woven, they also tend to wear more quickly. Yarn slippage may occur especially at seams or points of stress. Examples of basket-weave fabrics include hopsacking, monk's cloth, and oxford cloth.

Seersucker. **Seersucker fabric** is created by **slack-tension weaving**. Two warp beams are used in this process. One beam is held at normal tension while the other is held loose. As the filling is inserted and beaten into the cloth, the loose warp yarns create a permanent puckered or crinkled effect on the fabric that cannot be ironed out. Seersucker is usually made of cotton or cotton blends and is used for lightweight summer clothing.

TWILL WEAVE

Twill weave can be identified by diagonal lines on the fabric surface. In the simplest twill weaves these lines, or **wales**, are created by inserting the filling yarn over two warp yarns and under one warp yarn. The next filling yarn also passes over two warp yarns and under one, but the pattern starts one warp yarn farther in. A yarn that crosses more than one yarn at a time is called a **float**.

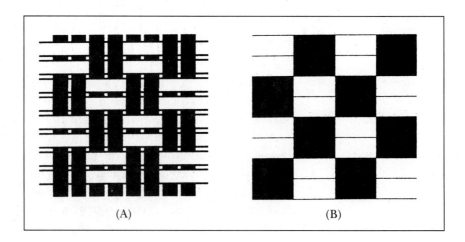

(A)   (B)

FIGURE 10–6

(A) Basket weave

(B) Basket weave

diagrammed on point paper

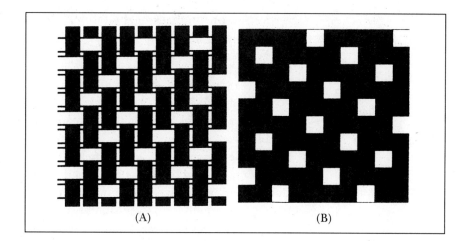

FIGURE 10–7

(A) Twill weave; (B) Twill weave diagrammed on point paper

(A)   (B)

When diagrammed on graph paper, or point paper, the twill weave looks like a series of steps (see Figure 10–7). Twill weaves are described as 2/1, 3/2, and so on. The first number refers to the number of filling yarns crossed by the warp; the second number refers to the number of filling yarns the warp passes under.

Twill lines may be very steep, reclining, or regular. Most twill is regular. A **regular twill** has a 45° angle. There are several different variations of twill weaves, including:

Right-hand twill. Twill lines run from the lower left to the upper right. Right-hand twills are the most common twill weave.

Left-hand twill. Twill lines run from the lower right to the upper left.

Even-sided twill. An equal number of warp and filling yarns are exposed on both sides of the fabric. The filling yarn crosses over two or three warp yarns and under two or three warp yarns.

Warp-faced twill. Warp yarns predominate on the face of the fabric.

Filling-faced twill. Filling yarns predominate on the face of the fabric. Few filling-faced twills are made because they have poor durability resulting from usually weak filling yarns.

CHARACTERISTICS OF TWILL WEAVES.   Twill fabrics are generally woven closely because they have fewer yarn interlacings. They are usually strong and have good abrasion resistance. They also drape well and shed soil easily. It is important to establish the face of a twill fabric. Usually the wale dominates the face of the fabric. Because the twill line is reversed on the back of the fabric, all garment parts must have the same side showing.

Following are some examples of twill weaves.

Chino is a warp-faced, steep twill that is usually made with combed two-ply yarns.

Denim is a warp-faced twill, usually made of yarn-dyed cotton or cotton blends.

Drill, a piece-dyed, medium- to heavyweight warp-faced twill fabric, is generally used in work clothes and industrial fabrics.

Gabardine is warp-faced steep twill with a prominent wale.

Herringbone twill is an even-sided twill in which the twill line periodically reverses to form a chevron pattern.

Houndstooth check is a yarn-dyed twill fabric with a pointed-check effect.

Jean is a piece-dyed, medium-weight warp-faced twill that is lighter than drill.

Serge is an even-sided twill with subdued wale.

Surah or **foulard,** a top-weight, even-sided twill, is made of filament fibers.

SATIN WEAVE

Satin-weave fabric is created by allowing the warp yarns to float over four or more filling yarns. The filling yarn passes under four warp yarns, then over one warp yarn. The warp yarn may float over as many as twelve filling yarns. These interlacings are never adjacent. Instead they are spaced regularly so the fabric appears to be smooth.

Satin fabrics are frequently made from filament yarns with low twist. The filament yarns plus the weave's few interlacings give satin its characteristic luster. The term *satin* refers to a weave structure and to fabric constructed of filament yarns in a satin weave. **Sateen fabric,** a variation of satin, is made when filling yarns float over warp yarns. Sateen is usually made from cotton or cotton blends. (See Figure 10–8.)

CHARACTERISTICS OF SATIN WEAVES.   The long floats of the satin weave make it susceptible to snagging and wear from abrasion. Durability can be improved with appropriate fiber choice and high

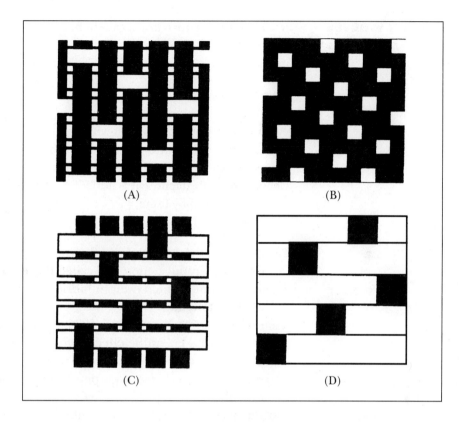

FIGURE 10–8

(A) Satin weave; (B) Satin weave diagrammed on point paper; (C) Sateen weave; (D) Sateen weave diagrammed on point paper

thread counts. The smooth surface of satin sheds soil easily. Satins are used frequently for garment linings because they are smooth and slide over other garments.

Following are some examples of satin weaves.

Antique satin is a fabric with floats on its face and surface slubs on its back. The back of the fabric is frequently used as the decorative side.

Crepe-back satin is a fabric with low twist warp floats on its face and high twist crepe yarns on its back.

Double-faced satin is a fabric woven with two warps and one filling so both sides have satin characteristics. See additional discussion under Interwoven Fabrics in this chapter.

Peau-de-soie is a heavy, semidull, satin-weave fabric.

Satin, a medium- to heavyweight satin-weave fabric, is made from filament yarns.

Special Weaves

In addition to basic weave fabrics, there are numerous special weaves.

DOBBY WEAVE

A **dobby weave** is characterized by small, repeated geometric patterns. Because the patterns are created by long floats, dobby weaves are subject to snagging and have poor abrasion resistance. To make the weave, a **dobby attachment** is added to a sixteen-harness loom, which is then called a **dobby loom**.

Examples of dobby weaves include:

Birds-eye. Cloth in which long floats create a small diamond pattern with a dot in the center; also called **diaper cloth.**

Huck. Medium- to heavyweight fabric with a pebbly surface; usually used for toweling.

Pique. Medium- to heavyweight fabric with a pronounced surface pattern. May have a waffle effect or a cord effect; usually made of cotton. Stuffer yarns may be used to increase the design effect. **Stuffer yarns** are extra filling or warp yarns used to add weight or thickness to a fabric.

Shirting madras. Fabric with a small geometric design in a striped pattern; frequently used for men's dress shirts.

Waffle cloth. Dobby-weave fabric with a honeycomb effect.

LENO WEAVE

The **leno weave** can be identified by pairs of warp yarns which twist around filling yarns in a figure 8 pattern. Some thermal blankets, casement curtains, netting, and bagging are leno weaves.

To create a leno weave, a plain or dobby loom is fitted with a doup harness which alternately twists the warp threads. The doup harness is also called a leno harness.

Leno weaves include:

Grenadine. An open-weave fabric made from hard twisted yarns.

Marquisette. A sheer, lightweight leno-weave fabric frequently used for curtains; usually made with filament yarns.

JACQUARD WEAVE

Beautifully patterned Jacquard fabric can be created on a **Jacquard loom**. The first Jacquard loom was invented by Joseph-Marie Jacquard in 1801. The loom originally used punched cards to control each warp yarn independently. Modern, high-speed Jacquard looms are controlled electronically. In **Jacquard weaving**, the Jacquard loom often used long floats of yarn to create its designs. The long floats are subject to snagging and abrasion, so the fabric may not be durable. Fabrics with shorter floats are more durable.

Examples of Jacquard weaves are:

Brocade. A richly patterned fabric. Designs are created by floats of varying lengths on a plain-, twill-, or satin-weave background. The floats are often of colored yarns. Brocades are used in evening wear, draperies, and upholstery fabrics.

Brocatelle. A fabric very similar to brocade except that its design is raised. Stuffer yarns are often used to create this three-dimensional effect. Brocatelle is used primarily for draperies and upholstery fabrics.

Damask. Fabric with a flat design usually done in one or two colors. The design is created by floats which cross four to seven yarns. Damask fabrics are made of many fiber contents and in many weights. End uses include table linens, furnishings, and apparel.

Tapestry. Originally a handwoven fabric with a filling yarn design completely covering the warp yarns. Now mass produced on Jacquard looms.

EXTRA-YARN WEAVES

Extra warp or filling yarns may be used to create designs which resemble embroidery. **Dotted swiss** is an example of extra-yarn weaves. The durability of extra-yarn weaves is determined by the closeness of the weave and whether the design is created by spot or swivel weaving. There are three methods of incorporating extra yarns into cloth: spot weaving, swivel weaving, and lappet weaving.

SPOT WEAVING. In **spot weaving**, the extra filling or warp yarns that form the design on the face of the fabric are long floats on the back, which may be trimmed. Sometimes the back of the fabric is used as the outside for design effects.

SWIVEL WEAVING. In **swivel weaving**, fabrics are made on looms with an attachment which holds tiny shuttles of filling yarns. Swivel-weave fabrics are more durable than spot weaves because their design yarns are wrapped around the warp yarns several times. Swivel-weave, dotted-swiss fabrics are expensive and therefore are seldom seen in the United States except as imports.

LAPPET WEAVING. In **lappet weaving**, extra warp yarns are used to create a zigzag design. This weave is seldom seen in the United States except in imported Swiss braids.

WOVEN-PILE WEAVES

Pile fabrics are created with three sets of yarns: warp ground yarns, filling ground yarns, and pile yarns. The warp and filling ground yarns form the base fabric, or **ground**. The pile yarns may be either extra filling yarns or extra warp yarns. Warp pile fabrics have an extra set of warp yarns; filling pile fabrics have an extra set of filling yarns. The extra yarns may be cut to form **cut-pile fabrics** such as **corduroy** or left uncut to form fabrics such as **terry cloth**.

The durability of pile fabrics is determined by the count of the ground fabric, the interlacing of the pile, the density of the pile, and the height of the pile. The tighter the weave of the ground, the less likely the uncut pile will snag and pull, and the less likely the cut pile will shed and pull. Grounds of twill are more durable than plain-weave grounds because more yarns per inch are possible in twill weaves. These pile yarns may be interlaced in a V pattern or a W pattern. The W interlacing is considered to be more durable because it is harder for the pile yarns to be pulled out. The denser the pile, the more likely it will resist crushing. Higher piles require more care to prevent crushing or matting. Dry cleaning and special pressing procedures may be recommended. The direction of the pile in a product is also important because the pile of each piece should face the same way to avoid shading differences.

There are four methods for creating pile weaves: wire, filling pile, double cloth, and slack tension.

WIRE METHOD. The **wire method** used two sets of warp yarns and one set of filling yarns. Wires are inserted between the extra warp yarns

FIGURE 10–9

*Overwire construction
of pile weaves*

and the ground. (See Figure 10–9.) If the wire has a sharp edge, the pile will be cut. If the wire is smooth, the pile will be uncut. Sometimes waste picks are used instead of smooth wires to make uncut pile fabrics. The wires are removed before the fabric is taken off the loom; waste picks are removed after the fabric is removed from the loom.

Following are fabrics made by the wire method.

Frisé. A heavy, durable upholstery fabric which may have an uncut pile or a combination of cut and uncut piles. Also called **frieze**.

Velvet. A warp pile fabric usually made of filament yarns. Velvets may be made by the wire method but are more commonly made by the double-cloth method. The double-cloth method is discussed later in this chapter.

FILLING-PILE METHOD. The **filling-pile method** uses two sets of filling yarns and one set of warp yarns. The extra filling yarns create long floats over the ground. These floats are cut after weaving and then brushed up to form the pile. Following are examples of filling-pile fabrics.

Corduroy. Filling-pile fabric with regularly spaced floats which are cut to form lengthwise rows, called wales. Wales may range from very fine to very wide. (See Table 10–6.) Corduroy is generally made from cotton or cotton-blend yarns.

Velveteen. Filling-pile fabric with irregularly spaced floats which are cut to form an overall pile. Velveteen is made from spun yarns.

DOUBLE-CLOTH METHOD. The **double-cloth method** is appropriate for cut-pile fabrics, not uncut pile fabrics. Two sets of warp and filling yarns are woven into two layers of fabric which are joined by an extra set of warp yarns. While the fabric is still on the loom, a sharp knife cuts the

TABLE 10–6 TYPES OF CORDUROY	
Type of Corduroy	**Number of Wales per Inch**
Featherwale	18 to 21
Pinwale (fine)	16 to 19
Midwale (medium or regular)	11 to 14
Widewale	2 to 9

two layers of cloth apart, creating two lengths of cloth with a cut pile. Velvet and plush fabrics are created by this method. This method is also used to create nonpile fabrics. (See discussion later in this chapter.)

Following are some fabrics made by the double-cloth method.

Crushed velvet. Velvet fabric which has been twisted mechanically to create random flat areas.

Panné velvet. Velvet which has had its pile pressed flat. One-direction pressing gives the fabric exceptional luster.

Plush. Warp pile fabric with a pile deeper than velvet. The pile is usually longer than $\frac{1}{4}''$.

Velour. Warp pile fabric usually made of cotton yarns. Used for draperies and upholstery fabrics. Knitted velours are discussed in Chapter 11.

Velvet. Warp pile fabric made by the double-cloth or wire method from filament yarns. The pile is $\frac{1}{16}''$ or shorter.

SLACK-TENSION PILE WEAVE OR TERRY WEAVE METHOD.
Slack-tension pile weaving is similar to slack-tension weaving, which creates seersucker. During slack-tension pile weaving, the ground yarns are held at tension while the pile yarns are allowed to relax or slacken. The looped pile forms when the filling yarns are beaten into the fabric.

Loops may appear on both sides of the fabric, or only on one. Sometimes the loops are sheared to create velour towels. Terry cloth is uncut pile toweling. Terry cloth is more durable than velour because the pile yarns in velour toweling pull out more easily. Terry cloth is also more absorbent than velour toweling because the pile yarns of the velour tend to become more compact and less porous.

INTERWOVEN FABRICS

Interwoven fabrics are woven from three or more sets of yarns. The three types of interwoven fabrics are double cloth, double weave, and double faced.

DOUBLE CLOTH. **Double cloth** is made using the double-cloth method to create velvet, except that the two layers of fabric are not cut apart. Melton and kersey are examples of double cloth. **Melton** is a double-cloth fabric used for winter coats. **Kersey**, also used for winter coats, is less smooth, heavier, and more lustrous than melton.

DOUBLE WEAVES. **Double weaves** are made with four sets of yarns (two warp and two filling). Two layers of fabric are created, but the yarns move from one layer to the other periodically. As a result, the layers cannot be separated without damaging the fabric. Double weaves are also called **pocket cloth** due to the small spaces that form between the layers of fabric. **Matelassé** is an example of a double-weave fabric.

DOUBLE FACED. **Double-faced fabrics**, which appear the same on both sides, are made with three sets of yarns (two sets of warp and one filling or one set of warp and two sets of filling). These fabrics include some blankets, double-faced satins, and double-faced coat interlinings.

MOMIE WEAVES

Momie weaves, also known as granite or crepe weaves, are a special class of weaves which have the appearance of small spots. They are made on a dobby loom and may be a satin weave variation. Following are examples of momie weaves.

Granite cloth. Momie weave with a grainy surface. It is a variation of the satin weave and is used in apparel and furnishings.

Moss crepe. A crepe-weave fabric made from high-twist crepe yarns and regular yarns. Moss crepe is used for apparel. Traditional crepe fabric is made of highly twisted crepe yarns. Crepe weaves look like, but are not, crepe fabrics. Moss crepe is an exception.

Sand crepe. Momie weave fabric with short, two-yarn floats. Made from spun or filament yarns.

LABORATORY ASSIGNMENTS

ASSIGNMENT 10–1   DETERMINE FABRIC FACE AND BACK

1. Gather the following materials:
   4 fabric samples, 3″ × 2″
   linen tester
2. Using Table 10–2 as a guide, determine the face and back of each swatch.
3. Mount each sample face up.

ASSIGNMENT 10–2   DETERMINE WARP AND FILLING YARNS

1. Gather the following materials:
   2 fabric samples, 3″ square
   linen tester
2. Using Table 10–3 as a guide, determine the warp and filling of each swatch.
3. Mount each sample with the warp yarns vertical and the filling yarns horizontal.

ASSIGNMENT 10–3   DETERMINE THE "UP" AND "DOWN" OF FABRIC

1. Gather the following materials:
   2 identical samples of corduroy, 3″ × 2″
2. Place both samples on a flat, well-lighted surface.
3. Lightly run your finger from top to bottom and then from bottom to top. Describe the difference.
4. Place one sample so its smooth (down) direction is toward you and one sample so its rough direction is toward you. Describe the difference you observe.
5. Hold up the samples. Describe the difference you observe.
6. Mount each sample, one in the up direction and one in the down (smooth) direction.
7. Identify the direction of each sample.

ASSIGNMENT 10–4   **DETERMINE THREAD COUNT**

1. Gather the following materials:
   2 samples of plain weave fabrics, 3″ × 2″
   linen tester
2. Look at each sample with its warp vertical and its filling horizontal.
3. Place the linen tester on the fabric sample with the calibrated edge along one warp yarn.
4. Count the number of threads in ¼″, and multiply that number by 4 to determine the number of threads in 1 inch.
5. Repeat steps 3 and 4 for the filling yarns.
6. Mount each sample, and indicate the thread count for each.
   _____×_____   _____×_____
7. Does either sample have a balanced weave? If yes, which one?
8. Why are balanced weaves more durable than unbalanced weaves?
9. Why is a larger number of yarns found in the warp direction of unbalanced weaves?
10. What household textiles are commonly labeled with thread counts?

ASSIGNMENT 10–5   **IDENTIFY PLAIN WEAVE AND PLAIN WEAVE VARIATIONS**

1. Gather the following materials:
   construction paper, at least 2 colors, cut into 1″ strips
   2″ squares of point paper
   plain weave samples from a purchased swatch kit or instructor-supplied swatches
2. Define *plain weave.*
3. Using point paper, diagram examples of plain weave, basket weave, and rib weave. Secure the diagrams in your notebook and label them.
4. Using construction paper, one color for warp and one color for filling, complete a 6″ × 8″ paper-weaving sample of the plain weave. Secure the sample in your notebook and label it.
5. Mount and label each plain-weave sample from your swatch kit or instructor-supplied swatches.

ASSIGNMENT 10–6   **IDENTIFY TWILL WEAVE AND TWILL WEAVE VARIATIONS**

1. Gather the following materials:
   construction paper, at least 2 colors, cut into 1″ strips

2″ squares of point paper
twill-weave samples from a purchased swatch kit or instructor-
supplied swatches

2. Define *twill weave*.
3. Using point paper, diagram a right-hand twill and a left-hand twill. Secure the diagrams in your notebook and label them.
4. Using construction paper, one color for warp and one color for filling, complete a 6″ × 8″ paper-weaving sample of the twill weave. Secure the sample in your notebook and label it.
5. Mount and label each twill-weave sample from your swatch kit or instructor-supplied swatches.

ASSIGNMENT 10–7   **IDENTIFY SATIN WEAVE AND SATIN WEAVE VARIATIONS**

1. Gather the following materials:
construction paper, at least 2 colors, cut into 1″ strips
2″ squares of point paper (see Instructor's Guide)
satin-weave samples from a purchased swatch kit or instructor-
supplied swatches
2. Define *satin weave*.
3. Using point paper, diagram a satin and a sateen weave. Secure the diagrams in your notebook and label them.
4. Using construction paper, one color for warp and one color for filling, complete a 6″ × 8″ paper-weaving sample of the satin weave. Secure the sample in your notebook and label it.
5. Mount and label each satin-weave from your swatch kit or instructor-supplied swatches.

ASSIGNMENT 10–8   **IDENTIFY JACQUARD WEAVE**

1. Mount and label the Jacquard weave samples from your swatch kit or instructor-supplied swatches.

ASSIGNMENT 10–9   **IDENTIFY DOBBY WEAVE**

1. Mount and label the dobby weave samples from your swatch kit or instructor-supplied swatches.

ASSIGNMENT 10–10   **IDENTIFY LENO WEAVE**

Mount and label the leno-weave samples from your swatch kit or instructor-supplied swatches.

ASSIGNMENT 10–11   **IDENTIFY PILE WEAVES**

Mount and label the pile-weave samples from your swatch kit or instructor-supplied swatches.

ASSIGNMENT 10–12   **IDENTIFY DOUBLE-CLOTH WEAVES**

Mount and label the double-cloth samples from your swatch kit or instructor-supplied swatches.

Knit Fabrics and Their Properties

OBJECTIVES

The student will be able to:

1. Differentiate between knit and woven fabrics
2. Identify and describe weft and warp knits
3. List the characteristics of warp and weft
4. Compare and contrast the characteristics of knit and woven fabrics
5. Continue to integrate fabric formation methods into the overall analysis of apparel, furnishings, and industrial textiles

Introduction

In simplest terms, **knitting** is interlooping yarn to create fabric, as opposed to weaving, which is interlacing yarns to create fabric. This looping structure contributes to the comfort and easy fit of knit fabrics and is responsible for increasing the popularity of knit apparel.

Historically knitting appears to have developed much later than weaving. Knit fragments from 250 B.C. have been found in the Middle

East. Knitting was probably introduced to Europe by the Arabs and did not become well known there until after 1000 A.D.

THE KNITTING INDUSTRY

The knitting industry can be divided into two main segments: knitted yard goods and knitted apparel. The knitted yard goods segment of the industry produces fabric which is sold to apparel manufacturers or retail fabric outlets. The knitted apparel segment of the industry produces complete knit garments, such as sweaters, hosiery, and t-shirts. Because specialized machinery is required to make knitted products, usually a mill produces only one type of product.

Advances in computer technology have allowed the knitting industry to respond quickly to changes in the fashion industry. Patterns are changed easily with computer-aided design (CAD), and electronically controlled machines are efficient and practical.

CATEGORIES OF KNITS

There are two main categories of knits: weft knits and warp knits. **Weft knits** are sometimes called **filling knits**. Both weft and warp knits are produced by interlooping yarns. In weft knits the loops are interlocked across the fabric. In warp knits the loops run the length of the fabric.

KNITTING MACHINES

In knitting, each loop is called a **stitch**. Knitting machines have needles to form stitches. In machine knitting each column of stitches is produced by a separate needle.

There are two basic types of knitting machines: flat and circular. **Flat knitting machines** produce flat fabric and are used to make both warp and weft knits. On flat knitting machines, needles are held in a flat needlebed (see Figure 11–1). Most warp knit fabrics are made on flat knitting machines. **Circular knitting machines** are used predominantly to make weft knits. The needles are set in a rotating cylinder, producing a tubular fabric (see Figure 11–2).

FIGURE 11–1

Flatbed knitting machine. (Courtesy of Vanguard Supreme.)

Weft Knits

Weft knits, or filling knits, can be made by hand or by circular or flat bed machine. Weft knit fabric is made with one continuous yarn which travels around the fabric on a circular knitting machine and across the fabric on a flatbed machine. Traditional hand knitting is a weft knitting process.

Examining the face of weft knit fabric reveals vertical columns of **knit,** or **plain**, **stitches**. These columns are called wales. The back of the

FIGURE 11–2

Circular knitting machine.
(Courtesy of Vanguard
Supreme.)

fabric shows horizontal rows of **purl**, or **reverse**, **stitches**, called **courses** (see Figure 11–3).

Common weft knits are **jersey knits**, **rib knits**, and **purl knits**. Yarn weight, cut, and variations of weft knit stitches can be used to create endless variety of weft knit fabrication. Cut is discussed later in this chapter.

WEFT KNIT STITCH VARIATIONS

In addition to knit and purl stitches, a wide variety of stitches can be used to create interesting textures and designs in knit fabric. The

(A)

(B)

FIGURE 11–3

Plain or jersey knit:

(A) Technical face;

(B) Technical back

most common variations are the miss or float stitch, tuck stitch, and open stitch, also called the transfer or spread stitch.

MISS OR FLOAT STITCH.   The **miss** or **float stitch** is used to create patterns or change colors. Instead of forming a stitch, the yarn is allowed to "float" across the back of the fabric. Miss or float stitches reduce the stretch of the fabric and are prone to snagging, especially if the yarn is allowed to float across the back of many stitches. When this stitch is used to change colors, the new color comes to the face of the fabric while the previous color floats across the back.

TUCK STITCH.   Like the miss stitch, the **tuck stitch** is used to create patterns in weft knit fabric. Two stitches are held on one needle and create an opening in the fabric. Tuck stitches add textured effects such as open lacy areas, bubbles, and puckers. Like miss stitches, tuck stitches reduce the stretch of weft knit fabrics.

OPEN, TRANSFER, OR SPREAD STITCH.   Like miss and tuck stitches, **open**, **transfer**, or **spread stitches** create interesting texture in weft knits. In this stitch, loops are transferred from one needle to the next. When used to create full-fashioned sweaters that are shaped to fit during the knitting process, these stitches are called **fashion marks**. Fashion marks occur where transfer stitches change the number and position of the yarns. Imitation or mock fashion marks do not shape the garment and are sometimes added to give the impression of a higher-quality garment.

JERSEY KNITS

Jersey knits, also called **single knits**, are very economical to produce. They are light- to heavyweight and have all knit stitches on the front and all purl stitches on the back. As a result, the front is smooth and flat with vertical wales. The back is more textured with horizontal courses.

CHARACTERISTICS OF JERSEY KNITS.   Jersey knits stretch both crosswise and lengthwise, but they have greater stretch in the crosswise direction. A common problem with jersey knits is they tend to **run** or **ladder** if a stitch breaks. Another problem is that the fabric is held under tension during production, which causes the fabric to curl when cut and to be less stable. However, special finishes can overcome curling and improve stability. If a jersey knit is to be printed, the printing is placed on the face because it is smoother.

END USES OF JERSEY KNITS.   End uses of jersey knits include sweaters, t-shirts, men's underwear, and hosiery. Following are some jersey knit variations:

Fleece. Jersey knit fabric with a brushed pile. The soft inside of a sweatshirt is fleece.

Intarsia. Decorative knitted design created without miss or tuck stitches. The color pattern is laid in and visible on both sides. Argyle is an example of an intarsia design.

Jacquard knits. Patterned jersey knits created with stitch and/or color variations. Float stitches are visible on the back.

Knitted terry. Jersey knit with an uncut loop pile on the purl side. Knitted terry looks similar to woven terry cloth. Although it is less stable and less durable, it has improved drape, increased absorbency, and stretch. Knitted terry is used for infant towels, beachwear, and robes.

Knitted velour. Jersey knit with a cut loop pile on the purl side. Knitted velour is similar to woven cut-pile fabrics such as velvet and velveteen, but it is softer, more supple, and has stretch. Knitted velour is used for sportswear and loungewear.

Sliver-pile knits. Jersey knits with a thick pile inserted on the purl side. The pile is formed from a sliver. The back of the fabric becomes the fashion face. Sliver pile knits are used for imitation furs and high-pile fabrics.

RIB KNITS

Rib knits are made such that knit and purl wales alternate across the fabric width. As a result, the machinery to create rib knits is more complex and slower than that used for jersey knits.

Rib knits are frequently described by the number of knit and purl wales. For example, a 2×2 rib knit has two rows of knit stitches and two rows of purl stitches alternating across the fabric. A 3×3 rib knit has three knit rows and three purl rows. (See Figure 11–4A and B.) If the same number of knit and purl wales alternate across the fabric, the front and back of the fabric is the same and the fabric is considered reversible.

CHARACTERISTICS OF RIB KNITS. Rib knits are more elastic than jersey knits, and they stretch more crosswise than lengthwise. The edges of rib knits do not curl. Laddering or running is a problem with rib knits, as it is with jersey knits.

END USES OF RIB KNITS. Rib knits are used for collars, necklines, cuffs, and bottom edges of sweaters. They are also used for knit hats and men's hosiery. Following are some rib knit variations.

Double knits. Produced on interlock machines or rib knit machines. Sometimes called "double jerseys." Both sides of a plain double knit resemble the face of a jersey knit. In contrast, complex double knits differ on each side. (See Figure 11–5.) In general, double knits are thicker and heavier than jersey knits, but lightweight double knits are available. Double knits have two-way stretch but are very stable and do not ladder. Although not currently in fashion, end uses for double knits have included a wide range of apparel for men, women, and children.

Interlock knits. Specialized 1 × 1 rib knits made on interlock machines. Both sides of an interlock knit resemble the face of a jersey knit. A knit stitch on the front has a matching knit stitch on the back. Interlock knits are more stable and smoother than regular rib knits. When compared to jersey knits they have similar elasticity but are heavier, more stable, and less likely to curl. Interlock knits ladder. End uses for interlock knits include underwear, blouses, and dresses.

PURL KNITS

Purl knits are created with alternate courses of knit stitches and purl stitches. One knit course alternates with one purl course. Both sides of a purl knit fabric resemble the back of a jersey knit. (See Figure 11–6.)

Special knitting machines called **links and links**, or links-links, are used to create purl knits. As a result, purl knits are sometimes called

(A)

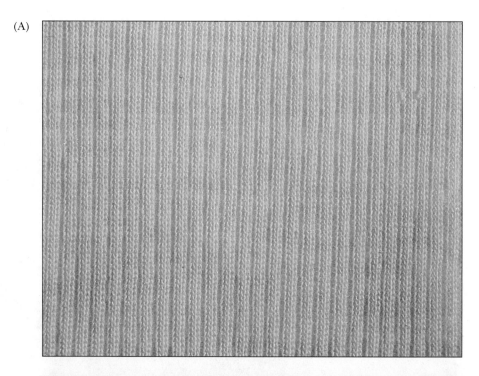

(B)

FIGURE 11–4

Rib knits: (A) Relaxed;
(B) Stretched to show
alternating rows

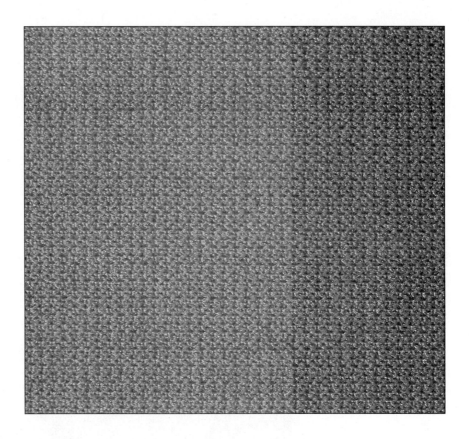

FIGURE 11–5

Double knit fabric

"links and links fabric." These machines are the slowest of the knitting machines, but they can create jersey, rib, and purl fabrics. Links and links machines are commonly used to produce sweaters.

Although purl-knit fabric has good stretch in all directions, it stretches out of shape easily. It tends to be thicker than jersey knits and does not curl. End uses for purl knits include infant and children's wear, sweaters, and scarves.

Warp Knits

As was mentioned earlier, warp knits are the second major category of knit fabrics. Unlike weft knits, where the yarn interloops across the width of the fabric, warp knits are characterized by vertical loops. Yarns zigzag along the length of the fabric. Each loop is created by a separate yarn.

(A)

(B)

FIGURE 11–6

Purl knit fabric:

(A) Front; (B) Back

Warp knitting, which is usually done on a flat knitting machine, is the fastest way to make fabric from yarns. Warp yarns are wound on a warp beam and then fed into the knitting machine. There are two main types of warp-knitting machines: tricot (pronounced tree-ko) and raschel. These two types of machines produce the overwhelming majority of warp-knit fabrics. (See Figure 11–7.)

Warp-knitting machines require extensive preparation for knitting, so it is difficult and time consuming to change patterns and designs. Recent innovations have created raschel machines which can be electronically controlled for easier and more efficient design changes.

The names of the two main types of warp knits correspond to the names of the machines used to make them: tricot and raschel. The term *tricot* may be used to refer to all warp knits. Milanese and simplex knits are similar to tricot but are less common.

TRICOT KNITS

Tricot knits account for the majority of warp knits. Due to the high speed of warp-knit production, high-quality, uniform, filament yarns are essential. The filament yarns can be smooth or textured.

Tricot knitting machines have bars that guide the movement of the yarns as the fabric is knit. These bars can be compared to harnesses in a weaving loom. One-bar, two-bar, three-bar, and four-bar tricots are available. The number of bars indicate the weight, and sometimes the quality, of the fabric. One-bar tricot is unstable and therefore seldom made. Lingerie is typically two-bar tricot. Three-bar and four-bar tricot are used for men's wear and dresses.

A wide variety of tricot fabrics are available. Weight, hand, pattern, and texture can be modified by programming the movement of the guide bars.

CHARACTERISTICS OF TRICOT KNITS.
The face of a warp knit resembles the face of a jersey knit, but the back of the warp knit is characterized by floats called **laps** or **underlaps**. The fabric is uniform in weight and appearance because uniform yarns are required. Tricot knits tend to be more tightly knit than weft knits and have less stretch, especially in the length. They may also be less resilient and lighter. The fabric does not ladder easily.

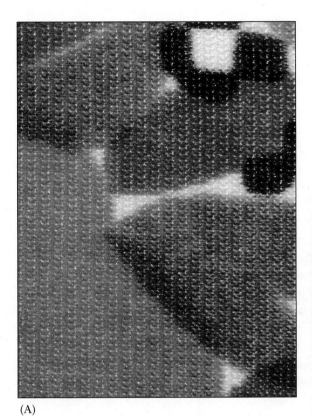

(A)

FIGURE 11–7

Tricot knits: (A) Warp knit fabric face; (B) Warp knit fabric back

(B)

END USES OF TRICOT.   Two-bar tricots are also called jersey tricots and are used extensively for lingerie, sleepwear, and lightweight women's blouses. Other end uses include uniforms, dresses, automobile upholstery fabrics, and men's shirts and slacks. Following are some tricot knit variations.

Brushed tricot. Tricot fabrics with long laps brushed to create a napped surface. Brushed tricot is usually made of nylon and is used for sleepwear, eveningwear, upholstery fabrics, and draperies.

Satin tricot. Nylon or polyester tricot fabric with long laps. The laps of satin tricot are longer than the laps of brushed tricot. Satin tricot is very smooth and has good crosswise stability.

Tricot jersey. Another name for two-bar tricot, the most common variety of tricot. Polyester jersey tricot is used for skirts, blouses, and so on. Nylon jersey tricot is used for lingerie. Backings for bonded fabrics are frequently made from acetate two-bar tricot.

Tricot-net fabrics. Fabric knitted with open spaces to create a meshlike effect. Lightweight tricot-net fabrics are used for lingerie or blouses. Heavier weights are used for curtains.

Tricot upholstery. Usually a two-bar jersey tricot made from heavy filament yarn. End uses include automobile and industrial upholstery fabrics.

RASCHEL KNITS

Raschel knits are similar to tricot knits but are available in a much wider variety of patterns and textures. A raschel knitting machine has up to forty-eight bars which control the position of the yarns and allow for great diversity in design. (See Figure 11–8.)

CHARACTERISTICS OF RASCHEL KNITS.   It may be difficult to distinguish tricot from raschel fabrics. In general, tricot fabrics are constructed from finer yarns, are relatively compact, and have smooth, simple designs. Raschel knits have more texture, open spaces, and are made from heavier yarns.

VARIATIONS AND END USES OF RASCHEL KNIT.   Variations and end uses of raschel fabrics include:

- warp knitted fabrics, which resemble woven fabrics

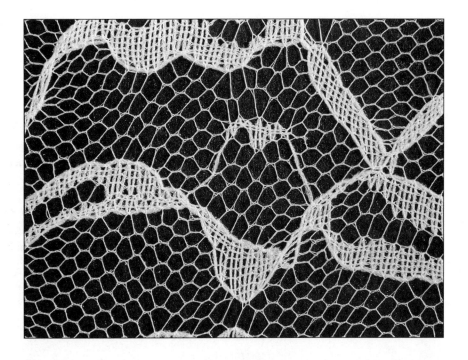

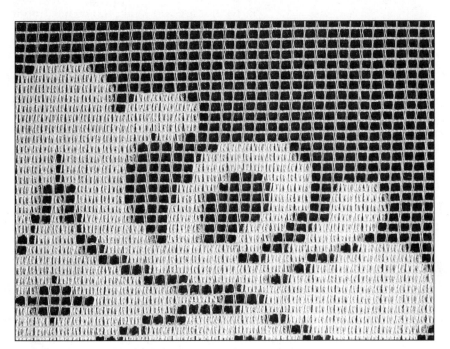

FIGURE 11–8

Rascel open structured knits

- fine laces and nets
- heavy carpet
- thermal underwear with a waffle effect
- power-net fabrics for swimwear and foundation garments (power-net fabrics are described later in this chapter)
- heavy blankets

WARP AND WEFT INSERTION YARN FABRICS OR LAID-IN YARN FABRICS

Extra yarns may be added to weft or warp knits to provide stability, decorative effect, additional stretch, or strength. These yarns are not knitted in but are simply laid in as the fabric is knitted.

Insertion warp knits include both tricot and raschel knits. Extra yarns may be inserted in the warp or the filling direction of warp knits. If they are inserted in the warp direction, they are called **inlay yarns**. A **power-net fabric** is a raschel knit with inlaid spandex yarns. The spandex provides additional stretch and comfort to swimwear and foundation garments.

Yarns that are too weak, too coarse, too irregular, or too inflexible for knitting may be used as laid-in yarns. The resulting fabrics may be used for apparel, home textiles, and industrial applications.

OTHER KINDS OF WARP KNITS

Simplex knits and Milanese knits are also warp knits.

SIMPLEX KNITS.   **Simplex knits** are a type of tricot knit which resemble a double knit. They are used for women's gloves and handbags.

MILANESE KNITS.   **Milanese knits** are a warp knit variation which are in limited production at this time. In general, milanese knits have been replaced by tricot.

Gauge and Cut

Gauge and **cut** are terms that refer to the relative fineness, or compactness, of knitted fabrics. The higher the gauge or cut number the finer the fabric.

Gauge describes the fineness of both warp knits and hosiery. Gauge units of measure differ with the type of knit. The gauge is 2″ for warp knitted raschel, 1″ for warp knitted tricot and hosiery, and 1½″ for full-fashioned sweaters. Cut refers to the fineness of weft knits. Cut indicates the number of wales or stitches per inch.

Gauge and cut numbers are machinery measurements and therefore indicate the number of needles in the unit of measure (i.e., 1″ for hosiery). The wales per measurement in actual fabric may differ due to subsequent stretching or shrinkage.

Comparing Knit and Woven Fabrics

It is important to realize that there are many varieties of knit and woven fabrics and that both knits and wovens are available in a wide range of quality. Despite these many differences, some generalizations can be made about the advantages and disadvantages of each type of fabric.

COST OF KNITS AND WOVENS

Knits are cheaper to produce than wovens but require higher-quality yarns, so the cost of the yarn offsets the savings in production. Knitting yarns must be uniform so thin spots do not form in the fabric.

COMFORT OF KNITS AND WOVENS

Knits are well known for their comfort and ease of fit. Their looped structure allows for stretch and recovery as the body moves. In general, woven fabrics are more rigid and less able to conform to the body. Using stretching yarns in woven fabrics can improve comfort.

Because knits are bulky, they provide good insulation and are warmer in still air than wovens. Tightly woven fabrics provide superior resistance to wind.

APPEARANCE RETENTION OF KNITS AND WOVENS

The wrinkle recovery of knits is superior to that of wovens, but wovens can be set with sharper pleats and creases.

A very significant problem with knits is their tendency to stretch out of shape. Therefore, it is important that knit garments, especially loosely knitted garments, be folded, not hung, during storage. Hanging can cause the garment to lengthen, and "hanger marks" can occur. Sagging or "bagging" can occur at stress points like knees and elbows. Sometimes the original shape of a garment can be restored with proper cleaning procedures.

Another serious problem with knits is their tendency to snag. The looped structure of knits, especially of weft knits, makes them susceptible to being caught on sharp objects. Sometimes snags can be worked back into the fabric, but unsightly pulls, holes, and laddering usually result from snagging.

Because knits also exhibit more shrinkage than wovens, the consumer must read labels carefully to determine if the fabric has been pretreated appropriately.

LABORATORY ASSIGNMENTS

ASSIGNMENT 11–1 **IDENTIFY COURSES AND WALES**

1. Gather the following materials:
   2 samples of jersey knit fabric, each 2″ × 2″
   linen tester
   pick
2. Examine both sides of each sample with the linen tester and determine the courses and wales of each.
3. Mount one sample with the wales showing and one sample with the courses showing.
4. Which is usually considered the back of the fabric, courses or wales?

ASSIGNMENT 11–2 **IDENTIFY THE CUT OF WEFT KNIT FABRICS**

1. Gather the following materials:
   two samples of jersey knit, 2″ × 2″, one tightly knit and the other loosely knit

linen tester

pick

2. Determine the stitches per inch by first placing the linen tester on the right side of the fabric with one edge along a vertical column of loops. Count the number of vertical stitches in 1 inch; and record the number.

3. Repeat Step 2 with the second fabric sample.

ASSIGNMENT 11–3   IDENTIFY WARP AND WEFT KNITS

1. Gather the following materials:
   samples of weft, rib, tricot, and raschel knits,
       3″ × 3″
   linen tester
   pick
   small scissors

2. Identify each sample.

3. Using the linen tester, determine the face of each sample.

4. Cut a yarn in the center of each sample. Gently pull at the hole to determine if a run will start. Which sample(s) run(s)?

5. Refer to the diagrams of warp weft knits in the chapter. Explain why some samples resisted running.

6. Mount and label each sample.

ASSIGNMENT 11–4   EVALUATE THE RELATIVE STRETCH OF KNIT FABRIC

1. Gather the following materials:
   samples of jersey, rib, tricot, and raschel knits,
       1½″ in the filling and 2½″ in the warp
   linen tester
   pick
   stretch gauge

2. Identify each sample.

3. Using the stretch gauge, evaluate the stretch of each sample.
   a. Place the sample between Line A and Line B. It should fit exactly.
   b. With your left hand, hold the left side of the sample so it aligns with Line A.

    c. Gently stretch the sample with your right hand until the top edge begins to curl.

    d. Identify the line at which you stopped pulling and record the stretch percentage.

4. Which sample had the greatest stretch? Which sample had the least?

5. Mount and label each sample with its stretch percentage.

ASSIGNMENT 11–5   **IDENTIFY KNIT FABRICS**

Mount and label the knit samples from your swatch kit or instructor-supplied swatches.

Nonwovens and Other Methods of Fabric Construction

OBJECTIVES

The student will be able to:

1. Characterize nonwovens and suggest appropriate end uses
2. Compare the properties of nonwoven fabrics to those of woven and knit fabrics
3. Discuss the formation of cohesive structures and briefly list the steps in forming wet, dry, and polymer laid nonwovens
4. Describe other fabric formation methods and suggest appropriate end uses
5. Further integrate nonwovens and other fabric formation methods into the overall analysis of apparel, furnishings, and industrial textiles

Introduction

The term **nonwoven** can be confusing because it has two definitions. In one sense refers to any textile that is not woven. This definition includes a knit as a nonwoven. More commonly, however, the term nonwoven is used in the textile industry to refer to any textile product that is created directly from fibers and is held together by bonding or entanglement. This second definition is used in this book.

Nonwovens are the fastest-growing segment of the textile industry. Figure 12–1 lists many products that use nonwoven fabrics.

The general characteristics of nonwovens are they:

1. Have many applications in apparel, furnishings, and industry.
2. Are made directly from filament or staple fibers.
3. Are relatively inexpensive compared to woven or knitted fabrics.
4. Have no grain and do not ravel or run.
5. Have the properties of the fibers from which they are made. These properties can be modified by adding other materials.
6. Are held together by bonding or entanglement.

TAPA CLOTH — EARLY NONWOVEN

Some authorities believe that **tapa cloth**, or **bark cloth**, was the first fabric made by man. Early man created this nonwoven fabric from the inner bark of mulberry, fig, or breadfruit trees. The bark was softened in water, beaten, and then smoothed flat. The resulting fabric was very similar to soft paper. Use of tapa cloth in apparel is limited because it does not drape well and is difficult to sew. It is still made in the South Pacific for use in religious ceremonies and as a handcraft.

DURABLE AND DISPOSABLE NONWOVENS

The two major classifications of nonwovens are durable and disposable. **Durable nonwovens** are designed for multiple uses. As their name implies, they are not thrown away after each use but are used again and again. Polyester, olefin, and rayon are the major fibers used to produce durable nonwovens. Examples of durable nonwovens include apparel interfacings, blankets, carpet backings, furniture padding, reservoir linings, subroofing materials, and erosion and weed-control covers.

Disposable nonwovens are designed to be discarded after a single use or, sometimes, after a few uses. Rayon is the primary fiber used to make disposable nonwovens. Examples of disposable nonwovens include medical garments, filters, tea-bag covers, and disposable diapers.

Agriculture
- Seed strips
- Greenhouse covers

Automotive
- Sound and heat insulation
- Interior trim
- Battery separators
- Vinyl roofs
- Upholstery
- Carpet backing

Civil Engineering
- Road and railroad beds
- Soil stabilization
- Drainage
- Dam and stream embankments
- Golf and tennis courts
- Artificial turf
- Sedimentation and erosion control

Clothing
- Interfacings
- Skiwear
- Insulated clothing, gloves
- Swimwear
- Imitation fur
- Underwear
- Bra and shoulder padding
- Robes
- Handbags
- Tailors' patterns
- Shrouds, casket liners
- Shoe liners, insoles
- Rainwear

Construction
- Roofing and tile underlayment
- Acoustical ceilings
- Insulation

Home Furnishings
- Upholstery backings and webs
- Slipcovers

- Wallcovering backings
- Quilts, blankets, bedspreads
- Mattresses, mattress covers, tickings
- Pillows, pillowcases
- Lampshades
- Window shades
- Draperies
- Carpet backings

Household
- Wipes (wet, dry, polishing)
- Aprons
- Scouring pads
- Glove liners
- Laundry softeners and antistatics
- Dust cloths, mops
- Tea and coffee bags
- Doormats, bathmats
- Garment bags
- Placemats, napkins
- Ironing-board pads
- Laundry bags
- Washcloths
- Tablecloths
- Cheese wrap

Industrial, Military
- Coated fabrics
- Filters
- Clean room apparel
- Air conditioning
- Military clothing
- Abrasives
- Parachutes
- Cable insulation
- Reinforced plastics
- Tapes
- Protective clothing, labcoats

Leisure, Travel
- Sails, kites
- Sleeping bags
- Tarpaulins, tents
- Artificial leather, luggage

- Art canvases
- Airline headrests
- Fiberglass boats

Health Care
- Surgical: caps, gowns, masks, shoe covers
- Sponges, dressings, wipes
- Orthopedic padding
- Bandages, tapes
- Dental bibs
- Drapes, wraps, packs
- Sterile packaging
- Bedpan covers
- Instrument pads
- Privacy curtains
- Bed linen, underpads
- Examination gowns, slippers
- Filters for IV solutions, blood oxygenators, and kidney dialyzers
- Transdermal drug delivery

Personal Care and Hygiene
- Buff pads
- Diapers
- Sanitary napkins, tampons
- Incontinence products
- Dry and wet wipes
- Cosmetics applicators, removers
- Bibs
- Vacuum-cleaner bags
- Tea, coffee bags

School, Office
- Bookcovers
- Mailing envelopes, labels
- Maps, signs, pennants
- Floppy-disk liners
- Towels
- Promotional items

FIGURE 12–1

Products that use nonwovens. (Courtesy INDA, Association of the Nonwoven fabrics Industry. Material originally printed in INDA's Nonwoven Fabrics Handbook. Copyright, INDA.)

GEOTEXTILES

Textiles use is growing dramatically in geotechnical applications. **Geotextiles** are fabrics designed for use in civil-engineering projects. Often a geotextile is custom-made to meet the specific requirements of its end use. Figure 12–2 lists the uses of geotextiles. Geotextiles are divided into three categories: layer separation, filtration or drainage, and reinforcement.

While the geotextile may be woven or knitted, predominantly it is nonwoven. Most nonwovens used for geotechnical applications are created by heat fusion or entanglement. Heat fusion or entanglement are discussed later in this chapter.

FORMING A COHESIVE STRUCTURE

Before discussing the production of nonwovens, it is important to understand how the fibers are held together in a cohesive structure. There are two main methods: entanglement and bonding.

ENTANGLEMENT. **Entanglement** is the process of interlocking fibers. Fibers may be entangled when they are dry or when they are wet. Needle punching is an example of dry entanglement (see Figure 12–3).

FIGURE 12–2

Functions of geotextiles in various applications. (Courtesy of Textiles, *a publication of The Textile Institute.)*

Applications	Geotechnological functions		
	Layer separation	Filtration/drainage boundaries	Reinforcement
Coastal and river protection	●	●	◐
Road and railway bases	●	◐	◐
Land drainage	◐	●	○
Embankments			
— internal reinforcement	○	●	●
— surface reinforcement	○	◐	●
Land reclamation	◐	●	◐
Earth/asphalt reinforcement	○	○	●

● Major function   ◐ Minor function   ○ Not important

Wet or fluid entanglement is done with high-speed water jets. When the water hits the fibers, they curl around each other to form a cohesive structure (see Figure 12–4).

BONDING. There are three types of **bonding:** adhesive, chemical, and heat. Adhesives may be used to "glue" fibers together. They are applied in a coat, producing a stiff fabric. Printing the adhesive in a pattern creates a softer fabric. The adhesive and the fibers must be compatible, however.

In chemical bonding, the fibers are sprayed with a dilute chemical solution and heated. The heat causes the fibers to dissolve and the chemicals to evaporate. The fibers resolidify in a cohesive structure. Again, the chemical spray and fibers must be compatible.

Thermal bonding or heat fusion is appropriate for thermoplastic fibers. Heat causes these fibers to melt and fuse. Blends of thermoplastics

FIGURE 12–3

Needlepunch felt or dry entanglement. (Courtesy INDA, Association of the Nonwoven Fabrics Industry. Material originally printed in INDA's Nonwoven Fabrics Handbook. Copyright, INDA.)

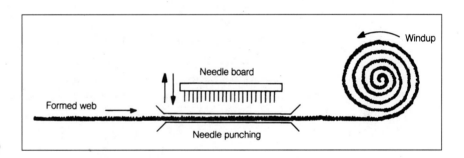

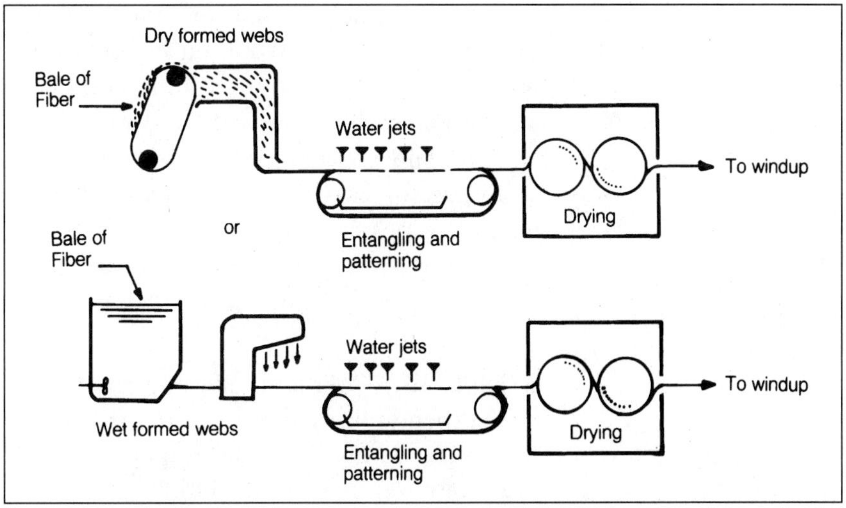

FIGURE 12–4

Wet entanglement. (Courtesy INDA, Association of the Nonwoven Fabrics Industry. Material originally printed in INDA's Nonwoven Fabrics Handbook. Copyright, INDA.)

and nonthermoplastic fibers can be heat fused, but they are less cohesive. In blends of two different thermoplastic fibers, the fibers must be compatible.

METHODS OF CREATING A NONWOVEN

The first step in creating a nonwoven is forming a web of fibers. There are three methods of forming fiber webs: dry laid, wet laid, and polymer laid. Both staple and filament fibers may be processed into nonwovens, but they require different processes.

DRY LAID. Dry laid, or dry formed, the most commonly used method, forms webs when the fiber is dry. Staple fibers are dry laid. There are two main methods of dry laying: carding and **air laying**. In the carding method the carded web is produced by the carding machine. Air-laid webs are created when the fibers are dispersed by air and then collected on a screen. After the web is formed it is held together by entanglement or bonding.

There are two main types of dry laid nonwovens: needle-punch nonwovens and dry-laid bonded-web nonwovens. **Needle-punch nonwovens** are held together by entanglement (see Figure 12–3). Barbed needles pass continuously through the fiber web until a cohesive mass forms. If the fibers are thermoplastic, they are sometimes heat fused to add strength.

An example of needle-punch nonwovens is mechanical or **needle-punch felt**, which is used for indoor/outdoor carpeting, carpet backings, and craft felts. Wool felt is discussed later in this chapter. Other end uses for needle-punch nonwovens include blankets, geotextiles, apparel interlining, and filters.

Dry-laid bonded-wed nonwovens are held together by chemical, adhesive, or heat bonding. Examples of dry-laid bonding fabrics include wipes, interlining, insulation, filters, and backings for quilted fabrics. Some bonded webs are wet laid. See the following section for a discussion on wet-laid, bonded-web nonwovens.

WET LAID. Wet-laid, or wet-formed, webs are created when fibers are suspended in water and then collected on a screen. This process, which is used less, is similar to paper making (see Figure 12–4). Staple fibers are wet laid. Bonded-web and spun-laced nonwovens are examples of wet-laid fabrics.

Wet-laid bonded-wed nonwovens are known for their uniformity. After the web is formed it is bonded by heat fusion, chemicals, or adhesives. Examples include filters, interlining, insulation, roofing substrates, and wipes.

Spun-laced nonwovens are sometimes called **hydroentangled fabrics** or **water-needled fabrics**. High-speed jets of water force through the fiber web, causing the fibers to entangle. No adhesives are used. Examples of spun-laced fabrics are mattress pads, sanitary products, medical gowns, wall coverings, protective clothing, and filters.

POLYMER LAID. **Polymer-laid fabrics**, also called **direct-laid fabrics**, are produced as thermoplastic fibers are extruded from a spinneret. There are two types of polymer-laid nonwovens: spun-bonded nonwovens and melt-blown nonwovens. **Spun bonding** is the second most widely used method of producing nonwovens. Polyester and olefin are the most commonly used fibers for this method. As the filament is extruded from the spinneret, it is blown onto a collection surface. The still-molten fibers bond as they contact the surface. They may be subjected to additional bonding or entanglement.

In general, spun-bonded fabrics are easy to sew and possess the properties of the fiber from which they are made. Their end uses include geotextiles, carpet backings, wall coverings, protective apparel, filters, insulation, and shoe linings.

Melt-blown nonwovens form from molten synthetic fibers that are broken into short lengths by a stream of air as they leave the spinneret. Coor air distributes the fibers onto a collection surface where they are held together by bonding or entanglement. (See Figure 12–5.) Polyester and olefin are often used for this method.

FIGURE 12–5

Melt blowing. (Courtesy INDA, Association of the Nonwoven Fabrics Industry. Material originally printed in INDA's Nonwoven Fabrics Handbook. Copyright, INDA.)

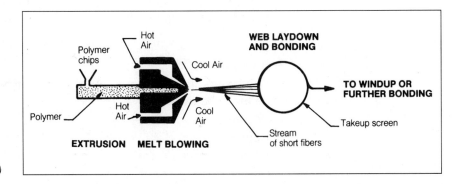

Melt-blown nonwovens tend to have low strength and low abrasion resistance. End uses for melt-blown nonwovens include hospital and medical supplies, filters, and insulation.

Other Methods of Fabric Construction

In addition to weaving, knitting, and nonwoven formation, other methods can create many interesting, beautiful, and useful textile products. This section starts with a discussion of felt, a very old textile product, and concludes with fiber-reinforced composites textiles, a new development in textile technology.

FELT

Some authorities believe felt is the oldest textile, while others believe tapa cloth is the oldest. **Felt** is not included in the nonwoven portion of this chapter because technically it is not a nonwoven. It has many of the characteristics of a nonwoven, but it is formed by the interlocking structure of the wool fiber, not through the entanglement of fibers. Note the difference between **mechanical** or **needle-punch felt** and **wool felt**. Mechanical felt is considered a nonwoven, while wool felt is not. In this text, the term *felt* means wool felt.

Wool fiber is used to make felt. The wool fibers are pressed into a flat sheet and then subjected to moisture, heat, and agitation. The scaly structure of the wool fiber causes the fibers to interlock and mat. Because felt is a relatively weak fabric, **scrim**, loosely woven fabric, is sometimes added to the felt to improve the fabric's strength. Other fibers, usually cotton or rayon, may be added to decrease cost. The characteristics of felt are it:

- Does not fray.
- Is easy to cut.
- Can be molded into shapes. Adding other fibers decreases the wool's ability to be molded.
- Provides warmth.
- Repels water.
- Has poor stretch recovery and poor strength.

- May pill.
- Has poor drape.

End uses for felt include hats, fashion accessories, and crafts. Its industrial end uses are soundproofing, insulation, and filters.

FILMS, FOAMS, AND LAMINATED AND BONDED FABRICS

Films, foams, and laminated and bonded fabrics are included in this chapter because they are made from chemicals that are similar to those used in traditional textile products or because they are combinations of films, foams, and traditional textile products.

POLYMER FILMS.   **Polymer films** are synthetic polymers that are extruded in sheets or cast onto a drum. Polymer films used in apparel or furnishings are commonly made from vinyl or polyurethane. These films are categorized as:

Plain or **nonreinforced films**, like sandwich bags.
Expanded films, which incorporate tiny air cells into the compound.
Reinforced or **supported films**, which are plain or expanded films that
    have been laminated to a woven, knit, or nonwoven. Laminated fab-
    rics are discussed later in this chapter.

The characteristics of polymer films are they:

- Have poor strength unless supported.
- Repel water. Some expanded films have less repellency.
- Resist soil.
- Are not air permeable. Some expanded films have improved air per-
  meability.
- Have poor drape.
- Can be finished to simulate other products, like leather.
- Are low cost.

Films are used for metallic yarns, leatherlike fabrics for apparel and upholstery fabrics, packaging, and garment bags.

FOAMS.   **Foams** are created when air is incorporated into rubber or polyurethane. Chemical compounds that are mixed with the rubber or polyurethane cause air cells to form and give foams their sponginess. Foams vary in their sponginess. End uses for foams include furniture padding, carpet backing and padding, stuffing for pillows and toys, and apparel.

LAMINATED FABRICS. **Laminated fabrics** are layered structures in which two or more fabrics are fused. Each layer maintains its identity. The two types of laminates are foam and film.

Foam Laminates. **Foam laminates** have two or three layers and are usually used for insulation. In this structure, a polyurethane layer is fused to a face fabric. Sometimes a third fabric, usually a tricot knit, is fused to the foam, sandwiching the foam layer in the middle. End uses for fabric and foam laminates include winter coats and sportswear.

Film Laminates. **Film laminates**, or **coated fabrics**, are created when a film is laminated to a knit or woven fabric. Rubber, polyurethane, and polyvinal chloride films are commonly used. Coated fabrics are often created to resemble leather. They are used for upholstery fabrics, wall coverings, and apparel. Sometimes film laminates are discussed as chemical-finishing treatments. Coated fabrics vary in their degree of consumer acceptance. They tend to be stiff and uncomfortable.

GORE-TEX®, a **microporous film laminate**, is an example of a traditional fabric laminated with a very thin film. The GORE-TEX® film is a fluorocarbon membrane with very small pores that transmit water vapor but not water (see Figure 12–6). As a result, it is used extensively for rainwear and skiwear.

Another name for microporous film laminates like GORE-TEX® is poromeric fabrics. **Poromeric fabrics** have wider consumer acceptance than traditional film laminates because they are waterproof, transmit water vapor, and drape well. In addition to rainwear and skiwear, they are used in medicine, tents, sleeping bags, and swimwear.

BONDED FABRICS. **Bonded fabrics** are two-layer structures in which the layers are joined with an adhesive. The adhesive does not add thickness to the fabric, but it may add body. Usually the face fabric is bonded to a tricot. Bonded fabrics offer the benefits of shape retention and possible self-lining. Their end uses include draperies, apparel, and tablecloths.

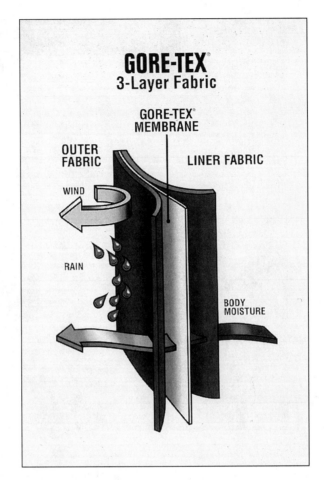

FIGURE 12–6
GORE–TEX® fabric construction. (Courtesy of W. L. Gore and Associates, Inc.)

MALI OR STITCH-BONDED FABRICS

Mali or **stitch-bonded fabrics**, alternatively referred to as **stitch-through** or **stitch-knitted** fabrics, are created when yarns or fibers are sewn with needles and thread (see Figure 12–7). A major advantage of mali fabrics is they can be produced faster than traditional knit or woven fabrics. There are three types of mali fabrics:

Malimo®, the most common type of mali fabric, is a flat fabric which is similar to conventional cloth. Its end uses include furnishings such as wall coverings, draperies, and household linens.

FIGURE 12–7

Malimo fabric

The **Malipol system** produces a pile fabric. Its end uses include upholstery, carpeting, and a terry cloth substitute.

Maliwatt fabric is **batting** used for insulation. The Maliwatt machine
stitches the batt of fibers.

TUFTED FABRICS

The **tufting** process creates pile fabric quickly and efficiently. In the
United States, tufting is the primary method of producing carpeting.
Large needles stitch yarns into a woven primary fabric. Over 1,000 needles work simultaneously to create carpeting that may be up to 18 feet
wide. The tufts may be cut to create a cut-pile effect. After the fabric is

tufted it is stabilized with a coating of latex. Sometimes a secondary fabric is applied to the latex. (See Figure 12–8.)

The tufting process is used primarily to create carpeting, but tufted bedspreads, blankets, and upholstery fabrics are available.

LACE AND OTHER OPENWORK FABRICS

There are numerous varieties of lace and other openwork fabrics.

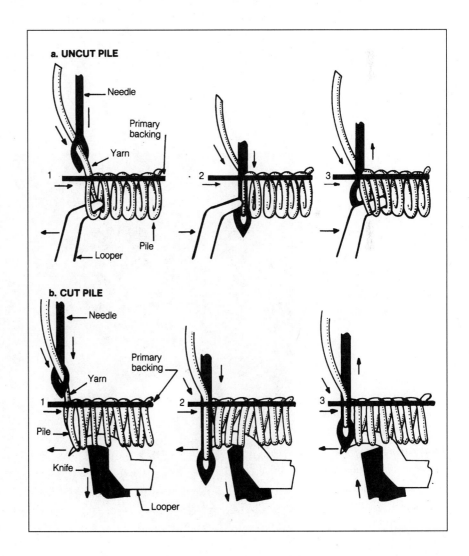

FIGURE 12–8

The tufting process:
(A) Uncut pile; (B) Cut pile

LACE. **Laces** are beautiful openwork fabrics that may be created either by hand or by machine. There are two categories of lace: bobbin lace and needlepoint lace. **Bobbin lace**, also called **pillow lace**, is created with twisted and plaited threads that are worked over a pillow. (See Figure 12–9.) **Needlepoint lace** is similar to embroidery. Embroidery is discussed later in this chapter. Needlepoint designs are stitched over base threads. Typical designs are flowers and birds.

Originally all laces were made by hand. Now most lace fabric is made by the Levers machine. **Knitted** or **raschel laces** may be made on the raschel knitting machine. Some lacelike fabrics are created on the Schiffli embroidery machine. Schiffli embroidery is discussed later in this chapter.

Traditionally laces were named for the towns in which they were developed.

FIGURE 12–9

The Lacemaker *by Nicolas Maes, 17th century Dutch painter. (Courtesy of The Metropolitan Museum of Art, the Friedsam Collection, Bequest of Michael Friedsam, 1931 [31.100.5].)*

Lace Vocabulary

The following describes these laces.

Alençon. A needlepoint lace with a hexagonal mesh background and a
solid design outlined with cord. (See Figure 12–10A.)

Chantilly. Delicate French lace, frequently of flower or vine design.
(See Figure 12–10B.)

Cluny. French bobbin lace, usually in medium- to heavyweight. (See
Figure 12-10C.)

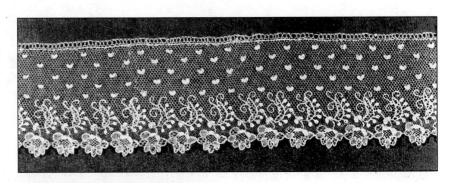

FIGURE 12–10A

*Point d'Alençon—French
needlepoint lace border from
the late 18th century.
(Courtesy of The
Metropolitan Museum of Art,
Bequest of Emma Townsend
Gary, 1937 [37.20.271].)*

FIGURE 12–10B

*Chantilly—French bobbin lace shawl
from the 19th century. (Courtesy of
The Metropolitan Museum of Art,
Bequest of Josephine Van Devenier
Smith, 1922 [22.73.2].)*

FIGURE 12–10C

Cluny—French bobbin lace edging. (Courtesy of The Metropolitan Museum of Art, Gift of Richard C. Greenleaf, 1923 [23.199].)

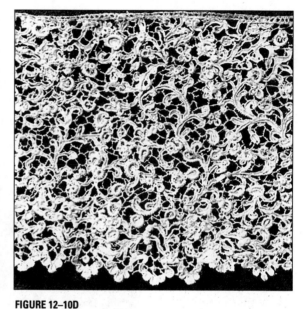

FIGURE 12–10D

Rosepoint—French or Italian needlepoint lace border from the 17th century. (Courtesy of The Metropolitan Museum of Art, Gift of Mrs. Edward S. Harkness, 1930 [30.135.136].)

Cordonnett. Lace in which the pattern is outlined in cord; also called reembroidered lace.

Levers. Lace made on the Levers machine. It is usually expensive.

Nottingham. A machine-made lace with large designs, commonly used for tablecloths.

Rosepoint. Needlepoint lace with elaborate raised patterns. (See Figure 12–10D.)

OTHER OPENWORK FABRICS.   Due to their openwork structure, netting, macramé, crochet, tatting, and hairpin lace are commonly discussed with laces. They are created by knotting and looping yarns, but they are typically coarser than traditional lace. Most are handcraft techniques. Following are brief descriptions of each.

Crochet. Crocheting involves using a crochet hook to loop yarns together. The techniques for making Irish crocheted lace were brought to the United States by Irish immigrants during the 1800s.

Hairpin lace. Hairpin lace is a variation of crocheting in which yarns are wound around a frame before being crocheted together.

Macramé. Decorative knots are used to make macramé. Beautiful wall hangings are created by this hand technique.

Netting. Nets are open-mesh structures that are created by looping and knotting yarns together by hand or by machine. They may be as lightweight as **tulle** or as heavy as fishing net. Netting can be embellished with fancy stitches, seed pearls, and gems.

Tatting. A tatting shuttle is used to create knotted laces.

QUILTED FABRICS

Most **quilted fabrics** are made with three layers: a face fabric, a backing fabric, and filling or batting sandwiched between. Some quilted fabrics are made with two face fabrics and are reversible. The three layers of most quilts are held in place by small machine or hand stitches which form decorative patterns. (See Figures 12–11 and 12–12.) Higher-quality quilted fabrics are stitched with thread. Some lower-end goods are bonded with adhesives or heat in a pattern that mimics the decorative patterns of stitched quilted fabrics. Quilted fabrics are prized for their warmth and decorative stitching.

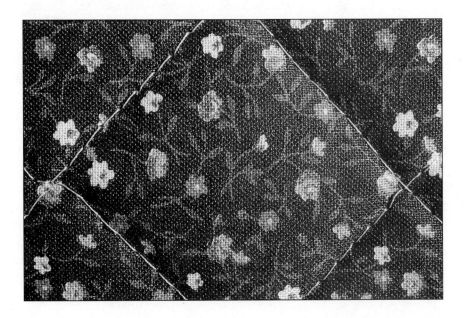

FIGURE 12–11

Modern machine quilted fabric

FIGURE 12–12

American crazy quilt—New England, ca. 1885. The top is silk and silk velvet with cotton and chenille embroidery; the back is cotton. (Courtesy of The Metropolitan Museum of Art, Gift of Reverend and Mrs. Karl Nielsen, 1962 [62.143].)

EMBROIDERY

Embroidery is not a fabric structure. It is a technique for adding decoration. It is sometimes discussed as an aesthetic finish. **Embroidered fabrics** are decorated with patterns of flat surface yarns. Fabrics can be embroidered by hand or by machine. In hand embroidery many intricate stitches are used to create beautiful historic, ethnic, and modern, nontraditional designs.

As mentioned earlier, machine embroidery is done on the Schiffli embroidery machine or a multihead embroidery machine. Only a limited variety of stitches and patterns are possible with this method, however. **Eyelet** is one example. (See Figure 12–13.) More intricate patterns are achieved on a multihead embroidery machine. This machine is used to stitch designs onto garments and to create patches that are later sewn onto garments.

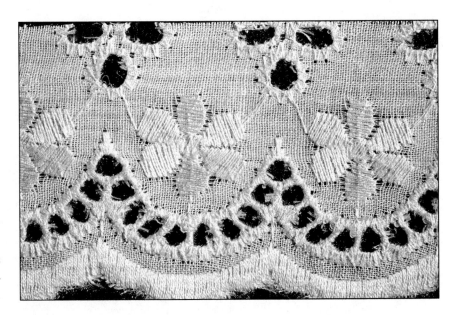

FIGURE 12–13

Schiffli machine made embroidered eyelet.

BRAIDING

Braids are narrow fabrics made of three or more yarns plaited in a diagonal pattern. Braided fabrics are frequently used as trims in apparel or furnishings, and they may also be used to make rugs. Shoelaces are tubular braids.

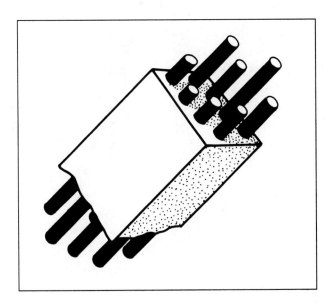

FIGURE 12–14

Fiber reinforced composites

FIBER-REINFORCED COMPOSITES

Fiber-reinforced composites (FRCs) are high-technology combinations of textiles and resins. Most commonly aramid, carbon or glass fibers, yarns, or fabrics are imbedded in or impregnated with epoxy, phenolic, or polyester resins. (See Figure 12–14.) FRCs have superior strength, are lightweight, and can be molded into desired shapes. They therefore have great potential for use in sporting equipment, the automotive industry, and space exploration.

LABORATORY ASSIGNMENTS

ASSIGNMENT 12–1   PROVIDE DEFINITIONS

1. Define the term *nonwoven*.
2. Define *durable nonwoven* and *disposable nonwoven* and give an example of each.

ASSIGNMENT 12–2   IDENTIFY MALI FABRICS

Explain how mali fabrics differ from other types of nonwovens.

ASSIGNMENT 12–3   IDENTIFY NONWOVEN AND OTHER FABRIC CONSTRUCTIONS

Mount, label, and list one end use for each nonwoven and other fabric construction sample in your swatch kit or instructor-supplied swatches.

Dyeing and Printing

OBJECTIVES

The student will be able to:

1. Discuss the importance of aesthetics and permanence of color and design
2. Define *colorfastness* and relate it to the end use of a textile product
3. Compare and contrast dyes and pigments
4. List the advantages and disadvantages of each of the five stages at which dyeing can be done
5. Discuss roller, screen, heat transfer, and special printing techniques
6. Integrate color and design into the overall performance of apparel, furnishings, and industrial textiles

Introduction

In general, the consumer expects two things: (1) fashionable, aesthetically pleasing colors and prints, and (2) permanent colors. As trends change, however, styles sometimes demand that garments appear aged after several washings.

THE IMPORTANCE OF AESTHETICS

Most authorities agree that the color or printed design of a fabric is the most important factor in the customer's decision to purchase apparel or furnishings.

COLOR PERMANENCE

Colors that are permanent are considered to be **colorfast**. Colors that are fast will not:

Bleed. Lose color in water. Bleeding may produce both color loss and staining. When a red T-shirt is washed with white underwear, for example, the T-shirt may bleed, losing its color and staining the white underwear.

Crock. Transfer color due to abrasion or rubbing.

Fade. Lose color.

Frost. Lose color due to localized abrasion. (See Figure 13–1.)

Migrate. Color shift that occurs when the moisture lifts color and redeposits it in another area. Most often seen in the underarm area.

FIGURE 13–1

Frosting on jeans

TABLE 13–1 COLOR CHANGE FACTORS AND POSSIBLE EFFECTS	
Color Change Factor	**Effect(s)**
Abrasion during wear	Frosting (localized loss of color)
Abrasion during cleaning	Overall loss of color
Exposure to sunlight	Loss of color
Atmospheric fumes	Loss of color, change of color
Detergents	Loss of color
Chlorine bleaches	Loss of color
Dry-cleaning chemicals	Loss of color, change of color
Perspiration	Loss of color, change of color, color migration
Antiperspirants	Change of color
Laundering	Loss of color, especially if hot water is used

Color permanence can be affected by abrasion during wearing and cleaning, exposure to sunlight, atmospheric fumes, detergents, bleaches, dry-cleaning chemicals, perspiration, and some antiperspirants. See Table 13–1 for a list of the possible effects of these color-change factors.

The end use of a textile product is an important determinant of the coloration process because the color must be colorfast under the conditions in which it is being used. For example, curtains and draperies are particularly susceptible to fading from sunlight exposure. Upholstery fabrics are susceptible to fading from abrasion and possibly sunlight exposure. In clothing, colorfastness to washing and perspiration are important.

Dyes and Pigments

Colorants are chemical agents which produce colors. The colorants used to add color to textiles are dyes and pigments. **Dyes**, also referred to as **dyestuffs**, and are the most common way to add color to fabric. Until the mid 1800s only natural dyes were available. They were made from various animal, vegetable, and mineral substances. In general, natural dyes have poor colorfastness. Synthetic dyes were discovered in 1856 by William Perkin, an English chemist. Because synthetic dyes have better colorfastness than natural dyes, very few natural dyes are used commercially.

In the dyeing process, most dyes are dissolved in water and absorbed into fibers during the dyeing process, although some are dissolved in solvents. In most cases the dye chemically bonds with the fiber. After the fibers are immersed in the dye bath or the design is printed, the excess dye and processing chemicals must be washed away. If left in these chemicals can reduce fiber strength. If the dye has been printed on it must be **aged**, or set with steam, to make the color permanent. The word **set**, in this case, means "to make permanent."

Unlike dyes, **pigments** do not dissolve in water and are not absorbed into the fiber. They do not adhere to fabric without a **resin binder**. This binder, which is usually mixed with the pigment, acts like an adhesive. Pigments are applied in a bath or printed on the fabric. The colored fabric must undergo **curing**, or heating, to adhere the pigment to the fabric permanently. See Table 13–2 to compare the characteristics of dyes and pigments.

The hundreds of colorants available to the modern textile chemist are divided into twelve major categories. They can be further classified according to their use with specific fibers. See Table 13–3 for very brief descriptions of the major dye classifications.

TABLE 13–2 COMPARISON OF DYES AND PIGMENTS

Dyes
- Bond chemically with the fiber
- In general, are more colorfast than pigments
- Crocking and fading are less of a problem than with pigments
- Do not affect the texture of the fabric
- Can be used on fibers, yarns, fabric, and garments
- Printed colors must be aged with steam or heat
- Washing and rinsing are required to remove chemicals and excess dye

Pigments
- Cheaper and more efficient to apply than dyes
- May stiffen the fabric
- With dark colors, crocking and loss of color in laundering may occur
- Any color can be applied to any fabric, but not on formed fibers or yarns
- Can be added to manufactured fibers before extrusion
- Easier to obtain a color match because the color is on the surface
- Can only be applied as a solid color or as a print
- Colors must be cured

TABLE 13–3 MAJOR DYE CLASSIFICATIONS

Cellulosic Fibers

Azoic dyes (also called naphthol dyes)
Wide range of colors; launder well, but dark shades may crock

Direct dyes (also called substantive dyes)
Wide range of colors, but less intense than basic or acid dyes; may lose color in laundering

Direct-developed dyes
Same as direct dyes, but improved colorfastness

Reactive dyes
Very bright colors possible; good colorfastness; difficult to match; used on protein fibers and nylon

Sulfur dyes*
Wide variety of colors but dull shades; used especially for navy, black, and brown

Vat dyes*
Considered the best dye for colorfastness; smaller color range than other dyes; used on acrylics, modacrylics, and nylon

Pigment dyes
See discussion of pigments in Table 13–2

Protein Fibers

Acid dyes
Wide range of bright colors but colorfastness varies; used on nylon, spandex, and some acrylics

Premetalized acid dyes
Duller colors than acid dyes but better colorfastness

Chrome dyes (also called mordant dyes)
Not as bright and smaller color range than acid dyes; may bleed

Pigment dyes
See discussion of pigments in Table 13–2

Manufactured Fibers

Cationic dyes (also called basic dyes)
Bright colors with excellent colorfastness when used on synthetics

Disperse dyes
Good color range but colorfastness varies; fume fading on acetate (shades of blue turn pink)

Pigment dyes
See discussion of pigments in Table 13–2

If they are not completely washed out, some vat and sulfur dyes may cause tendering in cotton fabrics. Tendering is the weakening of a fiber due to exposure to chemicals used in dyeing or finishing or to other degradants.

The dyeing and printing processes have a significant impact on the environment. Large amounts of water and energy are used with dyes. Pigments, in contrast, require much less water and energy. Some techniques, such as heat transfer printing, produce less waste and pollution than others. The industry is continuing to research environmentally friendly methods.

Dyeing

Color may be added to textiles at different times during the production process. Often the decision as to when to add color is determined by the end use of the product. The stage at which the color is added affects colorfastness. The earlier in the production process the color is added, the more colorfast the color will be.

Another factor governing when to add color is current fashion trends. Because color is a major factor in the consumer's buying decision, and because color styles change frequently, it is cost effective to delay adding color until the last stage of production. Doing so allows the manufacturer to more accurately meet the expectations of the customer, lower inventories, and avoid costly overruns of poor-selling colors. Unfortunately, delaying color application may result in poor colorfastness.

THE DYEING PROCESSES

Textiles can be dyed at several different stages during production. The stage at which the product is dyed determines which process is used. The five processes for dyeing are:

1. Solution dyeing
2. Stock or fiber dyeing
3. Yarn dyeing
4. Piece dyeing
5. Product and garment dyeing

The advantages and disadvantages of each process are summarized briefly in Table 13–4.

SOLUTION DYEING. Solution dyeing occurs at the prefiber stage and can only be done to manufactured fibers. Pigments are added to the fiber solution, or dope, before extrusion. Solution-dyed fibers are also called spun-dyed fibers, dope-dyed fibers, and mass-pigmented fibers.

STOCK DYEING. The process of adding color at the fiber stage is called **stock** or fiber **dyeing.** Fibers for use in worsted yarns may be top dyed. **Top dyeing** occurs at the sliver stage after all short fibers have been combed out.

TABLE 13–4   SUMMARY OF THE ADVANTAGES AND DISADVANTAGES OF THE DYEING PROCESSES

Solution Dyeing
    Advantages: Excellent colorfastness, excellent for hard-to-dye fibers such as olefin
    Disadvantages: The color decision is made very early in production, only appropriate for manufactured fibers

Stock Dyeing
    Advantages: Excellent for producing fibers to create tweed or heather effects, good dye penetration
    Disadvantages: Relatively expensive, early color decision

Yarn Dyeing
    Advantages: Excellent for use in woven or knitted stripes, plaids, ginghams, chambray; excellent dye penetration
    Disadvantages: More expensive than piece dyeing but less expensive than stock dyeing, early color decision

Piece Dyeing
    Advantages: More cost effective than stock or yarn dyeing, both knits and wovens can be piece dyed, color decision is delayed
    Disadvantages: Can achieve only solid colors (except for cross dyeing and tone-on-tone), dye penetration may not be as good as yarn or stock dyeing

Product Dyeing
    Advantages: Color decision delayed as long as possible so the process is actually cost effective, process can be used to overdye garments or other textile products from a previous season
    Disadvantages: More costly than piece dyeing, all components must be compatible (polyester thread in a cotton T-shirt accepts dye differently than the cotton), sizing and shrinkage may be a problem, penetration of color may be poor, colorfastness may be poor.

YARN DYEING. **Yarn dyeing** occurs after fibers have been spun into yarn but before the yarns are woven or knitted into fabric. **Space dyeing** is a special yarn-dyeing technique that produces a multicolor effect along the length of the yarn. There are three methods of yarn dyeing: skein, package, and beam. In **skein dyeing**, the yarns are wound in loose hanks, or bundles, before dyeing. In **package dyeing**, the yarns are wound onto perforated cones or tubes before dyeing. The perforations allow the dye to circulate through the cones or tubes. In **beam dyeing** the yarn is wound on the warp beam before immersion in the dyebath.

PIECE DYEING. **Piece dyeing**, or fabric dyeing, is the most common method for dyeing solid-colored fabric. There are six methods of dyeing fabric: beam, beck, jet, jig, pad, and foam.

Beam dyeing is used for lightweight, open-weave fabrics. This method is very similar to the beam method for dyeing yarns. The fabric is wound on large perforated beams and then immersed in the dye bath.

In **beck dyeing**, sometimes called box or winch dyeing, the fabric to be dyed is stitched end-to-end and circulated through the dyebath. This method is used for knits and wool fabrics because little stress is placed on the fabric, and the fabric maintains its original hand.

Jet dyeing is similar to beck dyeing, but it involves using streams of pressurized dye in an enclosed system. Jet dyeing is faster and more economical than beck dyeing.

Jig dyeing places considerable tension on the fabric, so it is only used on stable fabrics that have flat surfaces, such as taffeta and lining fabrics. The fabric is stretched flat and passed through the dye bath.

Like jig dyeing, **pad dyeing** stresses the fabric and is suited only to stable fabrics. This method uses pads to squeeze the dye into the fabric. Pad dyeing is the only method appropriate for use with pigments.

Foam dyeing has been used on a limited basis in the carpet industry. This method uses foam to apply the dye to the surface of wet fabric.

Special Piece-Dyed Effects. There are three variations of piece dyeing: cross, union, and tone-on-tone. These variations are used to achieve specific results when dyeing blends (i.e., polyester/cotton).

Cross dyeing is used to create a multicolored effect in a blend. Differently colored dyes are selected for their affinities for particular fibers. These dyes are then combined into one dye bath. When the blended fabric is dyed, each fiber picks up a different color. For example, a blue/gray heather effect is possible in fabric made of polyester/cotton blended yarns if the dye bath includes blue dye for the polyester and gray dye for the cotton. When single fiber yarns are combined with other single fiber yarns, a striped or plaid effect can be achieved. Cross dyeing achieves stock-dyed and yarn-dyed effects at lower cost.

The purpose of **union dyeing** is to achieve a solid color in a blend. In this process, the dyebath is prepared with dyes that will produce the same color in each fiber of the blend. For example, two different dyes will be needed to dye a polyester/wool blend one solid shade of red.

Tone-on-tone dyeing is frequently used on carpeting. The same manufactured fiber can be varied to have different affinities for dyes. When these fiber variants are used in the same fabric, one dyebath yields a shaded effect.

PRODUCT AND GARMENT DYEING.

Product or **garment dyeing** is dyeing garments or other textile products, like towels or sheets, after they have been constructed. This process is most often used for sweaters, pantyhose, T-shirts, sweatshirts, towels, and bed linens.

COLOR CONSISTENCY

The textile colorist is challenged constantly to achieve uniform color throughout a dye batch with no streaking or blotching. The colorist must also ensure the color is consistent from one end of the bolt to the other, and from one bolt to the next. The textile products buyer, whether purchasing in a personal or professional capacity, should examine all products for consistent color.

Printing

Printing uses the pigments and dyes employed in dyeing and applies them in a pattern or design. Printed textiles are subject to the same aesthetics and performance coloration guidelines as dyed textiles. In general, dyed textiles have better colorfastness than printed textiles because the dyeing process allows for better dye penetration.

In printing, the pigments or dyes are thickened with gums or starches to provide more control during application. The thickened dye or pigment is called **print paste**. Some dyes are not suited for use as print paste. **Wet prints** are fabrics that have been printed with dye. They are so named because steam is required to set the color, and processing chemicals and excess dyes must be washed out.

Fabrics printed with pigments are called **dry prints** because the dry heat of the curing process sets the color. Washing is not needed. In general, printing with pigments is cost effective, provides good colorfastness to light, but poor colorfastness to crocking and cleaning. Printing with pigments frequently stiffens the fabric in the printed areas. Fabric printed with dyes maintains its original texture. Tables 13–1, 13–2, and 13–3 summarize the color change factors, dye and pigment characteristics, and major dye classifications.

PRINTING METHODS

Printed designs may be applied to yarns, fabric, and, in some cases, completed garments. Most commercial prints are produced by screen or roller printing methods.

SCREEN PRINTING. **Screen printing** developed from the hand technique of stenciling. Stenciling is discussed later in this chapter. In screen printing, fine mesh screen is first mounted on a frame and treated with a photosensitive film. Next the film in the design area is removed with photochemicals. Each color in a design requires a separate screen. Therefore, a three-color design requires three screens and three applications of print paste. The screen is then laid on the fabric and print paste is applied. The design appears on the fabric where the film was removed. Screen printing is sometimes referred to as "silk-screen printing" because original screens were made of silk. Now meshes of synthetic fibers or metal are used. There are three commercial screen-printing methods: hand, automatic or flatbed, and rotary.

Although **hand-screen printing** is slow, it is easier to set up than other methods and is cost effective for small orders. It is used for printing designs on garment parts or on ready-made garments like T-shirts and sweatshirts.

Automatic screen printing, also called flatbed or flat-screen printing, is an automated version of hand-screen printing. This method is especially appropriate for creating limited qualities of high-fashion fabrics and for print designs to be test marketed. It can be used to print lengths of fabric but not ready-made garments or garment parts. (See Figure 13–2.)

FIGURE 13–2

Automatic flat screen printing machine. (Courtesy of MASTERS OF LINEN/U.S.A.)

Rotary screen printing is the fastest screen printing method. In this process the screen is a cylinder instead of the flat screen used in hand- or automatic screen printing. The dye is forced through holes in the cylinder as it rolls over the fabric. This method is becoming the most popular. It is not as fast as roller printing (see following), but its setup is quicker and easier.

ROLLER PRINTING.   **Roller printing**, or **machine printing**, is similar to the process of printing a newspaper. Copper rollers or cylinders are engraved to reproduce the desired design. Each color pattern in a design is engraved on a separate roller. Therefore, a three-color design requires three rollers. The cloth to be printed is imprinted with each roller. (See Figure 13–3.)

This process is fast and efficient, but its setup is very time consuming, costly, and difficult. Roller printing is therefore usually only done for very large orders. Rotary screen printing is becoming the preferred method because it is easier and less time consuming to set up.

TYPES OF PRINTING.   Each of the previously discussed methods of printing can be used for various types of prints, including:

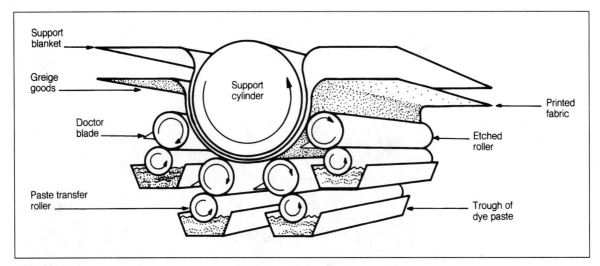

FIGURE 13–3

Roller printing

1. **Direct printing** is applying dye or pigment directly onto white or previously dyed cloth. **Blotch printing** is a variation of direct printing in which both the background color and the design are printed on the fabric. This technique eliminates predyeing white fabric to achieve a colored background.

2. In **discharge printing** piece-dyed fabric is printed with a chemical solution to remove the fabric's original color. An example of a discharge print is black fabric with white polka dots. Sometimes additional printing steps add color to the bleached areas.

3. **Resist printing** yields results similar to discharge prints except that a resist is applied to the fabric before dyeing to prevent the dye from penetrating the fibers. Resist printing is done more frequently as a handcraft. Resist printing is discussed further later in this chapter.

4. **Duplex printing** creates a printed pattern on both sides of the fabric. The designs can be the same or different. If both sides are printed with the same pattern, the fabric can appear to have a woven-in design. This method is expensive. Jacquard and dobby fabrics have nearly replaced duplex prints.

5. **Warp printing** creates beautiful, subtle designs. The warp yarns are printed before the fabric is woven. Warp-printed fabrics are usually expensive, but transfer printing the warp yarns has lowered their

cost. **Ikat** is the hand technique of warp printing. Transfer printing is discussed in more detail later in this chapter.

6. In **flock printing** an adhesive is applied to the fabric in a specific patterns. Short fibers are then scattered over the surface and adhere in the desired pattern. The fibers can be vibrated mechanically to arrange the fibers in an upright position. **Electrostatic flocking** uses an electrical charge to orient the fibers vertically. Electrostatic flocking is slower but provides more luxurious flocking.

7. **Deluster printing** involves using **delustering** agents to reduce the luster of shiny fabrics. The delustering agents are printed on the fabric to create shiny and dull patterns.

8. **Burn-out printing** uses chemicals that destroy fibers and create a pattern of holes in the fabric. The resulting fabric is weak and not durable.

SPECIAL PRINTING TECHNIQUES.   Special printing techniques include heat-transfer printing and jet printing.

Heat-Transfer Printing.   In **heat-transfer printing**, also called thermal transfer printing or sublistatic printing, a design is printed on special paper with disperse dyes. This printed paper is then laid on the fabric and the design transfers to the fabric through heat and pressure. (See Figure 13–4.) The procedure is similar to applying decals. This process is limited to disperse dyes and is appropriate only for fibers with an affinity for disperse dyes. These fibers include nylon, polyester, acrylic, and acetate.

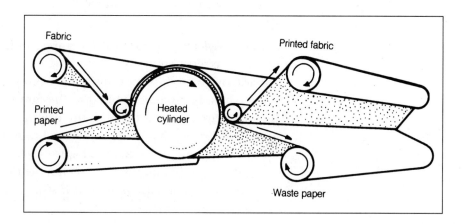

FIGURE 13–4

Heat transfer printing

Heat-transfer printing can be used on fabrics, garment parts, or ready-made garments. It allows the print to be inspected before printing and therefore reduces the incidence of second-quality merchandise. No additional step is needed to set the color, and environmental effects are minimal.

Jet Printing. **Jet printing** is a computerized process that is used primarily on carpets, pile upholstery, and toweling. Small jets control the flow of dye streams. (See Figure 13–5.)

PROBLEMS WITH PRINTING

Accuracy in printing is essential to producing quality goods. Second-quality merchandise increases cost and reduces efficiency. Common printing problems include out-of-register prints and off-grain prints. **Out-of-register prints** have edges that do not line up correctly. The colors may overlap or not meet exactly.

Off-grain prints do not follow the lengthwise or crosswise grain of the fabric. Garments cut from off-grain prints cannot be both matched and cut on grain. If the print is matched, the garment will be off-grain and will not hang properly. If the garment is cut on grain, the print will not match. Except for very low-end goods, out-of-register prints and off-grain prints are unacceptable to the customer.

HANDCRAFT PRINTING TECHNIQUES. Many attractive, one-of-a-kind textile designs are created by hand. Several of these printing techniques are introduced here briefly, but the serious textile-design student may enjoy further study of these beautiful methods of creative expression.

Resist Methods. A resist protects areas of fabric from dye. Following are some resist methods.

Batik originated in Indonesia. It involves a series of waxings and dyeing baths. Hot wax is applied to the fabric in the desired design. The waxed area does not absorb the dye in the dyebath. Subsequent waxings and dyebaths create additional design details. Solvents are required to remove the wax. (See Figure 13–6.)

Tie-dyeing or bound resist is a technique many people have experienced. Areas of fabric are bound with string or rubber bands or knotted before being dyed.

FIGURE 13–5

Millitron® injection dyed area rugs. Computer controlled micro jets inject dye into the face of the carpet with surgical precision. (Courtesy Milliken & Company.)

Stenciling originated centuries ago in Japan and developed into the modern-day version of screen printing. A stencil is made by cutting a pattern in special paper or thin metal sheets. The stencil is held over the fabric, and dyes or pigments are brushed or sprayed on with an air gun.

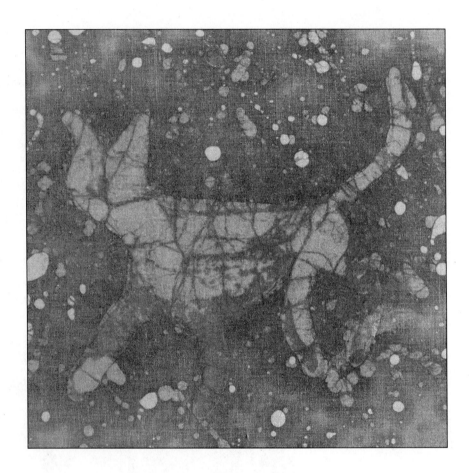

FIGURE 13–6

Batik

Block Printing.   In **block printing**, a design is drawn on a block, and the surface of the block around the design is carved away. The raised area is coated with dye paste and pressed into fabric to apply the design. Sometimes several blocks are carved to create more intricate designs. These blocks may be reused many times.

Hand Painting.   In **hand painting**, thickened dyes and pigments are used on fabric much like oils are used to paint on canvas. Unthickened dyes are very similar to watercolors, and similar effects can be achieved. Pigments must be mixed with textile binders to adhere properly to fabric, however.

Airbrushing.   **Airbrushing** is another technique that can be adapted for use on fabric. Dyes and pigments are used instead of paint.

LABORATORY ASSIGNMENTS

ASSIGNMENT 13–1   **DETERMINE THE EFFECTS OF FIBER ABSORBENCY**

1. Gather the following materials:
   samples of white fabric (greige cotton, greige polyester, cotton/
   polyester blend), $2\frac{1}{2}'' \times 1\frac{1}{2}''$
   dyestuff (Ritt® or Tintex®)
   250-ml beaker
   container to prepare the dyebath
   hot plate (if necessary)
   enamel pan (if necessary)
   tongs
2. Immerse the fabric samples in hot water for 15 minutes to remove
   any starch, oil, or waxy finishes.
3. Prepare the dyebath according to the instructions on the package.
4. Place the samples in the dyebath for 5 minutes, stirring constantly.
5. Rinse well, and allow the samples to dry.
6. Mount and label each sample with its fiber content.
7. Answer the following:
   a. Which sample appears to be the most absorbent?
   b. Which sample appears to be the least absorbent?
   c. Describe the appearance of the blend.
   d. Explain how fiber absorbency affects dye penetration.

ASSIGNMENT 13–2   **EXPERIMENT WITH CROCKING**

1. Gather the following materials:
   samples of white cotton, $2'' \times 2''$
   variety of printed samples to be tested for crocking, $3'' \times 3''$ (Sugges-
   tion: unwashed samples of dark colored calico and inexpensive
   printed fabric)
   flat-top pen or pencil (optional)
   water
2. Place the samples to be tested on a flat surface.
3. Fold the white cotton fabric over the forefinger or the flat top of
   the pen or pencil.

4. Firmly rub across the test specimens twenty times.
5. Examine the white fabric to determine if any dry crocking has occurred.
6. Repeat steps 2 to 5 using a damp white cloth.
7. Mount each sample and rate its staining:
   1 = No crocking
   2 = Slight crocking
   3 = Considerable crocking

ASSIGNMENT 13–3 **EXPERIMENT WITH CROSS DYEING**

1. Gather the following materials:
   multifiber test strip, samples cut 1″ wide
   samples of unknown griege fabrics, 2″ × 3″
   250-ml beakers
   hot plate
   Textile Identification Stain (TIS)
   distilled water
   enamel pan
2. Place the fabric samples in the beakers and cover them with hot water for 15 minutes to remove any starch, oil, or waxy finishes.
3. Prepare the dye solution using 1 gram of TIS for each 100 ml of water.
4. Place the stain solution in the enamel pan and bring the solution to a boil.
5. Add the fabric samples and the multifiber test strip to the pan.
6. Maintain the temperature and boil for 5 minutes.
7. Remove the samples and rinse well in 120° F water.
8. Allow samples to dry.
9. Compare the color of the samples to the multifiber test strip.
10. Mount and label each sample with its generic fiber content.

ASSIGNMENT 13–4 **CREATE HEAT TRANSFER PRINTS**

1. Gather the following materials:
   fabric crayons
   polyester fabric samples, 6″ × 6″
   bond paper

iron

2. Create a design on the bond paper with the fabric crayons. The printed design will appear as a mirrored image of the design drawn. Therefore, be careful with letters.
3. Preheat the iron to the temperature indicated on the fabric crayon box.
4. Place the design face down on the fabric.
5. Slowly and carefully iron the design onto the polyester sample.
6. Mount the sample.

ASSIGNMENT 13–5   **IDENTIFY DYED AND PRINTED SAMPLES**

Mount and label each dyeing and printing sample from your swatch kit or instructor-supplied swatches.

C h a p t e r

14

Finishes

OBJECTIVES

The student will be able to:

1. Discuss the function of finishes and give examples of their positive and negative effects
2. Explain the purposes of finishes and the ways in which finishes may be classified
3. Define and list preparatory finishes
4. Define and list aesthetic finishes
5. Define and list performance finishes
6. Integrate finishes into the overall performance of apparel, furnishings, and industrial textiles

Introduction

Finishes function to give fabrics properties they do not possess naturally. Almost all apparel and furnishings textiles have been subjected to some type of finishing process and frequently have more than one finish. While most finishes are beneficial, some are not. For example, a durable-press resin finish makes cotton easier to care for, but it also

255

reduces its wear life by as much as 50 percent. This chapter primarily discusses finishes that are applied to fabrics, but finishes can be part of any production stage. For example, delustering agents can be added to manufactured fibers before extrusion.

In general, the purposes of finishes are to prepare fabric for further processing and enhance the aesthetics and/or performance of the final product. If finishing is not done by the manufacturer, it is typically done by converters. As a result, finished goods are sometimes called converted goods. The dyer or printer also does finishing.

Classifying Finishes

There are several different ways to classify finishes:

Temporary/renewable/durable/permanent
Chemical/mechanical
Preparatory/aesthetic/functional

TEMPORARY/RENEWABLE/DURABLE/PERMANENT FINISHES

Finishes can be classified by their degree of permanence. **Temporary finishes** are removed by washing or dry cleaning. For example, simple calendering, which is similar to the process of ironing, is removed during washing. Calendering is discussed later in this chapter.

Renewable finishes are temporary finishes that can be reapplied. The starch removed during washing can be reapplied before ironing. Water-resistant and soil-resistant finishes are other examples of renewable finishes.

Durable finishes are expected to be effective during the life of the product. However, this effectiveness decreases. Semidurable finishes last through several cleanings.

Permanent finishes are uniform and do not diminish during the lifetime of the product.

CHEMICAL/MECHANICAL FINISHES

Finishes can be categorized as mechanical or chemical, and sometimes both.

Chemical finishes are sometimes called **wet finishes** because they are applied to fabric in a water or other liquid bath. **Resins**, the chemicals used in wet finishes, are the most-used chemicals in the textile industry. They are used in wrinkle- and crease-resistant finishes, and frequently on cellulosics and cellulosic blends. Resins are a durable treatment, not a permanent treatment. Two commonly used resins are formaldehyde compounds and dimethyl urea glyoxal compounds. See Tables 14–1 and 14–2 for a summary of the advantages and disadvantages of these compounds.

The steps in applying a resin finish are:

1. Padding. The fabric is wetted with the finishing solution. Pads are used to squeeze out excess water.

TABLE 14–1   ADVANTAGES AND DISADVANTAGES OF FORMALDEHYDE RESIN TREATMENTS

Advantages
Add firmness and stiffness (though may also be a disadvantage)
Provide wrinkle resistance and crease retention
Provide shrink resistance
Reduce moisture absorption, dry more quickly

Disadvantages
Weaken cellulosics by as much as 50 percent
Reduce moisture absorption, less comfortable to wear
May produce a "fishy" odor in the fabric, which usually disappears fairly quickly
Oil-based stains are difficult to remove, treatment with soil-release or soil-resistant finishes may reduce this problem
Suspected carcinogen

TABLE 14–2   ADVANTAGES AND DISADVANTAGES OF DIMETHYL UREA GLYOXAL (COMPARED TO FORMALDEHYDE COMPOUNDS)

Advantages
Softer hand
Less loss of fabric strength
Not suspected carcinogen

Disadvantages
More costly
Crease resistance and wrinkle resistance are less effective

2. Drying. The fabric is dried.

3. Curing. Dry heat is used to set the finish. (See Figure 14–1.)

Water-bath finishing is costly in terms of water pollution and energy consumption. **Foam finishing**, a process in which finish is applied in a foam, is a newer method which reduces water pollution and uses less energy. The fabric does not get as wet, so water pollution is reduced and less energy is needed to dry it. Solvent finishing is another alternative to water-bath finishing, but it is not as common due to the costs and hazards of working with solvents.

Mechanical finishes are called **dry finishes** because the fabric does not need to be wet. These finishes involve a physical treatment which changes the appearance and/or hand of the textile product.

PREPARATORY/AESTHETIC/FUNCTIONAL FINISHES

This text categorizes finishes according to the preparatory/aesthetic/functional classification because this system emphasizes customer benefits of the finish. It is important to note that finishes may serve multiple purposes. A durable-press finish may be considered aesthetic because it improves the appearance of the fabric, and it may also be considered functional because it makes the fabric easier to care for. Some preparatory finishes also serve multiple purposes. For example, mercerization improves the strength of cotton and also enhances its luster and absorbency.

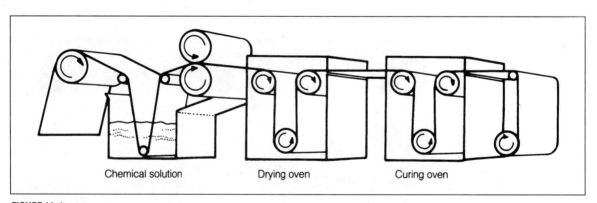

Chemical solution   Drying oven   Curing oven

FIGURE 14–1

Pad-dry-cure textile finishing

Preparatory finishes are routinely given to fabrics. The purpose of these basic finishes is to prepare the fabric for further processing. For example, cotton is routinely bleached to produce white fabric, but bleaching also prepares the fabric for dyeing and printing. The customer frequently is not aware of these treatments.

The purpose of **aesthetic finishes** is to improve the appearance and/or hand of the product. The moiré effect, a watermark design which may be seen in fabrics as well as ribbons, is an example of an aesthetic finish.

Functional finishes improve the overall performance of the product. For example, water-resistant finishes make polyester/cotton poplin suitable for use in raincoats.

Preparatory Finishes

Preparatory finishes can be further grouped according to their purposes: those that clean fabrics, those that enhance aesthetics, and those that improve performance.

PREPARATORY FINISHES THAT CLEAN FABRIC

It is necessary to remove dirt, impurities, and any sizing agents and lubricants applied to fibers or yarns before weaving and knitting. There are several methods used to do so. The characteristics of the fiber(s) determine the appropriate cleaning method.

BOILING OFF.   The **boiling-off** process is similar to laundering with detergents and soaps, although some shrinkage will occur. The wet fabric may go directly into a dye bath. **Boiling off** is used with cottons, cotton blends, and manufactured fibers.

BLEACHING.   The purpose of **bleaching**, which is usually done during boiling off, is to produce white fabric or to prepare fabric for dyeing or printing. Usually chlorine bleaches or peroxygen bleaches are used.

CARBONIZING.   Carbonizing removes any leaves or twigs that might remain in wool. Sulfuric acid is used to destroy the vegetable matter.

DEGUMMING. **Degumming** is similar to boiling off. It removes the sericin, or gum, from silk fabrics and makes the silk softer and whiter.

DESIZING. Sizing agents are used to strengthen warp yarns to withstand the stress of weaving. In **desizing**, the sizing agents are removed by washing in an enzyme solution so that the fabric may properly absorb later finishes and dyes.

SCOURING. **Scouring** removes impurities from wool and is similar to boiling off. (See Figure 14–2.)

SOLVENT SCOURING. **Solvent scouring** is a dry-cleaning procedure done on knits to remove oils added to aid the knitting process.

TENTERING. **Tentering** straightens the grain of the fabric by making the warp yarns and filling yarns perpendicular. To do this, the fabric is stretched widthwise on a tentering frame. The small holes frequently found along the selvages of fabric are the result of the hooks of the tentering frame. It is important that the fabric be on grain before printing.

FIGURE 14–2

Scouring. (Courtesy of WestPoint Stevens.)

FIGURE 14–3

Singeing. (Courtesy of WestPoint Stevens.)

PREPARATORY FINISHES THAT IMPROVE APPEARANCE OR HAND

Singeing, optical brighteners, fulling, and delustering are finishes that improve apperance or hand.

SINGEING. **Singeing** removes any fiber ends that may be protruding from the fabric surface. The fabric is passed quickly over a gas flame or heated copper plate and then immersed in a water bath. Singeing improves the clarity of prints and helps prevent pill formation. (See Figure 14–3.)

OPTICAL BRIGHTENERS. **Optical brighteners**, or fluorescent whiteners, are added to bleached fabrics to intensify their whiteness and brightness.

FULLING. Fulling, a controlled felting process which causes fabric to shrink, increases the density of wool fabrics.

DELUSTERING. In delustering, fibers and fabrics are treated to reduce their luster. Manufactured fibers frequently have high luster.

Titanium dioxide pigment can be added to the spinning solution before extrusion to reduce fiber luster. Fibers can also be etched or scratched to reduce luster. Fabric luster can be reduced by delustering agents that adhere to fabrics with resin binders and by mechanical finishes such as napping (discussed later in this chapter).

PREPARATORY FINISHES THAT IMPROVE PERFORMANCE

Cottons can be mercerized and silk can be weighted to improve performance.

MERCERIZATION.   Only cotton or cotton blends are mercerized. In this technique, the fabric or yarns are treated with sodium hydroxide while held under tension. Mercerization increases luster, improves strength, and increases absorbency.

WEIGHTING OF SILK.   Silk fabrics can be weighted with metallic salts. Weighting increases the body of the silk. Heavily weighted silks have poor abrasion resistance, however.

Aesthetic Finishes

The industry uses numerous finishes to improve the aesthetics of fabrics.

BEETLING

Beetling, a process in which fabric is beaten with hammers, creates a smooth, lustrous surface on linens and fabrics intended to look like linens. This finish is temporary unless the fabric has been treated with a resin before beetling.

BRUSHING

Brushing is often done following napping, sueding, or shearing. These procedures are discussed later in this chapter. The purpose of brushing is to brush the nap or pile of the fabric in one direction. **Shearing** may leave loose fibers on the fabric. They can be removed by brushing.

BURN-OUT DESIGNS

Burn-out designs are created when fabrics are printed with a chemical solution which destroys some of the fibers. For example, if a cotton fabric is printed with sulfuric acid, the acid destroys the fabric in the printed area. This technique can also be used on blended fabrics. In this case, one fiber is destroyed in the printed area. Burn-out designs are also discussed in Chapter 13.

CALENDERING

Calendering is a mechanical finishing process used to smooth the fabric and/or impart interesting surface designs. Almost all fabrics are calendered. In this procedure, fabric passes through two or more heated rollers. If the fabric is coated with a resin before calendering, the finish will be durable. Using other sizing agents, such as gums or starches, produces a temporary, or possibly semidurable, finish. Calendering thermoplastic fabrics produces a permanent finish. For example, surface designs can be heat set into fabrics made of thermoplastic fibers. Following are variations of the calendering process.

SIMPLE CALENDERING. **Simple calendering** is a temporary finishing process similar to ironing or pressing, in which dampened fabric is fed through heated rollers. As a result, wrinkles are smoothed and the fabric develops a slight sheen. Simple calendering does not usually produce a lasting effect.

GLAZING. Fabrics produced by **glazing** have a highly polished surface and are produced on a friction or chasing calender. One of the rollers, called the friction roller, is made of highly polished steel and rotates faster than the fabric moves. The friction creates the glazed surface. Examples of glazed fabrics are chino, chintz, and polished cotton.

CIRÉING. **Ciré** fabric is a highly polished fabric which is often described as looking wet. It is produced on a friction calender, but the friction roller rotates much faster than when producing glazed fabric. Note that ciré is a finish, not a fabric. Fabric with a ciré finish is appropriately termed ciré fabric or ciréd fabric.

EMBOSSING.   Calender rolers with engraved designs are used to create embossed fabrics. As the fabric is passed through the calender it is imprinted with a design. It is especially important to use thermoplastic fabrics with this process or pretreat the fabrics with resins for design permanence. **Embossing** can be used to create a plissé effect. See the discussion of plissé later in this chapter. Embossed fabric should not be ironed because the design will be removed.

MOIRÉ.   **Moiré** is a special kind of embossing in which the roller is engraved with a watermark or wood-grain pattern. This special effect can also be created by pressing two lengths of ribbed fabric, such as taffeta, together. Great pressure is needed to flatten the ribs and create the mioré effect, however. (See Figure 14–4.)

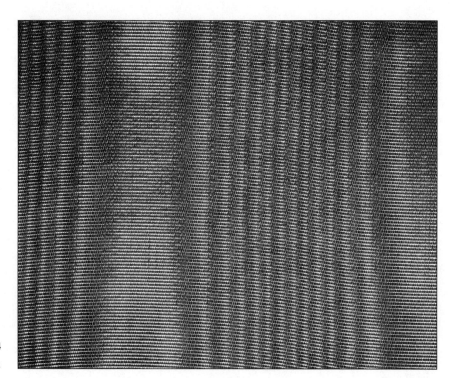

FIGURE 14–4
Moiré finish

SCHREINERING.   **Schreinering** produces a soft luster and soft hand. The fabric is embossed with from 180 to 360 diagonal lines per inch. Examples of fabrics that may have this finish are damask table linens, cotton and polyester/cotton sateens, and nylon tricot.

CHEMICAL OR ABRASIVE WASHING

The fashion trend for garments that appear worn or faded and/or have a very soft hand has led to the development of special washing processes that use chemicals and/or abradants to create these effects. Acid washed and stone washed denim, and sanded silk are examples of chemical- or abrasive-washed fabrics.

CHEMICAL WASHING.   In **chemical washing**, chemicals such as alkalis, oxidizing agents, and enzymes are used to partially destroy fabric. **Acid-washed fabrics** are chemically washed fabrics. Note that the name is a misnomer because acid is not used in the process.

ABRASIVE WASHING.   In **abrasive washing**, fabric or garments are tumbled with abrasive materials, such as pumice, which have been combined with chemicals. **Stone-washed denim** and **sanded silk** are produced this way.

FLOCKING

In flocking, adhesives are used to adhere short fibers to the surface of fabric. The effect is similar to that of pile fabric. The fibers may be flocked in a pattern, such as polka dots, or all over the fabric. Flocking is also discussed in Chapter 13.

NAPPING AND SUEDING

Napped and **sueded fabrics** have a pile or nap which has been brushed up from the surface of the fabric. Napped and sueded fabrics should not be confused with pile fabrics.

NAPPED FABRICS.   Napped fabrics have a longer pile than sueded fabrics. They are usually made from fabrics with loosely twisted yarns so the pile can be brushed easily. Both knits and wovens can be napped. In the napping process, also called **gigging** or **raising**, rollers with small, fine hooks pass over fabric, catch fibers, and pull them to the surface. **Flannel** is an example of napped fabric.

SUEDED FABRICS. Unlike napped fabrics, sueded fabrics have a very low pile. To create sueded fabric the surface of fabric is exposed to an abradant material resembling sandpaper. Both knits and wovens can be sueded.

PLISSÉ

The term **plissé** refers to both the finishing process and the resulting fabric. In plissé, fabrics are treated with chemicals which cause them to shrink. For example, cotton fabric is printed with a paste of sodium hydroxide, causing it to shrink where the chemical was applied. Untreated areas pucker. If the sodium hydroxide is applied in a striped pattern, the fabric will resemble a woven seersucker.

Plissé is considered durable but not permanent because ironing flattens the puckers. Fibers other than cotton can be treated with appropriate chemicals to create a plissé. Embossing can be used to create a less expensive, and less durable, plissé effect.

SHEARING

In shearing, which has been compared to the gardening task of mowing the lawn, the nap or pile of a fabric is cut to uniform length. A design or sculptured effect may be sheared into the pile or nap. Sometimes fabrics are sheared to remove unwanted surface fibers or yarn ends.

SOFTENING

Fabric softeners are applied to reduce harshness in softening. An undesirable hand may be caused by tightly twisted yarns, tightly woven fabrics, durable press, heat setting of some manufactured fibers, and finishing of some acrylics. Durable press is discussed later in this chapter. Silicone compounds, which are durable, are the most commonly used softeners. Temporary softeners are used in home and commercial laundries.

STIFFENING

Many fabrics need stiffening to improve body and hand. Starches, gelatins, resins and acids are used to stiffen fabric. Starches, gums, and gelatins are temporary finishes that must be reapplied. Resins are durable and provide longer-lasting stiffening than sizing agents. Acids provide permanent stiffness. **Acid stiffening**, or **parchmentizing**, is the process of exposing fabric to an acid and then immediately neutralizing the acid. Organdy is an example of an acid-stiffened fabric.

Functional Finishes

For ease of discussion, functional finishes are separated into three main divisions: shrinkage control, resistant, and others.

SHRINKAGE-CONTROL FINISHES

Before shrinkage control an be presented, it is necessary to review the various types of shrinkage.

Relaxation shrinkage occurs because fabrics are held under significant tension during manufacturing and processing. During laundering, moisture encourages the fibers to relax and contract. Relaxation shrinkage does not usually occur during dry cleaning unless the garment is wet processed. Most relaxation shrinkage occurs during the first laundering, but it may continue up to the fifth laundering.

Consolidation shrinkage occurs during tumble drying of washables and during dry cleaning in coin-operated machines. The mechanical action of tumbling causes the fiber to return to a more natural shape, shorter and wider, and the fabric does the same.

Progressive shrinkage occurs every time the fabric is laundered. Rayon and wool are particularly susceptible to progressive shrinkage.

Residual shrinkage is the small amount of shrinkage that may occur after fabrics have been preshrunk properly.

Shrinkage-control methods have been developed to address the various forms of shrinkage. Heat setting and mechanical and chemical treatments are used to control shrinkage. Mercerization, discussed under preparatory finishes, is a chemical shrinkage-control method. Other methods are summarized briefly in the following.

COMPRESSIVE SHRINKAGE. **Compressive shrinkage** is a mechanical method of relaxation in which dampened fabric is overfed onto a roller to encourage the fibers to relax and shrink. Residual shrinkage is usually 1 percent or less. Comprehensive shrinkage is used on tubular knit and woven cottons, woven linens, and HWM rayon. Sanforized® is one registered comprehensive shrinkage process.

CHEMICAL SHRINKAGE. Resin treatments are used to chemically control shrinkage of wools, rayons, and cottons in **chemical shrinkage**. Wools are also treated with chlorine. The method is determined by the fiber content of the fabric.

Chlorination. In **chlorination**, wool fabric is treated with chlorine, which partially dissolves the scales of the fiber and limits its capacity to felt. This method is seldom used because it causes the fabric to lose strength and imparts a rough hand.

Resin Treatment for Cottons and Rayons. Compressive shrinkage followed by a resin treatment is effective for cottons and rayons. This method has the advantage of providing crease resistance.

Resin Treatment for Wool. To shrink fabric chemically, the fabric is coated with a resin, which flattens the scales of the fiber and/or binds them in place. Several different procedures have been developed. The most successful combine chlorination and resin treatments.

HEAT SETTING. The most effective way to control shrinkage in thermoplastic fibers is heat setting. Dimensions are set by exposing the fabric to temperatures that are near, but not above, the melting point of fiber. Both woven and knitted thermoplastics can be heat set.

SPONGING. **Sponging**, also referred to as **London shrinking, damp relaxing,** or **steam relaxing**, is used to control relaxation shrinkage in wool fabrics. The fabric is dampened thoroughly with water or steam and allowed to dry slowly in a relaxed state. Sponging wools does not make them washable or control progressive shrinkage because the fiber will still felt.

RESISTANT FINISHES

Resistant finishes are designed to overcome a negative trait of the fiber or fabric. Most resistant finishes are chemical treatments, but some, like durable press finishes, are both chemical and mechanical. Most of these finishes are durable but may be affected by environmental conditions or care procedures.

ABRASION-RESISTANT FINISHES.   The **abrasion resistance** of a fabric can be improved by applying a resin. Because the resin causes the fabric to soil more easily, **abrasion-resistant finishes** are seldom used.

ANTIMICROBIAL FINISHES.   **Antimicrobial finishes**, sometimes called **antibacterial** or **antiseptic finishes**, inhibit the growth of bacteria and other germs. These finishes are chemical agents that prevent odors and damage from perspiration. They are also especially useful in medical applications where they help reduce infection and help control the spread of disease. Antimicrobial finishes are used on underwear, diapers, and health-care textiles and in the restaurant/hotel industry.

ANTIROT AND ANTIMILDEW FINISHES.   Cellulosics are particularly susceptible to rotting and mildew. Chemicals such as phenol, formaldehyde, and pentachlorophenol inhibit the growth of microorganisms. These chemicals can be applied to fabrics to provide resistance to mildew and rotting.

ANTISTATIC FINISHES.   The buildup of electrical charges is especially objectionable in synthetic fibers. It can be controlled by applying **antistatic finishes**. Commercial fabric softners and antistatic sprays are available to the consumer, but these finishes are not durable and must be reapplied after cleaning. An effective means of controlling static electricity is modifying the fiber before extrusion to increase absorbency. An even more effective means is using metal or metalized fibers or biconstituent fibers containing carbon. These specialized fibers effectively dissipate electrical charges.

DURABLE-PRESS FINISHES. **Durable-press finishes** have significantly reduced the time and effort required to care for apparel and home furnishings. These finishes, commonly known as durable press or **permanent press**, have drawbacks but in general are very popular with consumers. The terms *durable press* and *permanent press* are used interchangeably, but the former may be more accurate because some finishes are only effective for 40 to 50 launderings.

Durable press finishes serve two purposes:

1. Protect garments and other finished textile products, such as bed linens, tablecloths, and curtains, from wrinkles that occur during laundering and use.
2. Maintain creases and pleats that have been deliberately pressed into the fabric.

There are three methods to achieve durable press:

1. Heat setting thermoplastic fibers
2. Resin finishes
3. Liquid ammonia finishes

Heat setting was presented previously, and liquid ammonia treatments are seldom used due to excessive cost. As a result, this discussion emphasizes resin finishes. Resin finishes are predominantly used on cellulosics and cellulosic blends.

Fabrics treated with resin finishes may be precured or postcured (see Figure 14–5). **Precuring** is the more common. The first step in both processes is to saturate the fabric with resin. Precured fabrics are cured before being cut and sewn. Postcured fabrics are cured after being cut and sewn so the entire garment is cured in the desired shape. **Postcuring** is generally considered superior because wrinkle resistance and crease retention are more permanent. Table 14–3 summarizes the common problems of durable-press finishes.

Special **wrinkle-resistant (WR) treatments** have been developed for use in 100-percent cotton fabrics. The fabrics must be tightly woven, and made of premium cotton fibers that have been twisted tightly into yarns for maximum strength. Because less resin is applied, there is less damage to the cotton and the fabric retains a softer hand. However, WR treatments are far less durable than traditional durable-press treatments.

Crease-resistant finish (CRF) is another term for a wrinkle-resistant finish, but it usually refers to finishes that reduce wrinkles during wear. Ironing is needed after laundering. CRFs are used on cotton, rayon, and flax. Because much less resin is applied, the fabrics maintain more of their abrasion resistance and a softer hand.

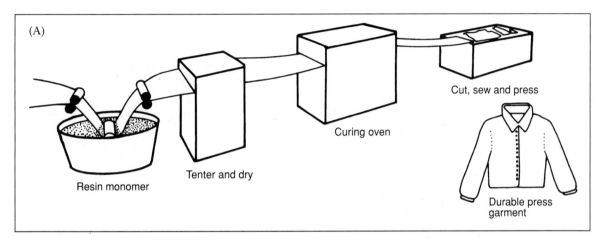

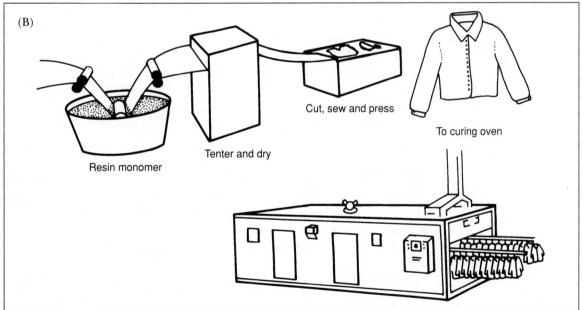

FIGURE 14–5

(A) Precuring process; (B) Postcuring process

TABLE 14–3   COMMON PROBLEMS ASSOCIATED WITH DURABLE PRESS

1. Increased cost to the consumer.
2. Puckered seams (alleviated by adjusting stitch length and tension and using special thread).
3. Stiff fabric.
4. Loss of strength and reduced abrasion resistance in cotton (blends of cotton and polyester compensate for strength loss in the cotton fiber).
5. Reduced abrasion resistance may result in frosting. The weaker cotton fibers wear away, leaving the polyester. Because the absorbency of each fiber is different, a color change is noticeable.
6. Alterations to lengthen or enlarge a garment may be difficult or impossible. Hem creases cannot be removed.
7. Laundering procedures must be followed carefully to obtain satisfactory results. Warm-water washing, cool rinsing, tumble drying, and prompt removal from the dryer are recommended.
8. Soil and stain removal may be difficult. Both polyester and resins have an affinity for oily stains and reduced absorbency. Soil-release finishes (see discussion later in this chapter) have been developed to address this problem.
9. A "fishy odor" may be noticeable in new fabrics, although it usually disappears quickly.
10. The resin reduces absorbency and may make the garment uncomfortable in warm, humid weather.
11. The controversy over acceptable levels of exposure to formaldehyde, a component in durable-press resins, is unresolved. Research and development of alternative processes continues.

FLAME-RESISTANT FINISHES.   The Flammable Fabrics Act of 1953 and its various amendments prohibit the sale and use of highly flammable fabrics. Of particular concern are fabrics used for children's sleepwear, mattresses, carpeting, and upholstered furniture.

Flame-resistant fabrics can be achieved three ways:

1. Using flame-resistant fibers such as glass, aramid, and modacrylic.
2. Using manufactured fibers that have had flame-resistant chemicals added before extrusion. Acetates, polyesters, nylons, and rayons are produced in flame-resistant variants.
3. Treating fabrics with fire-resistant finishes.

The flame-resistance issue is very complex, in part because many different finishes are available. Flame-resistant finishes are wet finishes. The choice of finish is determined by fiber content, yarn and fabric construction, and projected end use. Care procedures affect the performance and durability of the finish. Brand names of flame-resistant finishes include: Pyroset® and Pyrovatex®. Table 14–4 lists problems commonly associated with fire-resistant finishes.

MOTHPROOF FINISHES. Most wool and animal hair fibers are mothproofed permanently with a chemical that is applied during dyeing. **Mothproof finishes**, which are relatively low cost, protect the fabric from both moths and carpet beetles.

SLIP-RESISTANT FINISHES. Filament yarns have a tendency to slip and move over one another. This phenomenon, called yarn slippage, is especially noticeable near seams (seam slippage). Yarns can also shift in loosely woven fabrics. **Slip resistant finishes** hold filament yarns in place.

SOIL-RELEASE FINISHES. Problems with cleaning and removing stains from durable-press fabrics have prompted the development of

---

TABLE 14–4   COMMON PROBLEMS WITH FIRE-RESISTANT FINISHES*

1. Loss of fabric strength.

2. Harsh, unpleasant hand.

3. The effectiveness of finish may depend on specific care procedures. Chlorine bleach, nonphosphate detergents, and soaps may make the finish ineffective. Phosphate detergents are recommended for use on fabrics with some fire-resistant finishes, but these detergents contribute to water pollution and are banned in many areas. Unfortunately, the most effective finish for children's sleepwear must be washed with high phosphate detergents to remain effective.

4. Dry cleaning may destroy the finish.

5. Finishes vary in their effectiveness on single fiber fabric and on blends. For example, the finish appropriate for polyester may be rendered useless when the polyester is blended with cotton.

*Note that not all fire-resistant finishes exhibit all of these problems.

soil-release finishes such as Visa®. These finishes make the fabric easier to clean by improving absorbency. However, they should not be confused with **soil-resistant finishes**, which prevent the fabric from becoming soiled.

Most durable-press fabrics are polyester/cotton blends. Combining polyester, which is hydrophobic, and resin finishes, which reduce absorbency, creates fabrics that do not "wet out" in laundering. Soil, especially oily soil, cannot be removed if the fabric does not become completely wet.

Soil-release finishes are usually applied during resin treatment. These finishes are durable and gradually wash out in laundering. Additional benefits of soil-release finishes are increased wearing comfort in warm, humid weather; reduced static electricity; and a softer hand.

SOIL AND WATER-RESISTANT FINISHES. Soil- and **water-resistant finishes** are discussed together because the chemicals used are similar. These finishes prevent water and stains from being absorbed into fabric. The liquid remains on the surface.

It is important to note that these finishes vary in effectiveness and durability. Some soil-release finishes protect against oily substances such as gravy, and some protect against waterborne stains such as juice and coffee. These finishes may be durable or temporary and may be applied commercially or in the home. A well-known durable finish that repels both water and oil is Scotchgard®. Temporary finishes can be reapplied.

It is important to note that water-resistant fabrics are not waterproof. Water penetrates these fabrics. These fabrics, however, are more comfortable to wear than the slicker-type raincoat because they allow vapor to escape.

WATERPROOF FABRICS. Completely waterproofed fabrics can be made by laminating or coating the fabric with vinyl or polyurethane. These fabrics tend to be stiff and uncomfortable to wear because water vapor cannot escape.

GORE-TEX®, a popular new development for outdoor clothing, is a waterproof, breathable, laminated fabric. A fine membrane of PTFE fluorocarbon is laminated to the back of the fabric to provide complete waterproof protection while allowing water vapor to escape.

OTHER FINISHES

Various other finishes prepare fabrics for some highly specialized functions.

ABSORBENT FINISHES.   The absorbency of cellulosics can be increased by treating them with aluminum compounds. Fabrics with these **absorbent finishes** are especially useful in underwear, toweling, and diapers. Other finishes, such as soil release and antistatic, also improve the absorbency of synthetic fibers.

ANTIPESTICIDE FINISHES.   Protective clothing can be treated with special finishes which prevent the penetration of pesticides. These **antipesticide finishes** also assist in completely removing the pesticides during laundering.

CORONIZING.   **Coronizing** is a special treatment for glass fibers which improves drape and wrinkle resistance. The fibers are heat set, dyed, and finished in one operation.

LIGHT-REFLECTANT FINISHES.   Microscopic reflecting beads can be applied to fabrics to create a **light-reflectant finish**. This finish is an important safety feature for Halloween costumes, joggers, and bikers.

HEAT-REFLECTANT FINISHES.   **Heat-reflectant finishes** are usually fine coatings of metal and resins. They can be engineered to reflect heat from the body to keep it cool, or they can reflect heat toward the body to provide warmth. Draperies can be engineered to function this way.

LIGHT-STABILIZING FINISHES.   The ultraviolet rays of the sun destroy many fibers. Treating these fibers with ultraviolet absorbers or light stabilizers to create **light-stabilizing finishes** is important for furnishings, apparel, and industrial textiles that are used predominantly outdoors. Outdoor furnishings and car interiors are particularly susceptible to damage from ultraviolet rays.

LABORATORY ASSIGNMENTS

ASSIGNMENT 14–1   **REVIEW FINISHES**

1. Describe the general function of a finish.
2. List one example of each of the following types of finish:
   a. Permanent
   b. Temporary
   c. Mechanical
   d. Chemical
   e. Functional
   f. Aesthetic
   g. Preparatory

ASSIGNMENT 14–2   **COMPARE PERMANENT AND TEMPORARY FINISHES**

1. Gather the following materials:
   two samples of sheer fabric sized with household starch, 2″ × 2″
   two samples of permanent-finished organdy, 2″ × 2″
   pint jar with lid
   detergent
2. Set aside one organdy and one starched sample to use as controls.
3. Fill the pint jar with warm water and ½ teaspoon detergent.
4. Place the test samples in the jar and secure the lid.
5. Shake the jar for 1 minute.
6. Allow the jar to stand for 5 minutes, then shake for 1 minute.
7. Remove the samples from the jar, rinse them thoroughly, and allow them to dry.
8. Compare the treated specimens to the control samples.
9. Mount and label all samples.
10. Answer the following:
    a. Which of the samples had a permanent finish? Which had a temporary finish?
    b. Could the temporary finish be replaced? If so, how?

ASSIGNMENT 14–3   COMPARE FINISH AND FABRIC FORMATION

1. Gather the following materials:
    one sample of woven seersucker, 3″ × 2″
    one sample of plissé, 3″ × 2″
    linen tester
    iron, preheated to the "steam" setting
2. Examine the samples with and without the linen tester.
3. Pull on each sample and observe what happens to the design.
4. Iron each sample.
5. Mount and label each sample.
6. Answer the following:
    a. What differences do you notice?
    b. How did pulling affect the samples?
    c. How did ironing affect the samples?
    d. Which sample has the puckered effect created by weaving?
    e. Which sample has the puckered effect created by a finishing procedure? Was the finish mechanical or chemical?

ASSIGNMENT 14–4   EXPERIMENT WITH WATER-REPELLENT FINISHES

1. Gather the following materials:
    two samples of prewashed muslin, 16″ × 16″
    soil-resistant spray, like Scotchgard®
    two 8″ embroidery hoops
    50 ml of water
    250-ml beaker
2. Following the directions on the can, spray one muslin sample with the soil-resistant spray and allow it to dry.
3. Place each sample in an embroidery hoop.
4. Holding the embroidery hoop at a 45° angle over a sink, pour 50 ml of water over the fabric.
5. Observe and record the results.
6. Draw conclusions.

ASSIGNMENT 14–5   EXPERIMENT WITH SOIL-REPELLENT FINISHES

1. Gather the following materials:
   two samples of prewashed muslin, 16" × 16"
   soil-resistant spray, like Scotchgard®
   assorted staining materials (e.g., ketchup, grape juice, motor oil,
       lipstick, salad oil, mustard)
   waxed paper
   ballpoint ink pen
2. Following the directions on the can, spray one muslin sample with
   the soil-resistant spray and allow it to dry.
3. Spread wax paper out to protect surfaces and lay the fabric samples
   on the waxed paper.
4. Apply small amounts of the staining substances to both samples.
5. Observe and record the effect of each stain.
6. Blot the stains with paper towel and observe the results.
7. Label each stain with a ballpoint ink pen.
8. Hand or machine wash and dry the samples.
9. Observe and record the results in the following tables.
10. Draw conclusions.

| | UNTREATED MUSLIN | | |
STAINING SUBSTANCE	IMMEDIATE OBSERVATION	AFTER BLOTTING	OBSERVATION AFTER WASHING

	TREATED MUSLIN		
STAINING SUBSTANCE	IMMEDIATE OBSERVATION	AFTER BLOTTING	OBSERVATION AFTER WASHING

ASSIGNMENT 14–6 **EXPERIMENT WITH FIRE-RETARDANT FINISHES**

1. Review laboratory safety procedures before conducting this assignment.
2. Gather the following materials:
   sample of regular flannel, 2″ × 4″
   sample of flannel labeled suitable for children's sleepwear, 2″ × 4″
   matches
   candles
   aluminum pie plate
3. Light a candle and allow a few drops of wax to collect in the bottom of the pie plate.
4. Stick the candle in the melted wax.
5. Slowly move the regular flannel sample into the flame.
6. Observe and record the results.
7. Slowly move the flannel that is suitable for children's sleepwear into the flame.
8. Observe and record the results. What are your conclusions?

ASSIGNMENT 14–7 **IDENTIFY FINISH SAMPLES**

Mount and label each finish sample from your swatch kit or instructor-supplied swatches.

Career Opportunities in Textiles

OBJECTIVES

The student will be able to:

1. Identify five general areas in textile-related careers
2. Discuss the variety of career opportunities in the textile industry
3. Describe why knowing textiles is important in each of the five general areas
4. Identify sources of information for conducting a career search in the textiles field
5. Discuss the role of product development

Introduction

The textile industry offers extensive career opportunities. Those who know and appreciate textiles find they can apply their knowledge to a wide variety of jobs. Some jobs, such as production, are concentrated in the southeastern Unites States. Marketing and corporate offices are in major cities like New York, Chicago, San Francisco, and Atlanta. Still more opportunities exist in small and large towns and cities across the nation.

International travel, as well as travel within the United States, is another opportunity. Offshore production and international sourcing are increasing the need for people who know textiles and are willing to travel.

The wide variety of end uses for textile products in apparel, furnishings, and industry provides additional opportunities for careers. Figure 15–1 describes some interesting career opportunities that require a knowledge of textiles.

Careers in textiles can be divided into five general areas:

science and technology
art and design
manufacturing and production
sales and marketing
product development

Each area relates to, and depends on, the other. It is important to understand that these areas function together and cannot operate effectively alone. Understanding the interrelatedness of these areas and their functions is critical to being successful in the textile industry.

Science and Technology

Careers in textile science and technology require strong preparation in college science courses such as general and organic chemistry. Courses in physics and statistics are also recommended. Someone who lacks a strong science background but has an interest in textiles might enjoy working as a technician in a laboratory. (See Figure 15–2.)

Many companies have research and development (R & D) departments where new products and technology are developed. For example, researchers working for chemical companies might study polymer chemistry or the environmental effects of new dyeing and finishing procedures. Other R & D departments might research more efficient fabrication methods and modification of manufacturing machinery. People in R & D departments often work closely with product developers.

The importance of water and air pollution control in the textile industry has created new opportunities for scientists.

Career Connections

Examples of careers obtained by students who have completed bachelor's programs in textiles and apparel-related fields

Title: Costume Designer
Company: Ringling Brothers, NY

Two years after graduation
Major: Apparel & Merchandising
Concentration: Apparel Design & Production

A costume designer for Ringling Brothers Circus. Has the opportunity to work with lots of jumbo spandex, rhinestones, and sequins.

Title: President
Company: Wolfman Outdoor Products, CO

Four years after graduation
Major: Apparel & Merchandising
Concentration: Apparel Design & Production

Apparel designer and owner of outdoor products company. Designs and manufactures motorcycle products as well as high quality kits for outdoor activities.

Title: Gift Shop Assistant
Company: Royal Carribean Cruiseline

Two years after graduation
Major: Apparel & Merchandising
Concentration: Merchandising

A gift shop assistant for the Royal Carribean fleet. Gets plenty of merchandising experience and world-wide travel.

Title: Costume Designer
Company: Warner Brothers, CA

Nine years after graduation
Major: Apparel & Merchandising
Concentration: Merchandising

A designer in the women's wardrobe department at Warner Brothers Studios. Recently completed first feature film credit as wardrobe supervisor.

Title: Style Manager
Company: Acme Boot Company, TN

Six years after graduation
Major: Apparel & Merchandising
Concentration: Apparel Design & Production

Designer of women's footwear for three brands. Job also includes sourcing from Mexico, Brazil, India, China, Dominican Republic, and Puerto Rico.

Title: Advertising Manager
Company: Hewlett Packard, CO

Twenty-one years after graduation
Major: Apparel & Merchandising
Concentration: Merchandising

Job involves marketing, communications, advertising, and trade shows. Also does market development and computer sales.

FIGURE 15–1

Career connections: examples of careers obtained by students who have completed bachelor's programs in textile and apparel-related fields. (Courtesy of International Textile and Apparel Association, Inc., developed by Jan Else for ITAA, Inc.)

Title: **Head** Designer
Company: **Stephanie Queller, NY**

Twelve years after graduation
Major: **Double Major in Design and Merchandising**

Head designer for a women's sportswear company. An expert in product development and design. Recently returned to alma mater as a guest lecturer.

Title: **Director of Quality Business Op.**
Company: **Target, MN**

Twenty-two years after graduation
Major: **Merchandising**

As director of quality business operations, the job involves quick response partnerships, total quality management, and electronic data interchange.

Title: **Buyer**
Company: **The Disney Store, Inc., CA**

Fourteen years after graduation
Major: **Apparel & Merchandising**
Concentration: **Merchandising**

An adult accessory buyer for The Disney Store, Inc. Area of work includes men's apparel, sportswear, and is also involved in developing a new line of women's accessories.

Title: **Vice President**
Company: **Dimitrios: A Design Archive, NY**

Nine years after graduation
Major: **Apparel & Merchandising**
Concentration: **Apparel Design & Production**

Vice President and Partner of textile design resource company, which is a vast collection of antique textiles, wallpapers, and original paintings from the apparel, home furnishings, and other related industries.

Title: **President/CEO**
Company: **Integrated Marketing Consultants, IL**

Twenty years after graduation
Major: **Apparel & Merchandising**
Concentration: **Merchandising**

Involved in marketing for the McDonald's Corporation. Also does consulting related to marketing and sales promotion.

Title: **Quality Assurance Manager**
Company: **Sportif USA, NV**

Ten years after graduation
Major: **Textiles and Clothing**
Concentration: **Textiles**

Quality control manager for sportswear company. Job involves travel to Hong Kong, Sri Lanka, and Mexico factories.

DEVELOPED BY:

International Textile and Apparel Association, Inc.
PO Box 1360
Monument CO 80132-1360, USA

FIGURE 15–1

Continued

FIGURE 15–2

Laboratory technician.
(Courtesy of Avondale Mills.)

Art and Design

Students who want to pursue careers in textile art and design should take additional fine art, art history, and art appreciation courses. A course in CAD would also be valuable. (See Figure 15–3.) History of costume coursework benefits apparel designers. Because textiles are the very "fabric" of apparel and furnishings, thoroughly understanding the properties of fibers and the interrelationship of yarn, fabric, coloration, and finish is essential to creating clothing and furnishings that are both beautiful and functional.

Textile and textile print designers are responsible for creating the fabrics apparel or furnishings designers use for their designs.

FIGURE 15–3

Computer-aided fabric design.
(Courtesy of Pendleton
Woolen Mills.)

Textile designers develop knitting and weaving patterns or select the yarns or fibers used in fabric production. (See Figure 15–4.) Textile print designers create the patterns and designs applied to fabrics. Both textile designers and textile print designers must be knowledgeable about using a flat, two-dimensional textile product (the fabric) as a covering for a three-dimensional shape (the human body). Even designers of home furnishings must be aware of the three-dimensional aspects of furnishings, especially upholstered pieces and bedding.

Design-related careers also exist in merchandising and retailing. Visual displays and customer service require an awareness of both the principles of design and the qualities of textiles.

The creativity of the designer builds on knowledge of new and improved products produced by science and technology. The niche or target market must be clearly understood so that products meet its needs and expectations. Price points and expected profit levels are the parameters within which the designer must work. The designer must also know the manufacturing requirements of the product. For example, the slippery nature of some fabrics, such as taffeta, require

FIGURE 15–4

Designer weaving a decorator fabric sample at Langdale Mill. (Courtesy of Textile World, *March 1995, Vol. 45, No. 3.)*

more sewing and handling time. Therefore, garments made from these fabrics are more expensive to construct.

RELATED OPPORTUNITIES IN ART AND DESIGN

Additional design opportunities exist in the field of entertainment. Costume and set designers work in the theater and on production sites. Self-employed artists and freelance designers frequently specialize in one field, such as tapestry weaving or silk painting. Due to their skills and reputations, these designers often teach their crafts.

Manufacturing and Production

Employment opportunities exist at all levels of production, from raw material to finished product. At each stage of processing (fiber, yarn, fabric, finish, and coloration) skilled technicians who know textiles are needed. Producing the final product, such as a pair of jeans, requires other skilled labor. Plant supervisors and managers must understand and solve problems encountered during production. (See Figure 15–5.) For example, garment construction techniques must be adapted to the properties of the fabric. Due to the complexity of equipment in the textile industry, appropriate maintenance and supervision during production provide additional job opportunities for skilled workers.

Industry emphasis on quality assurance has created many new careers in quality control. Engineers develop standards of performance, or specifications, that meet the cost and quality requirements of the company. Technicians monitor production to ensure all products meet expected levels of performance. Mills typically evaluate quality consistency. For example, a fabric producer may want to assure its customers that all its fabrics are within advertised ranges for weight and dimensional stability.

Quality control is also important when determining the suitability of a product for its expected end use. For example, a manufacturer or retailer must ensure that its purchases meet company standards. The manufacturer or retailer evaluates the products for end-use suitability as opposed to standards during production.

Sales and Marketing

Communication skills, the initiative to promote a product, and the ability to serve customers are essential to careers in textile marketing and sales. (See Figure 15–6.) Marketing and sales representatives provide a vital link by ensuring buyers and sellers along the product pipeline work together. They communicate the needs and desires of their customers to the companies they represent to ensure the goods

FIGURE 15–5

Plant manager checking decorator fabric at Langdale Mill. (Courtesy of Textile World, *March 1995, Vol. 45, No. 3.)*

and services are meeting expectations. This information is invaluable to product developers.

Sales representatives usually work closely with their clients and specialize in one area, such as men's wear or industrial textiles. Retail sales also provides many career opportunities. The competitive nature of retailing necessitates that sales personnel know the products they sell. Department manager, store manager, buyer, and fashion coordinator are related career options in retail.

Marketing is promoting a company's products to wide audiences. The textile marketer uses advertising and promotion to increase awareness and desirability of the company and its products. In textile marketing creativity, an awareness of trends, and solid textile knowledge are essential.

FIGURE 15–6

Sales presentation at Avondale Mills. (Courtesy of Avondale Mills.)

Product Development

Many textile companies, large and small, have created special product-development offices to do the research, merchandising, and styling they require to create or update their products. Product development is an outgrowth of the need to create textile products that meet the needs and desires of the marketplace. Sales and marketing specialists share their knowledge and expertise with product developers who create the products. These specialists must understand market research, quality control, production, and costing.

Product development is done at each step along the product pipeline, and often in close communication with research and development offices. The competitive, profit-driven nature of the textile industry requires innovation, flexibility, and speed.

The Keys to Success in the Textile Industry

The keys to success in the textile industry, whatever the phase, are creativity and innovation. Textiles is a demanding industry which is perpetually changing. It is on the cutting edge of new technology in R & D, challenged constantly to create new fashions to whet the appetite of the customer, and increasingly competitive. It is profit driven to reduce costs while still providing quality service and products.

Anyone entering the textiles field must understand the importance of staying current and up-to-date in the field. New technological developments, increasing global trade, and the ebb and flow of fashion and its demands on the textile industry are some of the phenomena that transform the industry daily.

LABORATORY ASSIGNMENTS

ASSIGNMENT 15–1   PREPARE A RESUME

Write or update your resume.

ASSIGNMENT 15–2   RESEARCH A CURRENT JOB

1. Read the current classified section of *Women's Wear Daily* or *Home Textiles Today*.
2. Select a job that interests you.
3. Research the job requirements and write a cover letter expressing your interest in the position.

ASSIGNMENT 15–3   CONDUCT CAREER RESEARCH

Research a company involved in one of the five areas of textiles using the following sources:

Dun's Million Dollar Directory
Standard and Poor's Register
Ward's Business Dictionary
America's Corporate Families

ASSIGNMENT 15–4   **USE YOUR COLLEGE'S RESOURCES**

Visit the campus career-development office to discuss possible internships or full-time jobs in the textile industry.

Appendix

Using the Linen Tester

The linen tester, also called a pick glass or pick counter, is a valuable tool for examining fibers, yarns, and fabrics under low magnification. The opening of the linen tester is usually ¼″ to 1″ in size. The sides of the opening are often calibrated for easy counting.

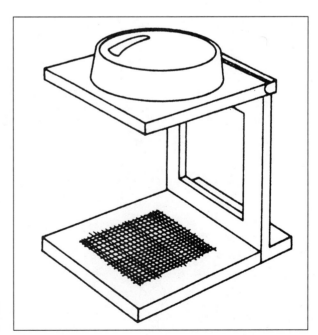

FIGURE A

The linen tester.

To use the tester to examine fibers or yarns, place the sample to be examined on a white piece of paper in a well lighted area. Place the tester over the sample and view the sample through the glass.

Thread count can be determined with the linen tester. In a well lighted area, place the sample on a flat surface. Place the opening of the linen tester over the sample and align the sides with the warp and filling yarns. View the sample through the glass and count the number of warp and filling yarns in one inch. Or count the number of warp and filling yarns in ¼″ and multiply that number by 4.

Knitted fabrics are examined similarly. Align the edges of the linen tester opening with the wales on the face of the fabric. Count the number of stitch rows in 1″ across the fabric to determine the wales per inch. Courses per inch, counted on the back of the fabric, are the number of stitch rows in 1″ running vertically down the fabric.

A pick needle, which resembles a pencil with a long needle extending from one end, is often used with a linen tester to help count threads or to separate yarns or fibers.

Glossary

Abrasion resistance The ability to withstand the effects of rubbing or friction.

Abrasion-resistant finish Resin finish which improves the ability of the fabric to resist abrasion. Because the resin causes the fabric to soil more easily, this finish is seldom used.

Abrasive washing Process in which fabrics or garments are tumbled with abrasive materials, such as pumice, that have been combined with chemicals to produce stone-washed and sanded fabrics.

Absorbency The ability of a fiber to take in moisture.

Absorbent finishes Finishes that increase absorbency.

Acid stiffening *See* **parchmentizing**.

Acid-washed denim Denim that has been washed with an oxidizing chemical to produce a worn look.

Acid-washed fabrics Chemically washed fabrics. Note that the name is a misnomer because acid is not used in the process. *See* **chemical washing**.

Aesthetic finishes Finishes that improve the appearance and/or hand of the product.

Ageing The process of setting colors with steam.

Airbrushing Process in which dyes and pigments are applied to fabric with an airbrush.

Air-jet loom A shuttleless loom that uses a jet of air to propel the filling yarn across the shed.

Air laying Forming a web of fibers using air to disperse the fibers on a screen.

Alençon A needlepoint lace with a hexagonal mesh background and a solid design outlined with cord.

American Egyptian Type of high-grade cotton. *See* **long-staple fiber.**

Antibacterial finishes *See* **antimicrobial finishes**.

Antimicrobial finishes Special finishes that inhibit the growth of bacteria and other germs. Chemical agents that prevent odors and damage from perspiration; also called antibacterial or antiseptic finishes.

Antimildew finishes *See* **antirot finishes.**

Antipesticide finishes Finishes that prevent the penetration of pesticides and assist in completely removing pesticides during laundering.

Antique satin Fabric with floats on its face and surface slubs on its back; the back is frequently used as the decorative side.

Antirot finishes Finishes that resist mildew and rotting, made of chemicals (such as phenol, formaldehyde, and pentachlorophenol) that inhibit the growth of microorganisms.

Antiseptic finishes *See* **antimicrobial finishes**.

Antistatic finishes Finishes that control the buildup of electrical charges. Not durable and must be reapplied after cleaning.

Artificial silk The name given the first rayon fiber; marked the beginning of the manufactured-fiber industry.

Automatic screen printing An automated version of the hand screen printing technique; also called flat bed printing or flat screen printing.

Balanced fabric Fabric with the same number of yarns in the warp and filling.

Bark cloth *See* **tapa cloth**.

Basket-weave fabrics Plain-weave variation that is loosely woven with two or more filling yarns interlaced with two or more warp yarns.

Batik Resist design method which originated in Indonesia; handcraft technique that involves a series of waxings and dyebaths.

Batiste Semi-opaque, soft, plain-weave fabric made from cotton, linen, or cotton blends.

Batt *See* **batting**.

Batting Sheet or roll of fibers matted together.

Beam dyeing Process of adding color to yarn or fabric that has been wound on large perforated beams and immersed in a dyebath.

Beck dyeing Process in which the fabric to be dyed is stitched end-to-end and circulated through the dyebath; also called box or winch dyeing.

Beetling Process in which linens and other fabrics intended to look like linens are beaten with hammers to create a smooth, lustrous surface; temporary unless the fabric has been treated with a resin before beetling.

Bicomponent fibers Fibers that are combinations of two separate polymers; the polymers may be variants of the same generic fiber or two different generic fibers.

Bicomponent-bigeneric Heterogeneous fibers of generically different fibers.

Biconstituent fibers *See* **matrix fibers**.

Bilateral fiber Bicomponent fiber in which two fibers are extruded side-by-side.

Birds-eye Dobby-weave fabric in which long floats create a small diamond pattern with a dot in its center; also called diaper cloth.

Bleaching Process that uses chlorine bleaches or peroxygen bleaches to produce white fabric or prepare fabric for dyeing or printing; usually done during boiling off.

Bleed Loss of color in water; may produce color loss and staining.

Blend Fabric or yarn made from two or more generically different fibers.

Block printing A handcraft technique in which a design is drawn on a block, the surface of the block around the design is carved away, the raised area is coated with dye paste, and the block is pressed into fabric. Sometimes several blocks are carved to create more intricate designs.

Blotch printing A variation of direct printing in which both the background color and design are printed on the fabric; eliminates predyeing white fabric to achieve a colored background.

Bobbin lace Fabric created with twisted and plaited threads worked over a pillow; also called pillow lace.

Boiling off Preparatory finishing process that resembles laundering with detergents and soaps.

Bombyx mori Cultivated silkworms.

Bonded fabrics Two-layer fabric structure in which the layers are joined with an adhesive. Adhesive does not add thickness to the fabric, but may add body. Usually the fabric is bonded to a tricot.

Bonding Use of adhesives, chemicals, or heat treatments to produce fabric directly from fibers; also a method of joining fabrics.

Bouclé yarns Ply yarns in which an effect yarn forms loops around the core yarn; the effect yarn is held in place by a binder; also called loop or curl yarn.

Bowed fabric Off-grain fabric in which the filling yarns curve.

Braids Narrow fabrics made of three or more yarns that are plaited; yarns are laced diagonally.

Break spinning *See* **open-end spinning.**

Brocade A richly patterned Jacquard-weave fabric in which designs are created by floats of varying lengths on a plain, twill, or satin-weave background; floats are often of colored yarns.

Brocatelle A Jacquard-weave fabric that is very similar to brocade except that its design is raised; stuffer yarns are often used to create the three-dimensional effect.

Brushed tricot Tricot fabric with long laps that are brushed to create a napped surface.

Brushing A finishing process that removes loose fibers on the fabric. Often done following napping, sueding, or shearing. Also used to brush the nap or pile of fabric in one direction.

Bulk yarns Yarns that have greater covering power or apparent volume than similar conventional yarns with normal twist.

Bulk-continuous-filament (BCF) yarns Textured multifilament yarns.

Bulky yarns Yarns created from fibers which, due to their inherent characteristics, cannot be closely packed together.

Burn-out printing Process of treating fabrics with chemicals that destroy fibers and create a pattern of holes in the fabric.

Byssinosis A serious lung disease caused by constant inhalation of cotton fibers, commonly known as "brown lung."

Cable yarns *See* **cord yarns**.

Calendering A mechanical finishing process used to smooth fabric and/or impart interesting surface designs.

Calico Percale fabric printed with small designs.

Carbonization Using sulfuric acid on wool to destroy cellulosic materials like leaves and twigs.

Carding Process of separating and aligning fibers to form a thin web.

Cellulosic fibers Fibers that come from plants (sometimes called vegetable fibers).

Challis Medium-weight, plain-weave fabric originally made of worsted wool, but now in fibers resembling wool.

Chambray Medium-weight, plain-weave fabric made with white warp yarns and colored filling yarns; made from cotton or cotton blends.

Chantilly Delicate French lace; designs are frequently flowers or vines.

Chemical finishes Finishes that involve chemicals; also called wet finishes.

Chemical shrinkage control Using chemical treatments to control shrinkage of wools, rayons, and cottons.

Chemical washing Process of using chemicals such as alkalis, oxidizing agents, and enzymes to partially destroy fabric and create a worn or abraded appearance.

Chenille Yarns with pile fibers sticking out all around; created by cutting leno-weave fabric into strips.

China grass Another name for ramie.

Chino Warp-faced, steep-twill fabric usually made with combed, two-ply yarns.

Chintz Percale fabric with printed stripes or floral designs; frequently glazed.

Chlorination Process of treating wool fabric with chlorine to partially dissolve the scales of fiber and limit its capacity to felt.

Circular knitting machine Knitting machine with the needles arranged in a circle on a cylinder to form tabular fabric.

Circular loom Specialized loom which weaves tubular fabric.

Ciré Finishing process that gives fabric a highly polished look often described as "wet," produced on a friction calendar. Note that ciré is a finish, not a fabric. Fabric with a ciré finish is appropriately termed ciré fabric or ciréd fabric.

Cloth *See* **fabric**.

Cloth beam Cylinder on which woven cloth is wound.

Cluny French bobbin lace, usually in medium to heavy weights.

Coated fabrics *See* **film laminates**.

Color migration Occurs when moisture lifts color and redeposits it in another area of the fabric.

Colorants Chemical agents that produce colors; dyes and pigments add color to textiles.

Colorfastness The capacity of a dye or pigment to retain its color during use and care.

Combing Process of further aligning fibers after carding. A comblike device removes shorter fibers and makes the remaining fibers more parallel.

Comfort stretch Term used to describe fabrics that provide elasticity. Used in, for example, lingerie, stretch lace, and leggings.

Compressional resiliency The ability of a fiber to return to its original thickness after being crushed.

Compressive shrinkage A mechanical method of relaxation shrinkage in which dampened fabric is overfed onto a roller to encourage the fibers to relax and shrink.

Consolidation shrinkage Shrinkage that occurs during tumble drying of washables and during dry cleaning in coin-operated machines. The mechanical action of tumbling causes fibers to return to a more natural shape, typically shorter and wider, and the fabric does the same.

Consumer textiles Group that includes both apparel and home furnishings and comprises about 75 percent of fiber consumption.

Conventional shuttle loom Loom that uses a shuttle to carry the filling yarn through the shed.

Converters Companies that purchase greige goods, arrange for finishing and dyeing or printing, and resell goods.

Cord Ribbed fabric with the rib running lengthwise.

Cord yarns Two or more ply yarns twisted together; also called cable yarn.

Cordonnett Lace in which the pattern is outlined in cord; also called reembroidered lace.

Corduroy Filling-pile fabric with regularly spaced floats cut to form lengthwise rows; generally made from cotton or cotton-blend yarns.

Core-spun yarns Yarns made by spinning a sheath of staple fibers around a filament core.

Corkscrew yarns *See* **spiral yarns**.

Coronizing A special treatment for glass fibers that improves drape and wrinkle resistance; fibers are heat set, dyed, and finished in one operation.

Cotton count Indirect weight system based on the number of hanks (hank equals 840 yarns) in 1 pound; the predominant system.

Courses The rows of loops on the traditional back of a weft knit.

Covered yarn Yarn made by wrapping a core yarn with another yarn.

Covering power The ability of a fabric to hide what is beneath it.

Crease-resistant finish (CRF) Another term for a wrinkle-resistant finish, but usually refers to finishes that reduce wrinkles during wear; ironing is needed after laundering.

Crepe Very high-twist yarns.

Crepe-back satin Fabric with low-twist warp floats on its face and high-twist crepe yarns on its back.

Cretonne Percale fabric with large floral designs.

Crimp The waves, bumps, or undulations of a fiber.

Crochet Process that involves using a crochet hook to loop yarns together.

Crocking The transfer of color due to abrasion or rubbing.

Cross dyeing Process used to create a multicolored effect in a blend. The dye bath is prepared so each fiber in the blend is dyed a different color.

Crushed velvet Velvet fabric mechanically twisted to create random flattened areas.

Cultivated silk Silk which is produced by cultivate silkworms in a controlled environment.

Curing Process treating with dry heat to set finishes or pigments.

Curl yarns *See* **bouclé yarns**.

Cut Refers to the relative fineness or compactness of weft knits.

Cut-pile fabric Fabric, such as velvet, with extra warp or filling yarns which are cut to form tufts.

Damask Jacquard-weave fabric with a flat design usually done in one or two colors. The design is created by floats that cross four to seven yarns.

Damp relaxing *See* **sponging**.

Decitex Refers to the weight in grams of 10,000 meters of filament yarn.

Degummed silk *See* **pure silk**.

Degumming Process that removes the sericin, or gum, from silk and makes the silk softer and whiter; similar to boiling off.

Deluster printing Process in which agents are used to reduce the luster of shiny fabric, delustering agents are printed on the fabric to create shiny and dull patterns.

Delustering Chemically or mechanically treating fibers and fabrics to reduce luster.

Denier Refers to the weight in grams of 9,000 meters of filament yarn.

Denim Warped-faced twill fabric, usually made of yarn-dyed cotton or cotton blends.

Derivative cellulosic fibers Fibers produced from cellulosic materials that cannot be used as fibers in their natural form. The cellulose is chemically changed during production so the resulting fibers are cellulose derivatives known as esters. Acetate and triacetate are derivative cellulosic fibers.

Desizing Removing the sizing agents (starches, gelatins, gums, or resins) used to strengthen warp yarns.

Diaper cloth *See* **birds-eye**.

Dimensional stability The ability of a fiber to maintain its original shape, neither shrinking nor stretching.

Direct-laid fabrics *See* **polymer laid**.

Discharge printing Printing piece-dyed fabric with a chemical solution to remove the original color. Sometimes additional printing steps add color to the bleached areas.

Disposable nonwovens Nonwoven fabrics designed to be discarded after a single use or, sometimes, a few uses.

Dobby attachment A mechanical attachment on a loom that allows small geometric patterns to be woven.

Dobby loom Loom with a dobby attachment.

Dope The spinning solution or liquid polymer forced through a spinneret to create a fiber.

Dope dyeing *See* **solution dyeing**.

Dotted swiss Sheer lightweight fabric, traditionally cotton, with small ornamental dots, created by extra yarn weaving. Imitation dotted swiss is made by flocking or printing.

Double knits Knits produced on interlock machines or rib-knit machines. Sometimes called double jerseys. Both sides of a plain double knit resemble the face of a jersey knit.

Double weaves Interwoven fabrics made with four sets of yarns (two warp and two filling). Two layers of fabric are created but the yarns periodically move from one layer to the other, so that the layers cannot be separated without damaging the fabric. Double-weave fabrics are also called pocket cloth due to the small spaces formed between the layers of fabric.

Doublecloth Interwoven fabric made with five sets of yarn, forming two layers of fabric which can be separated.

Double-faced fabrics Fabrics made with three sets of yarns (two sets of warp and one filling or one set of warp and two sets of filling); appears the same on both sides.

Double-faced satin Fabric woven with two warps and one filling so both sides have the characteristics of satin.

Doup harness A special harness which alternately twists warp yarns to create a leno weave.

Drape The ability of a fabric to hang in graceful folds, either on the body or some other shape. Flexibility of the fiber contributes to the drape of the fabric.

Drawing Stretching or elongating manufactured fibers, which increases strength; the step in staple yarn formation that blends and combines slivers.

Drill Piece-dyed, medium- to heavyweight warp-faced twill fabric, generally used in work clothes or industrial fabrics.

Dry finishes *See* **mechanical finishes**.

Dry laid Web formation method for staple fibers using carding or air laying.

Dry-laid bonded web Dry-laid nonwoven which is held together by chemical, adhesive, or heat bonding.

Dry prints Fabrics printed with pigments, so called because dry heat is required to set the color.

Dry spinning Fiber formation method in which the polymer is dissolved in a solvent and extruded in warm, dry air. The warm air evaporates the solvent and hardens the filaments.

Duck Stiff, heavy, plain-weave fabric.

Duoppioni silk Silk produced when two silkworms spin a cocoon together; resulting strand has a thick/thin appearance.

Duplex printing Process that creates a printed pattern on both sides of the fabric. Designs can be the same or different. If both sides are printed with the same pattern, the fabric can appear to have a woven-in design. This method is expensive. Jacquard and dobby fabrics have nearly replaced duplex prints.

Durable finishes Finishes that can be expected to be effective during the predicted life of the product, but that decrease in effectiveness during the product lifespan.

Durable nonwovens Nonwoven fabrics designed for multiple uses.

Durable-press finishes Finishes that maintain a flat, smooth, unwrinkled appearance in fabric.

Dye house Factory that dyes fabric; also called dye plant.

Dye plant *See* **dye house**.

Dyeing and printing Processes during which colors and or patterns of colors are added to a textile product.

Dyes Synthetics or natural organic compounds used to add color to textiles; also referred to as dyestuffs.

Dyestuffs *See* **dyes.**

Elastic recovery The ability of a fiber to return to its original length after being stretched.

Electrostatic flocking Using an electrical charge to orient flocking fibers vertically; *See* **flock printing** and **flocking.**

Elongation The lengthening or stretching of a fiber.

Embossing Using calender rollers with engraved designs to create embossed fabrics. As fabric passes through the calender, it is imprinted with the design.

Embroidered fabrics Fabrics decorated with patterns of flat surface yarns; can be embroidered by hand or machine.

Emulsion spinning A complex process that is used for insoluble polymers with high melting points. The polymer is dispersed in a carrier, extruded, and then heated to form the fiber.

Ends *See* **warp.**

Entanglement Process of interlocking fibers around each other.

Epitropic fiber Synthetic fiber that has small particles of carbon embedded in its surface to conduct electricity.

Even-sided twill Fabric in which an equal number of warp and filling yarns are exposed on both sides of the fabric.

Expanded films Result of incorporating tiny air cells into the film before extrusion or casting.

Eyelet Fabric decorated with cut-out areas surrounded by stitches.

Fabric Formed by assembling yarns and/or fibers into a cohesive structure. Most common structures are woven, knit, and nonwoven. Fabric may be called cloth, material, piece goods, or goods.

Fabric count *See* **thread count.**

Fade To lose color.

Fashion marks Created when open, transfer, or spread stitches are used to shape a full-fashion sweater.

Felt Fabric created directly from wool fibers. The wool fibers are pressed into a flat sheet and then subjected to moisture, heat, and agitation. The scaly structure of the wool fiber causes the fibers to interlock and mat.

Fiber-reinforced composites (FRCs) High-technology combinations of textiles and resins. Most commonly aramid, carbon or glass fibers, yarns, or fabrics are imbedded in or impregnated with epoxy, phenolic, or polyester resins.

Fibers Fine, hairlike substances that may be natural or manufactured; the smallest component of a textile product.

Fibrillation Process of drawing a film of polymer until it separates into a mass of fibers. Fibers are usually coarse and appropriate for use as twine; can be made into bagging or ropes or used in industry.

Filament fibers Long fibers measured in yards or meters.

Filature Factory where silk is reeled.

Filling knits *See* **weft knits**.

Filling-faced twill Fabric with filling yarns predominating on its face.

Filling-pile fabric Pile fabric in which the pile formed by extra filling yarns.

Film Synthetic polymer extruded in a sheet-like form or cast onto a drum.

Film laminates Created when a film is laminated to a knit or woven fabric; also called coated fabric.

Finish Any chemical or mechanical treatment or process that modifies the properties of a textile product.

Finishing mill Factory that finishes fabric.

Finishing plant *See* **finishing mill**.

Flake yarns Novelty yarns in which a binder secures small tufts of fiber to the core yarn; also called flock or seed yarn.

Flame-resistant finishes Treatments that reduce the flammability of fabrics.

Flannel Plain or twill weave fabric with a napped surface, usually of cotton or wool.

Flat knitting machine Knitting machine with needles held in a flat bed to form flat fabric.

Fleece Jersey-knit fabric with a cut pile that has been brushed.

Fleece wool Fleece sheared from the sheep.

Flexibility The ability of a fiber to bend or fold easily.

Float The warp or filling yarn that passes over several other yarns.

Float stitch Weft-knit stitch variation in which the yarn is allowed to "float" across the back of the fabric; also called miss stitch.

Flock printing Printing technique that uses an adhesive to attach short fibers to the fabric in a decorative design.

Flock yarns *See* **flake yarns**.

Flocking Process in which an adhesive is applied to the fabric and short fibers are then scattered over the surface and adhere to the adhesive.

Fly shuttle loom *See* **conventional shuttle loom**.

Foam dyeing Method that uses foam to apply the dye to the surface of wet fabric.

Foam finishing Newer method that reduces water pollution and uses less energy; finish is applied in a foam.

Foam laminates Two- or three-layer structures usually used to provide insulation. A polyurethane layer is fused to a face fabric. Sometimes a third fabric, usually a tricot knit, if fused to the foam, sandwiching the foam layer.

Foams Created when air is incorporated into rubber or polyurethane.

Foulard *See* **surah**.

Fox Fibre® Naturally colored cotton fiber, organically grown by Natural Cotton Colors, Inc.

Frieze *See* **frisé**.

Frisé Heavy, durable upholstery fabric that may have an uncut pile or a combination of cut and uncut piles. Also called frieze.

Frosting Color loss due to localized abrasion.

Fulling Controlled felting process that causes wool fabric to shrink.

Functional finishes Finishes that improve overall product performance.

Fur fibers Fibers from fur bearing animals such as fox, mink, beaver, and rabbit.

Gabardine Warp-faced, steep-twill fabric with prominent wales.

Garment dyeing *See* **product dyeing**.

Garnetting Mechanically shredding wool yarns or fabric into the fibrous state. The resulting fiber is weaker and of lower quality.

Gauge Refers to the relative fineness or compactness of warp knits and hosiery.

Gel spinning A hybrid of wet and dry spinning processes; used to create solvent spun rayon. Also called solvent spinning.

Generic name The name of a manufactured fiber that is based on chemical composition. Generic name categories are established by the Federal Trade Commission. Generic names begin with lowercase letters. Examples are olefin, nylon, acrylic.

Geotextiles Specialized industrial textiles used in civil-engineering projects such as dams, road beds, and erosion control.

Gigging Also called napping or raising. Process in which rollers with small, fine hooks pass over the fabric, catch fibers, and pull them to the surface.

Gingham Medium-weight, plain-weave fabric with a woven check or plaid; made from cotton or cotton blends.

Glazing Finishing process that creates a highly polished surface. Produced on a friction or chasing calender.

Goods *See* **fabric**.

GORE-TEX® A microporous film laminate. The GORE-TEX® film is a PTFE fluorocarbon membrane with very small pores that transmit water vapor but not water.

Grain Describes the relationship between the warp and filling yarns.

Grain perfect *See* **on grain**.

Granite cloth Momie weave with a grainy surface. It is a variation of the satin weave used in apparel and furnishings.

Grease wool Wool, sheared or pulled, before it is cleaned. It contains natural oils, dirt, and other impurities.

Greige goods Unfinished goods. Pronounced *gray*.

Grenadine Open-weave leno-weave fabric made from hard twisted yarns.

Grin through A flaw in fabric which occurs when broken spandex yarns appear on the surface of the fabric, or when the ground shows through on a pile weave.

Ground The base fabric in a pile weave.

Hairpin lace A variation of crocheting in which yarns are wound around a frame before being crocheted together.

Hand Refers to how the fabric feels, or the texture of the fabric.

Hand painting Thickened dyes and pigments can be used on fabric in much the same way that oils are painted on canvas. Unthickened dyes are very similar to watercolors and similar effects can be achieved. Pigments must be mixed with textile binders to adhere properly to fabric.

Hand-screen printing A hand printing method that uses prepared screens to apply colored designs to fabric. The process is similar to stenciling.

Hank A skein of standardized length. Spun yarns are traditionally sold in hanks.

Hard twist A comparative term used to describe the turns per inch in a yarn. Hard twist indicates a high number of turns per inch.

Harness A frame that holds the heddles in place during weaving.

Heat setting The controlled application of heat which allows creases and pleats to be permanently set in fabrics made from thermoplastic fibers; also improves the dimensional stability of thermoplastic fibers, yarns, or fabrics.

Heat-reflectant finishes Usually fine coatings of metal and resins which reflect heat.

Heat-sensitive fibers May be damaged by exposure to high heat; may also be heat set in desirable shapes with controlled application of heat.

Heat-transfer printing The design is printed with disperse dyes on special paper. The printed paper is laid on the fabric and the design is transferred to the fabric through heat and pressure. Also referred to as thermal transfer printing or sublistatic printing.

Heddles Cord or wire eyelets that hold the warp yarns in place for weaving. Heddles are held in position by the harness.

Herringbone twill An even-sided twill fabric in which the twill line periodically reverses to form a diagonal pattern.

Heterogeneous fibers Created when two or more different types of polymer, or variants of the same polymer, are extruded together.

High bulk yarns Combinations of manufactured fibers, usually two variants of acrylic which have different shrink potential. When the yarn is exposed to steam or boiling water the unstable fibers shrink, thus crimping the shrink resistant fibers. High bulk yarns do not usually have much stretch. These yarns have a soft, luxurious hand but tend to pill.

High-performance (HP) rayon *See* **High-Wet-Modulus (HWM) rayon**.

High-Wet-Modulus (HWM) rayon Rayon that resists deformation when wet; also called high-performance (HP) or polynosic rayon.

Hollow fibers Manufactured fibers with hollow centers.

Houndstooth check Yarn-dyed twill fabric with a pointed-check effect.

Huck Medium- to heavyweight dobby-weave fabric with a pebbly surface, usually used for toweling.

Hydroentangled fabrics Nonwovens created by using high-speed jets of water to entangle fibers; also called water-needled fabrics.

Hydrophilic fibers Fibers that can absorb moisture.

Hydrophobic fibers Fibers that do not readily absorb moisture.

Hygroscopic fibers Fibers that can absorb moisture without feeling wet.

Ikat The hand technique of warp printing.

Industrial textiles Woven, knitted, or nonwoven fabrics purchased for their strength, stability, and chemical resistance; used for items like filters, roofs, insulation, and storage tanks.

Inlay yarns *See* **insertion warp knits**.

Inorganic fibers Natural fibers that do not contain carbon and are obtained from minerals, such as glass, metal, asbestos, and ceramic.

Insertion warp knits Knits with yarns inserted in the warp or filling direction. Yarns inserted in the warp direction are called inlay yarns.

Intarsia Decorative knitted design created without miss or tuck stitches. The color pattern is laid in and visible on both sides. Argyle is an example.

Interlock knits Specialized 1 × 1 rib knits made on interlock machines. Both sides of an interlock knit resemble the face of a jersey knit. A knit stitch on the front has a matching knit stitch on the back.

Intermediate-staple fiber Fiber that is $^{13}/_{16}''$ to $1^{1}/_{4}''$ long. Upland is an intermediate-length cotton fiber.

Interwoven fabrics Fabrics that are woven from three or more sets of yarns, such as double cloth, double weaves, and double faced fabrics.

Jacquard knits Patterned jersey knits created with stitch and/or color variations. Float stitches are visible on the back.

Jacquard loom A loom with great versatility, which produces Jacquard fabrics.

Jacquard weaving Weaving system that allows for individual control of each warp yarn. Beautifully patterned fabric can be created on a Jacquard loom.

Jean Piece-dyed, medium-weight, warp-faced twill fabric that is lighter than drill.

Jersey knits Weft knit with no distinct rib; also called single knit. The front is smooth and flat with vertical wales. The back is more textured with horizontal courses.

Jet dyeing Process that is similar to beck dyeing but involves the use of pressurized streams of dye in an enclosed system. Faster and more economical than beck dyeing.

Jet printing Applying dye through small jets that control the flow of streams of dye; used primarily on carpets, pile upholstery fabrics, and toweling.

Jig dyeing Process in which the fabric is stretched flat and passed through the dyebath.

Jobber Person who purchases fabric from large mills or converters and sells small quantities of finished fabric.

Just-in-Time *See* **Quick Response**.

Kersey Double-cloth fabric that is rougher, heavier, and more lustrous than melton. Used for winter coats.

Knit stitches *See* **plain stitch**.

Knitted lace *See* **raschel lace**.

Knitted terry Jersey knit with an uncut-loop pile. The pile is on the purl side.

Knitted velour Jersey knit with a cut-loop pile. The pile is on the purl side.

Knitting Interlooping yarns to create fabric.

Knop yarns *See* **nub yarns**.

Knot yarns *See* **nub yarns**.

Laces Beautiful open-work fabrics created by hand or machine.

Ladder *See* **run**.

Lamb's wool First shearing from an animal under 7 months old. The wool is fine and soft.

Laminated fabrics Layered structures in which two or more fabrics are fused. Each layer maintains its identity.

Lanolin Oil recovered from wool during processing. A valuable natural by-product of wool that is used in soaps, cosmetics, and creams.

Lappet weaving Weaving process in which an extra wrap yarn forms a decorative embroidery-like design.

Laps Floats that occur on the back of a warp knit; also called underlaps.

Left-hand twill Twill fabric with wale lines running from the lower right to upper left.

Leno harness *See* **doup harness**.

Leno weave Identified by pairs of warp yarns that twist around filling yarns in a figure 8.

Levers lace Lace which has been made on the Levers machine.

Light-reflectant finishes Reflectant finishes with microscopic light-reflecting beads.

Light-stabilizing finishes Treatments that prevent damage from the ultraviolet rays of the sun.

Linen Fabric made from flax. Term is commonly used to refer to both fiber and fabric.

Linen count Yarn-count system based on the number of hanks in 1 pound. (1 hank equals 300 yards); also called linen lea count.

Linen lea *See* **linen count**.

Links and links machine Knitting machine used to produce purl or fancy knit fabric.

Links-links machine Knitting machine similar to the links and links machine.

Linters Short cotton fibers that are still attached to the cotton seed after ginning; unsuitable for spinning.

Loft The ability of a fiber to return to its original thickness after being crushed; also called compressional resiliency.

London shrinking *See* **sponging**.

Long-staple fiber Fiber that is 1½″ to 2½ ″ long. Sea Island Egyptian and pima (or American Egyptian) are examples.

Loom A machine that weaves fabric by interlacing vertical (warp) and horizontal (filling) yarns.

Loop yarn *See* **bouclé yarn**.

Loopy textured yarns Filament yarns which have been textured to have a bouclé effect and increased bulk but no stretch.

Loopy yarn *See* **loopy textured yarns**.

Lumen Central canal that runs longitudinally in some fibers.

Luster Amount of light reflected from a fiber.

Machine printing *See* **roller printing**.

Macramé Hand-knotting technique, often used to create wall hangings.

Mali fabrics *See* **stitch-bonded fabrics**.

Manufactured cellulosic fibers Fibers derived from cellulose (wood pulp and cotton linters) that cannot be used as textiles in their original form.

Manufactured fibers Fibers that are created through science and technology, as opposed to fibers that occur naturally.

Marquisette Shear, lightweight, leno-weave fabric frequently used for curtains; usually made with filament yarns.

Matelassé Double-weave fabric with a raised pattern or quilted effect.

Material *See* **fabric**.

Matrix fibers Heterogeneous fibers in which a polymer matrix is dispersed within another polymer before extrusion.

Mechanical felt *See* **needle-punch felt**.

Mechanical finishes Physical treatments that change the appearance and/or hand of the textile product; also called dry finishes because the fabric does not need to be wet during processing.

Melt spinning Fiber formation method in which the polymer is melted and forced through a spinneret. Upon extrusion, cool air solidifies the polymer into filaments.

Melt-blown nonwovens Fabrics formed from molten synthetic fibers that are broken into short lengths by a stream of air as they leave the spinneret. Cool air distributes the fibers onto a collection surface. The fibers are held together by bonding or entanglement.

Melton Heavy fulled wool double cloth with a very dense texture.

Mercerization Treating fabric or yarns with sodium hydroxide while holding them under tension. Increases luster, improves strength, and increases absorbency. Only cotton or cotton blends are mercerized.

Metric yarn count Indicates the number of 1,000-meter hanks in 1 kilogram.

Microdenier fibers *See* **microfibers**.

Microfibers Manufactured fibers that are less than 1 denier; also called microdenier fibers.

Micron (μ) One micron (or micrometer in S. I.) equals $\frac{1}{1000}$ of a millimeter.

Microporous film laminate *See* **poromeric fabrics**.

Migration *See* **color migration**.

Milanese knits Type of warp knit similar to tricot.

Mill Factory that produces yarn or fabric.

Miss stitch *See* **float stitch**.

Moiré A special kind of embossing in which the roller is engraved with a watermark or wood-grain pattern. This special effect can also be created by pressing two lengths of ribbed fabric, such as taffeta, together. High pressure is needed to flatten the ribs and create the effect.

Momie weaves A special class of weaves that appear to have small spots. Made on a dobby loom. May be a satin-weave variation.

Momme Unit of weight for silk fabrics. Also spelled mommie. Higher numbers indicate heavier fabrics.

Monofilament yarn One filament fiber.

Moss crepe Crepe-weave fabric made from high-twist crepe yarns and regular yarns. Moss crepe is used for apparel.

Mothproof finishes Permanently protect most wool and animal hair fibers with a chemical applied during dyeing.

Multicomponent fibers Combinations of more than two separate polymers into one fiber. The polymers may be different variants of the same generic fiber or two different generic fibers.

Multifilament yarn A yarn made up of a number of filament fibers. All fibers for one yarn are extruded at one time. Usually the number of fibers in yarn ranges from 20 to 120.

Multiphase loom Modern loom which forms sheds as the filling yarns are inserted, allowing as many as 20 pre-cut filling yarns to be inserted at the same time.

Muslin Generic term for any balanced, plain-weave fabric. Usually made from cotton in counts of 112, 128, and 140. Also refers to medium-weight, plain-weave fabric that is white or unbleached. Muslin sheets are made from carded yarns.

Napped fabrics Fabrics that have a pile or nap that has been brushed up from the surface of the fabric. Napped fabrics have a longer pile than sueded fabric.

Natural fibers Fibers that come from vegetable, animal, and mineral sources.

Needlepoint lace Lacemaking technique that is similar to embroidery. Designs are stitched over base threads.

Needle-punch fabric Nonwoven fabric created when needles are punched through a batt of fibers.

Needle-punch felt Nonwoven fabric created by the needle-punch technique; also called mechanical felt.

Needle-punch nonwovens *See* **needle-punch fabric**.

Netting Open-mesh structures created by hand or machine. May be as lightweight as tulle or as heavy as fishing net. Yarns are looped and knotted together.

Network yarns Yarns created from foamed polymers that are stretched until small connected fibers are formed.

New wool Previously unused wool.

Nonreinforced films *See* **film**.

Nonwoven Any textile that is not woven. In the textile industry the term *nonwoven* is used to refer to any textile product created directly from fibers and held together by bonding or entanglement.

Nottingham A machine-made lace with large designs, commonly used for tablecloths.

Novelty yarn Yarn with interesting or decorative effects, such as nubs, loops, or flakes.

Nub yarns Novelty yarns in which the effect yarn is twisted around the core yarn several times to create bumps at regular intervals. A binder holds the bumps in place.

Off grain Fabrics in which the warp and filling yarns are not aligned properly.

Off-grain prints Prints that do not follows the lengthwise or crosswise grain of the fabric. Garments cut from off-grain prints cannot be both matched and cut on grain.

Off-shore production Use of lower-cost foreign labor to assemble and finish garments.

Oleophilic Having an affinity for oil.

On grain Fabric in which the warp yarns are perpendicular to the filling yarns. Also called "grain perfect."

Open stitch Weft-knit stitch variation in which loops are transferred from one needle to the next; also called transfer or spread stitch.

Open-end spinning Method of spinning yarn from staple fibers. Fibers are fed into a roter where centrifugal force deposits them in a V-shaped groove. As yarn is pulled out, more fibers are added.

Optical brightners Compounds added to bleached fabrics to intensify whiteness. They cause the fabric to appear whiter and brighter; also called fluorescent whiteners.

Organdy Sheer, crisp, lightweight cotton plain-weave fabric.

Organza Sheer, crisp, lightweight plain-weave fabric made from filament yarns.

Out-of-register prints Prints that are out-of-register have edges that do not align correctly.

Over-the-counter fabrics Fabrics sold to retail stores for the home sewer.

Package dyeing Process in which yarns are wound onto perforated cones or tubes before dyeing. The perforations allow the dye to circulate through the cones or tubes.

Pad dyeing Dyeing method that uses pads to squeeze the dye into the fabric. Pad dyeing is the only method appropriate for dyeing with pigments.

Panné velvet Velvet that has had its pile pressed flat. One-direction pressing gives the fabric exceptional luster.

Parchmentizing Process of exposing the fabric to an acid and then immediately neutralizing the acid; also called acid stiffening. Organdy is an example of an acid-stiffened fabric.

Peau-de-soie Heavy, semidull, satin-weave fabric.

Percale Closely woven, medium-weight, plain-weave fabric that is made from carded yarns of cotton or cotton blends. Sometimes called utility percale. Percale sheets are made from combed yarns, usually in the thread counts of 180 to 200, and as high at 250. Combed percale is sometimes called true percale.

Permanent finishes Finishes that are expected to be uniform during the lifetime of the product. They do not diminish or fade during the lifetime of the product.

Permanent press A misnomer for durable press because the finish is not permanent; *See* **durable finishes.**

Picks *See* weft.

Piece dyeing Adding color to fabric; also called fabric dyeing. Most common method for dyeing solid-colored fabric.

Piece goods *See* **fabric.**

Pigments Inorganic compounds used to add color to textiles. Do not adhere to fabric naturally without a resin binder.

Pile Raised loops or cut loops (tufts) on the surface of fabric. Extra warp or filling yarns are used to create the pile.

Pilling The formation of little balls of loose fibers on the surface of a fabric.

Pillow lace *See* **bobbin lace.**

Pima cotton *See* **long-staple fiber.**

Pique Medium- to heavyweight dobby-weave fabric with a pronounced lengthwise cord. May have a waffle effect, usually made of cotton. Stuffer yarns may be used to increase the design effect.

Pirns *See* **quills**.

Plain films *See* **film**.

Plain stitch Knitting stitch that creates the wales on the face and courses on the back of a jersey knit; also called knit stitch.

Plain weave Simplest form of weaving. Made by passing a filling yarn over one warp yarn and then under one warp yarn at a time across the width of the fabric. The next filling yarn is inserted so the warp yarns that were under are now on top; also called tabby weave.

Plissé Refers both to the finishing process and to the resulting fabric. Fabrics are treated with chemicals that cause them to shrink where the chemicals are applied.

Plush Warp-pile fabric with a pile deeper than that of velvet. The pile is usually longer than ¼ ″.

Ply yarns Two or more single yarns twisted together. A two-ply yarn is two singles twisted together, a three-ply yarn has three singles twisted together, and so on.

Pocket cloth *See* **double weaves**.

Polymer Long chain-like compound with high molecular weight, used to create manufactured fibers.

Polymer films *See* **film**.

Polymer laid System for creating nonwoven fabric directly from thermoplastic fibers as they are extruded from a spinneret. Melt-blown and spun bonded fabrics are polymer laid.

Polynosic rayon *See* **High-Wet-Modulus (HWM) rayon**.

Poplin Unbalanced plain-weave fabric with a rib effect in the filling direction.

Poromeric fabrics Fabrics coated with a very fine, microporous film; also called microporous film laminates.

Power stretch Term used to describe stretch fabrics that provide holding power and elasticity, such as those used in foundation garments, swimsuits, and surgical support hose.

Power-net fabrics Raschel knit with laid-in spandex fiber or yarn.

Precuring Curing fabrics before they are cut and sewn.

Preparatory finishes Treatments that are routinely given to fabrics to prepare the fabric for further processing.

Print cloth Any unfinished, medium-weight, balanced, plain-weave fabric. Usually made of cotton or cotton blends.

Print house Factory that prints fabric.

Print paste Thickened dye or pigment used in printing.

Print plant *See* **print house**.

Product dyeing Process of dyeing complete garments or other textile products such as towels or sheets after they have been constructed.

Progressive shrinkage Shrinkage that occurs every time the fabric is laundered. Rayon and wool are particularly susceptible to progressive shrinkage.

Projectile looms Shuttleless looms which use a projectile to carry the filling yarn across the shed.

Protein fibers Silk and animal hair fibers.

Pulled wool Wool removed from an animal that has been slaughtered. Generally considered to be of lower quality than sheared wool.

Pure silk Silk after the sericin or gum has been removed. Degumming reduces the weight of the silk 20 to 30 percent.

Purl knits Knits created with alternate courses of knit stitches and purl stitches.

Purl stitches Knitting stitch that creates horizontal ridges across the fabric.

Quick Response Production and delivery that emphasizes speed and efficiency through computer use and automated manufacturing.

Quills Hold the filling yarn in the shuttle.

Quilted fabrics Fabrics made with three layers: a face fabric, a backing fabric, and a filling or batting sandwiched between. The three layers are held in place by small machine or hand stitches. Some lower-end goods are bonded together with adhesive or heat.

Raising *See* **gigging**.

Rapier looms Shuttleless looms which use a rapier or rod to carry the filling across the shed.

Raschel knits Warp-knit fabric, usually coarser than traditional warp knits, often with intricate designs.

Raschel lace Knitted lace made on a raschel knitting machine.

Ratiné yarns Novelty yarns that are very similar to bouclé yarns except that the loops are evenly spaced.

Raw silk Silk before the sericin is removed.

Raw wool *See* **grease wool**.

Recycled wool Wool yarns and fabrics that have been garnetted to a fibrous state and reused in products.

Reed A comb-like device that pushes filling yarns into place during weaving.

Reeling Process of unwinding the long silk fiber from the cocoon.

Regenerated cellulosic fibers Fibers produced from cellulosic materials that cannot be used as fibers in their natural form. These fibers retain their cellulosic properties. Rayon is a regenerated cellulosic fiber.

Regular twill A twill-weave fabric with wales on a 45° angle.

Reinforced films Plain or expanded films that have been laminated to a woven, knit, or nonwoven; also called supported film.

Relaxation shrinkage Shrinkage that occurs because fabrics are held under significant tension during manufacture and processing. During laundering, moisture encourages the fibers to relax and contract.

Renewable finishes Temporary finishes that can be reapplied. For example, the starch removed in washing can be reapplied before ironing.

Residual shrinkage The small amount of shrinkage that may occur even after fabrics have been preshrunk properly.

Resiliency The ability of a fiber to return to its original shape following bending, folding, or crushing; also called wrinkle recovery.

Resin binder A resin used to adhere pigments to the surface of a fabric.

Resins Compounds used in wrinkle and crease-resistant finishes. Frequently used on cellulosic and cellulosic blends. Resins are a durable treatment, not a permanent treatment.

Resist printing Process in which a resist is applied to the fabric before dyeing to prevent the dye from penetrating the fibers. Frequently done as a handcraft.

Reverse stitches *See* **purl stitches**.

Rib knits Knits made so that knit and purl wales alternate across the width of the fabric.

Ribbed fabric Unbalanced plain-weave variation, usually with noticeable lines or ribs on its surface. The line is created by using larger yarns or by grouping warp or filling yarns. In some ribbed fabrics, such as broadcloth, the rib line is almost invisible.

Right-hand twill Twill fabric with wale lines running from the lower left to the upper right. Right-hand twills are the most common of the twill weaves.

Ring spinning Method of spinning yarn from staple fibers. The roving is twisted and wound onto a bobbin in one operation.

Roller printing Printing method that uses engraved rollers to apply color to fabric. A three-color design requires three rollers. The cloth to be printed is imprinted with each roller.

Rotary screen printing The fastest screen-printing method. The screen is a cylinder instead of the flat screen used in hand or automatic screen printing. The dye is forced through the holes in the cylinder as it rolls over the fabric.

Roving The intermediate stage between sliver and yarn. The roving is slightly more cohesive than the sliver.

Roving frame Machine used to produce roving. It reduces the size of the sliver and adds slight twist.

Run Unraveled wale in a knit.

Sand crepe Momie-weave fabric with short two-yarn floats, made from spun or filament yarns.

Sanded silk Silk that has been washed with abrasive materials to produce a very soft hand.

Sateen fabric A variation of the satin weave, the filling yarns float over the warp yarns. Usually made of spun yarns.

Satin Medium- to heavyweight satin-weave fabric made from filament yarns.

Satin tricot Tricot fabric with long laps.

Satin weave Weave pattern that allows the warp yarns to float over four or more filling yarns. The filling yarn goes under four warp yarns and then over one warp yarn. The warp yarn may float over as many as twelve filling yarns. The interlacings are never adjacent but regularly spaced so the fabric appears to be smooth.

Schreinering An embossing calendering process that produces fabric with soft luster and soft hand. The fabric passes through a Schreiner calender and is embossed with 180 to 360 diagonal lines per inch.

Scouring Process done to wool that is similar to boiling off.

Screen printing Printing method that uses prepared screens to apply color in specific areas. Pigment or dye application is controlled carefully by the use of resist materials on the screens. Each color in a design requires a separate screen.

Scrim Loosely woven fabric often used to provide support for nonwovens and felt, as a backing or a lightweight fabric.

Scroop The rustle of silk as it rubs against itself.

Sea Island Egyptian High-grade cotton; *see* **long-staple fiber**.

Seed yarns *See* **flake yarns**.

Seersucker Puckered fabric that is created by slack-tension weaving.

Selvages Run parallel to the warp yarns and form the lengthwise edges of the woven fabric.

Semidurable finishes Finishes that last through several cleanings.

Serge Even-sided twill fabric with subdued wale.

Sericin Gummy protein substance that coats raw silk.

Sericulture The scientific production of silk.

Set To make permanent; the number of ends or warp yarns per inch in fabric.

Shattered silk Weighted silk that is disintegrating.

Sheared wool *See* **fleece wool**.

Shearing Finishing process that cuts the nap or pile of a fabric to uniform length. A design or sculptured effect may be sheared into the pile or nap.

Sheath-core fiber Bicomponent fiber in which one fiber forms a sheath around another fiber.

Shed The opening created by the warp yarns when the harnesses are raised and lowered. The shuttle inserts filling yarns in the shed.

Sheeting A plain-weave fabric usually made with carded yarns, traditionally but not exclusively from cotton.

Shirting madras Dobby-weave fabric with a small geometric design in a striped pattern, frequently used for men's dress shirts.

Short-staple fiber Fiber that is $\frac{3}{8}''$ to $\frac{3}{4}''$ long.

Shuttle A smooth, boat-shaped device that carries the filling yarn over and under the warp yarns during the weaving process.

Shuttleless looms Modern looms that use air, water, rapiers, or projectiles instead of shuttles to carry the filling yarn across the shed.

Silk noil Short fibers from broken cocoons and the outside of the cocoon that are of lower quality and lower luster than filament silk. Used to make spun silk; also called waste silk.

Silk-in-the-gum *See* **raw silk**.

Simple calendering Temporary finish process that is similar to ironing or pressing. The dampened fabric is fed through heated rollers to smooth wrinkles and impart the fabric with a slight sheen.

Simple yarn A yarn that is uniform and consistent in shape and size.

Simplex knits Tricot knit fabric that resembles a double knit.

Singeing Process of quickly passing fabric over a gas flame or heated copper plate and then immersing it in a water bath to remove any fiber ends that may be protruding from the surface of the fabric.

Single knits *See* **jersey knits**.

Single yarn A group of fibers twisted together to form a cohesive strand; if untwisted, a single yarn separates into individual fibers.

Sizing agents Starches, gelatins, gums, or resins used to add body, stiffness, smoothness, or weight to yarns or fabrics. Warp yarns are sized before weaving for added strength. Also called slashing agents.

Skein dyeing Dyeing method in which yarns are wound in loose hanks or bundles before dyeing.

Skewed fabric Off-grain fabric in which the filling yarns slant in a straight line.

Slack-tension pile weaving *See* **slack tension weaving**.

Slack-tension weaving Process using two warp beams. One beam is held at normal tension while the other is held at loose tension. As the filling is inserted and beaten into the cloth, the loose warp yarns create a pile or a puckered effect.

Slashing Process of sizing warp yarns.

Slashing agents *See* **sizing agents.**

Slip-resistant finishes Resin finishes used to hold filament yarns in place.

Slit-film yarns Yarns created when films are extruded, cooled, and then slit into narrow tapes.

Sliver Untwisted strand of somewhat parallel fibers.

Sliver-pile knits Jersey knits with a thick pile inserted on the purl side. The pile is formed from a sliver. The back of the fabric becomes the fashion face. Sliver-pile knits are used for imitation furs and high-pile fabrics.

Slub yarns Novelty yarns that are created by varying the amounts of twist in the yarn so some areas are thicker than others; also called thick-and-thin yarns.

Snarl yarns Novelty yarns in which the effect yarn and core yarn are held at unequal tension during twisting so the effect yarn forms unclosed loops; also called spike yarns.

Soft twist A comparative term used to describe the turns per inch in a yarn. Soft twist indicates relatively few turns per inch.

Softening Process of applying fabric softeners to reduce harshness.

Soil-release finishes Finishes that ease cleaning; should not be confused with soil-resistant finishes, which prevent the fabric from becoming soiled.

Soil-resistant finishes Finishes that prevent stains from being absorbed into the fabric. The soil remains on the surface.

Solution dyeing Adding pigment to the fiber solution, or dope, before extrusion. Solution-dyed fibers are also called spun-dyed fibers, dope-dyed fibers, or mass-pigmented fibers.

Solvent scouring Dry-cleaning-type procedure done on knits.

Solvent spinning *See* **gel spinning**.

Space dyeing Special yarn-dyeing technique that produces a multicolor effect along the length of the yarn.

Specialty hair fibers Fibers from animals other than sheep. Most specialty hair fibers come from animals in the goat or camel families.

Specific gravity Comparative measure of the mass of a fiber to an equal volume of water; also called density.

Spike yarns *See* **snarl yarns**.

Spinneret A device similar to a showerhead through which liquid polymer is extruded to form filament fibers. It resembles a thimble with tiny holes.

Spinners Companies that produce yarn from staple fibers.

Spinning Process of making a yarn from staple fibers; the process of extruding fiber-forming solutions through a spinneret.

Spiral yarns Novelty yarns that are created when two piles, differing in size, are twisted together.

Split film yarns Yarns created by drawing or stretching a film of polymer until it separates into a mass of fibers.

Sponging Process used to control relaxation shrinkage in wool fabrics. The fabric is thoroughly dampened with water or steam and allowed to dry slowly in a relaxed state; also referred to as London shrinking, damp relaxing, or steam relaxing.

Spot weaving Process in which extra filling or warp yarns form a design on the face of the fabric and are long floats on the back. The long floats may be trimmed. Sometimes the back of the fabric is used as the outside for design effect.

Spot yarns *See* **nub yarns**.

Spread stitch *See* **open stitch**.

Spun bonding Process of creating nonwoven fabric by blowing filaments onto a collection surface as they are extruded from the spinneret. The still-molten fibers bond as they touch. They may be subjected to additional bonding or entanglement.

Spun silk yarn Silk yarn made from short fibers; feels more like cotton than filament silk; *see* **silk noil**.

Spun-laced nonwovens *See* **hydroentangled fabrics**.

Staple fibers Short fibers that range from less than 1″ to 18″ long.

Steam relaxing *See* **sponging**.

Stenciling A handcraft that originated centuries ago in Japan. Screen printing is its modern version. The stencil is made by cutting a pattern in special paper or thin metal sheets. The stencil is held over the fabric and dyes or pigments are brushed or sprayed on with an air gun.

Stiffening Finish process that improves body and hand. Sizing agents, resins, and acids are used to stiffen fabric. Sizing agents are temporary finishes that must be reapplied. Resins are durable and provide longer-lasting stiffening than sizing agents. Acids provide permanent stiffness.

Stitch The loop of yarn formed by the knitting process; also produced by needle and thread, as in sewing.

Stitch-bonded fabrics Fabrics created when yarns or fibers are sewn together with needles and thread; also called mali fabrics, stitch-through, or stitch-knitted fabrics.

Stitch-knitted fabrics *See* **stitch-bonded fabrics**.

Stitch-through fabrics *See* **stitch-bonded fabrics**.

Stock dyeing Adding color at the fiber stage; also called fiber dyeing.

Stone washed denim Denim that has been washed with abrasive materials to produce a soft hand.

Stretch yarns Textured filament yarns that have a high degree of elastic stretch and rapid recovery. Stretch yarns should not be confused with elastomeric yarns or bicomponent yarns.

Striations Longitudinal markings on manufactured fibers that result from indentations or valleys in the cross section of the fiber.

Stuffer yarns Extra filling or warp yarns used to add weight or thickness to fabric.

S twist yarn A yarn with twist spirals that go from upper left to lower right.

Sueded fabrics Fabrics with a very low pile. The surface of the fabric is exposed to an abradant material which resembles sandpaper.

Supported film *See* **reinforced films**.

Surah Top-weighted, even-sided twill fabric made of filament fibers; also called foulard.

Swivel weaving Process of weaving with tiny shuttles of extra filling yarns to create designs resembling embroidery on fabric.

Synthetic fibers Fibers that are synthesized chemically, frequently from petroleum products.

Tabby weave *See* **plain weave**.

Tapa cloth Nonwoven fabric created by early man from the inner bark of mulberry, fig, or breadfruit trees; also known as bark cloth.

Tape yarns *See* **slit-film yarns**.

Tapestry Originally a hand-woven fabric with a filling yarn design that completely covered the warp yarns. Now tapestries are mass produced on Jacquard looms.

Tatting Using a tatting shuttle to create knotted laces.

Temporary finishes Finishes removed by washing or dry cleaning.

Tenacity Refers to fiber strength, usually describes the force needed to rupture the fiber.

Tendering The weakening of fiber due to exposure to the chemicals used in dyeing or finishing or other degradants.

Tentering Process of straightening the grain of the fabric by making the warp yarns and filling yarns perpendicular to each other. The fabric is stretched widthwise on a tentering frame.

Terry cloth Slack tension warp pile fabric with uncut loops on one or both sides, traditionally made of cotton.

Tex Unit of measure in the International System that refers to the weight in grams of 1,000 meters of fiber or yarn.

Texturing Modifying the surface of a fiber, or the process of adding bulk to yarns.

Thermoplastic fibers Fibers that melt or soften when exposed to heat.

Thermoplasticity The characteristic of a fiber to soften or melt when heated and harden when cooled.

Thick-and-thin yarns *See* **slub yarns**.

Thread Yarn that is used to sew garment pieces or other products together.

Thread count The number of yarns in 1 square inch of fabric; also called fabric count.

Thrown silk Reeled silk filament from four or more cocoons combined to make a yarn.

Tie-dying A handcraft resist technique. Areas of fabric or yarn are bound with string or rubber bands, or sometimes knotted before being dyed. Also called bound resist.

Tone-on-tone dyeing Process that produces a shaded effect on fabrics made from fiber variants of the same manufactured fiber. The variants are produced to have different dye affinities, so one dyebath yields a shaded effect.

Top Sliver made from tow or combed manufactured staple or wool fibers.

Top dyeing Adding color at the sliver stage after all short fibers have been combed out.

Tow A thick rope of thousands of filaments that can be cut into staple fibers; also referred to as short-linen fibers (less than 10″) or yarns made of short fibers and used in fabric when a coarse texture is desired.

Tow-to-top spinning Process of breaking or cutting tow into a sliver of staple fibers.

Trademark name Name used by a manufacturer to identify goods sold or made by that company. Trade names begin with uppercase letters; generic names begin with lowercase letters. Herculon® olefin, Dacron® polyester, and Lycra® spandex are examples.

Transfer stitch *See* **open stitch**.

Transgenic cotton Experimental cotton that has been genetically engineered to repel insects.

Traveler A U-shaped clip on a ring spinner which guides the twisting yarn onto the bobbin.

Triaxial loom Specialized loom that weaves three sets of yarn at 60° angles.

Tricot Warp-knit fabric made from filament yarns. The correct pronunciation of tricot is "tree-ko." The term *tricot* may be used to refer to all warp knits.

Tricot jersey Another name for two-bar tricot, the most common variety of tricot.

Tricot knits Warp-knit fabric, usually made of nylon, polyester, or acetate.

Tricot upholstery Usually a two-bar jersey tricot made from heavy nylon filament yarn.

Tricot-net fabric Fabric knitted with open spaces to create a meshlike effect.

True percale *See* **percale.**

Tuck stitch Welf-knit stitch variation in which two stitches are held on one needle to create an opening in the fabric.

Tufting Process in which needles are used to stitch pile yarns into a fabric backing.

Tulle A net structure used for veiling and eveningwear.

Turns-per-inch (TPI) Refers to the amount of twist in a yarn.

Tussah silk A variety a wild silk that is coarser and less lustrous than the silk produced by cultivated silkworms.

Twill weave Weave pattern identified by diagonal lines on the surface of the fabric. In the simplest twill these lines, or wales, are created by inserting the filling yarn over two warp yarns and then under one warp yarn. The next filling yarn also passes over two warp yarns and under one, but the pattern starts one warp yarn farther in.

Uncut pile fabric Fabric with loops of extra warp or filling yarns, such as terry cloth.

Underlaps *See* **laps.**

Union dyeing Process used to achieve a solid color in a blend. The dye bath is prepared so each fiber in the blend is dyed the same color.

Velour Warp-pile fabric, usually made of cotton yarns and used for draperies and upholstery fabrics. Knitted velours may be used for apparel.

Velvet Warp-pile fabric usually made of filament yarns.

Velveteen Filling-pile fabric with irregularly spaced floats that are cut to form an overall pile. Velveteen is made from spun yarns.

Virgin wool Previously unused wool.

Viscose rayon Refers to regular-strength rayon.

Voile Lightweight, plain-weave fabric with a two-ply warp. Made from cotton, cotton blends, or manufactured fibers.

Waffle cloth Dobby-weave fabric with a honeycomb effect.

Wales The diagonal lines created by the interlacing of the warp and filling yarns in a twill; the vertical columns of loops created during knitting; series of raised ribs (as in corduroy).

Warp Set of yarns that run lengthwise on a piece of woven fabric and parallel to the selvage; also called ends.

Warp beam Cylinder on which warp yarns are wound.

Warp knits Knits in which the loops interlock vertically. The face of a warp knit resembles the face of a jersey knit, but the back of a warp knit is characterized by floats called laps or underlaps.

Warp-faced twill Twill fabric with warp yarns predominating on the face of the fabric.

Warp-pile fabric Pile fabric in which the pile is formed by extra warp yarns.

Waste silk *See* **silk noil.**

Waterjet loom Shuttleless loom which uses a jet of water to carry the filling yarn across the shed.

Water-needled fabrics *See* **hydroentangled fabrics.**

Water-resistant finishes Finishes that prevent water from being absorbed into the fabric. The liquid remains on the surface. It is important to note that water-resistant fabrics are not waterproof.

Weaving The process of producing fabric by interlacing warp and filling yarns.

Weft The yarns that run horizontally across the width of a piece of woven fabric and are perpendicular to the warp yarns; also called filling yarns or picks.

Weft knits Knits in which the loops are interlocked across the fabric; sometimes called filling knit.

Weighted silk Degummed silk with metallic salts added to improve the fabric's body and drape. Weighted silks deteriorate more quickly than unweighted silks.

Wet finishes Finishes applied in a water bath or those that make the fabric wet; see chemical finishes.

Wet laid Web formation system for staple fibers, similar to papermaking.

Wet-laid bonded web Wet-laid nonwoven held together by chemical, adhesive, or heat bonding.

Wet prints Fabrics printed with dye. So called because steam is required to set the color and because processing chemicals and excess dyes must be washed out.

Wet spinning Fiber formation method in which the polymer is dissolved in a solvent and extruded into a chemical both which hardens the polymer into filaments.

Wicking The ability of a fiber to carry moisture along its surface.

Wild silk Coarse variety of silk produced by uncultivated silkworms.

Wire method Method for making pile fabric using two sets of warp yarns and one set of filling yarns. Wires are inserted between the extra warp and the base fabric to create the pile.

Wool Previously unused fiber from the fleece of lamb or sheep and specialty fibers such as camel hair. Also called virgin wool or new wool.

Wool felt *See* **felt.**

Woolen count Yarn count system based on the number of hanks in 1 pound (1 hank equals 1,600 yards).

Woolen yarns Soft, bulky yarns with fiber ends on the surface that are carded but not combed. Shorter woolen fibers and manufactured staple fibers may be processed into woolen yarns.

Worsted count Yarn count system based on the number of hanks in 1 pound (1 hank equals 560 yards).

Worsted yarns Yarns that are twisted more tightly, smoother, and stronger than woolen yarns. Longer wool fibers and manufactured fibers are processed in the worsted system.

Wrinkle recovery The ability of a fiber to return to its original shape following bending, folding, or crushing.

Wrinkle-resistant (WR) finishes Treatments that improve the wrinkle resistance of fabrics. Typically used on 100-percent cotton fabrics.

Yarn count system Indirect system for measuring the size of spun yarns.

Yarn dyeing Adding color to fibers after they have been spun into yarn but before the yarns are woven or knitted into fabric.

Yarns Groupings of natural or manufactured fibers combined to form a continuous strand which can be used to produce fabric.

Z-twist yarn Yarn with twist spirals which go from lower left to upper right.

Index